BALANCING TWO WORLDS

BALANCING TWO WORLDS

Asian American College Students Tell Their Life Stories

EDITED BY

Andrew Garrod and Robert Kilkenny

with an Introduction by Russell C. Leong
and an Afterword by Vernon Takeshita

Cornell University Press
Ithaca and London

First published 2007 by Cornell University Press
First printing, Cornell Paperbacks, 2007

Printed in the United States of America

Library of Congress Cataloging-in-Publication Data

Balancing two worlds : Asian American college students tell their life stories / edited by Andrew Garrod and Robert Kilkenny ; with an introduction by Russell C. Leong and an afterword by Vernon Takeshita.
   p. cm
   Includes bibliographical references.
   ISBN 978-0-8014-4595-8 (cloth : alk. paper) —
   ISBN 978-0-8014-7384-5 (pbk. : alk. paper)
   1. Dartmouth College—Students—Biography.   2. Asian American college students—New Hampshire—Hanover— Biography.   3. Asian American youth—Education (Higher)—New Hampshire—Hanover—Biography. I. Garrod, Andrew, 1937–   II. Kilkenny, Robert. LC2633.6.B35 2007 378.742'3—dc22
[B]   2007001104

Cloth printing   10 9 8 7 6 5 4 3 2 1
Paperback printing   10 9 8 7 6 5 4 3 2 1

In recognition of their bravery and insight, this book is dedicated to the fourteen student autobiographers whose essays are presented here.

Contents

Preface

"Asian Americans and Pacific Islanders (AAPIs) represent one of the fastest growing population groups in the United States. In March 2002, AAPIs were 4.4 percent of the U.S. population, up from 2.8 percent in 1990. The AAPI population continues to grow and is predicted to double by 2020."[1] Despite the burgeoning presence of Americans of Asian heritage in the United States and their relative success in the education system, few books have attempted to look qualitatively at their lives. Notable exceptions include *East to America*, an anthology of Korean American life stories edited by Elanie H. Kim and Eui-Young Yu, and the recently published *Asian American X: An Intersection of Twenty-first Century Asian American Voices*, edited by Arar Han and John Hsu.

Reading the personal stories of Asian Americans offers extraordinary insights into these writers' perspectives on both the United States and their parents' mother countries. It allows us to understand from the inside the developmental trajectory of a sometimes hybrid sense of self. The personal stories in *Balancing Two Worlds* are essentially memoirs in which the autobiographers—all students between the ages of eighteen and twenty-two who attended Dartmouth College—reflect on formative relationships and influences, life-changing events, and other factors that helped shape their values and their sense of personal identity. For the past ten years or so, incoming classes at Dartmouth have been between 13 percent and 14 percent Asian American. This means that between 140 and 150 Asian American students have been in each of the recent entering classes, which contrasts with the 8 percent to 10 percent that was typical more than ten years ago. The contributors to this book are of Indian, Pakistani, Burmese,

Vietnamese, South Korean, Chinese, Japanese, and Malaysian heritage. Selection of these authors was partly dictated by the representation of the different groups within the Dartmouth student population; for the class of 2009, 33 percent of those who self-identified as Asian American are of Chinese descent, 17 percent of Indian or Pakistani descent, 16 percent of Korean descent, and 4 percent of each of three groups—Vietnamese, Japanese, and Filipino. Though Dartmouth College was the site for the collection of the narratives, this book does not focus on Dartmouth per se or on its educational impact on our contributors, but rather on their evolving Asian American identities and youth culture.

Balancing Two Worlds offers a rare opportunity to explore the experiences of college-age students who, as Russell C. Leong quotes from a Dartmouth document from 1932 in the introduction, are "becoming aware of their own personality." Each author brings to this book his or her unique experience of growing up Asian American. It is our hope that readers of this anthology will be engaged by the particularity and detail of these stories, while at the same time connecting with the individual human experiences.

Almost all the essays in this book were written in the last four or five years. Only "Turning against Myself" and "Distilling My Korean American Identity" are older. All fourteen authors worked one-on-one with Andrew Garrod in weekly one-hour meetings over the ten-week term. Typically, a student would submit seven or eight pages to Garrod prior to each meeting; these pages then became the focus when they met. Teacher and writer also discussed how to proceed with the next portion of the narrative. Garrod made no assumption that the story was already formulated in the student's mind and conveyed to the student that each story had to be found, piece by piece. Because the emphasis was on process—helping writers with that most complex of tasks, finding their voice—no editorial interventions were made during the generative stage. Although the parameters were necessarily established by the editors, we encouraged the writers to develop their own themes and make sense of their experiences in ways that had significant meaning for their own lives. Not infrequently, a writer was halfway through the process before he or she came to understand what the essay's central concerns and themes were. "Memoir writers must manufacture a text, imposing narrative order on a jumble of half-remembered events," writes William Zinsser. "With that feat of manipulation, they arrive at a truth that is theirs alone, not quite like that of anybody else who is present at the same events."[2]

In helping our authors articulate their stories, we offered a few guiding questions: What gives purpose to your life? What relationships have been of major significance to you? When and how did you become aware of the concepts of race and ethnicity? How have you negotiated in your life your parents' language, religion, gender role and career expectations? What have been some of the major struggles in your life? How do you account for your academic success? What are the racial and ethnic backgrounds of some of your closest friends? Would you say that you were politically active in the college community? What role does your "Asianness" play in how you identify yourself? Is "Asian American" a useful categorization in your mind? We made no assumption that race was a vital element in the self-definition of every writer. Some only became aware that they were Asian or were viewed by others as such when they came to college.

The completed manuscripts were usually in the fifty to seventy page range. After careful consultation and discussion over months or occasionally even years, cutting and editing reduced and sharpened the text to a manageable length of eighteen to twenty-four double-spaced pages. Editors' changes to the text were minimal. Variations in tone, degree of self-analysis, and style of expression reflect our commitment to respect each writer's story and life.

After a draft had been reduced from around sixty to approximately twenty-five pages, it was sent to Robert Kilkenny, who had not worked with the students and therefore could offer a more objective reaction to their essays. This was done to bring the essays to another level of psychological cohesiveness in the hope that areas that seemed to be avoided or mysteriously unaddressed could be brought to the attention of the writers. Kilkenny suggested how and why a story would be better understood if some of these lacunae were explored more thoroughly. This was a conscious process of pushing writers to the edge of their ability to reflect on their own life histories. It was not unusual to have a writer balk or say that further exploration was too painful, or that they were genuinely unable to reflect further about experiences still subjectively raw and unresolved.

Almost all of the students in this book were enrolled in Andrew Garrod's various education classes, most of which are informed by a psychological developmental perspective. A few of the writers were recommended to the editors.

While fourteen essays—eight by men and six by women—appear in this book, they represent fewer than half of those developed and completed. Some students withdrew their essays from consideration for this anthology, because the writing of the essay and the self-reflection it had necessitated was the primary reason they embarked on the venture in the first place; others hesitated to make suggested changes or to engage in further self-exploration and editing. In such cases, we made an editorial decision as to whether the piece could stand on its own without further effort or whether it was insufficiently coherent to merit publication. Nevertheless, the editors are deeply grateful for all the essays so diligently worked on over the years, whether included in the book or not.

To encourage the frankest possible exploration of their lives and relationships, we offered the writers the option of remaining anonymous. For those who chose that option—often in deference to the dignity and feelings of other people in their narrative—details of identity and location have been altered. Many writers, however, chose to attach their name to their memoir.

For many of the authors, the process of putting their experiences into words has acted as a catalyst for further self-reflection on their life history. A life is often changed by such deep introspection. Over seventeen years of encouraging this type of work, the editors have consistently observed that the process of autobiographical writing can have a profound transformative effect on the spiritual, moral, and emotional domains of a writer's life. We have found would-be contributors overwhelmingly open to the invitation to make sense of their childhood and adolescent experiences, which up to then may have been inchoate and unintegrated. This opportunity to reflect can reconcile them to trauma and lend emotional resolution and understanding to the primary relationships and vicissitudes in their lives. As editors, we have felt deeply privileged to be guiding student writers through deeper levels of self-understanding and helping them gain purchase on the world through self-analysis and articulation.

Russell Leong's introduction organizes the essays by patterns and themes, and the editors have chosen to arrange the memoirs to reflect this organization. While certain motifs are indeed prevalent in the chapters identified in the introduction, each essay explores a multiplicity of themes. We want readers to appreciate the complexity of these as they play themselves out in the fourteen essays, which invited us to appreciate the courage, resilience, and insight of some remarkable young men and women.

The editors are deeply indebted to many friends and associates for the realization of this book. Nora Yasumura, the advisor for Asian and Asian American students at Dartmouth College, has been a staunch supporter of our project since its beginning and has offered, invaluably, names of potential contributors. Dean of Admissions Karl Furstenberg gave us priceless help and information. Dody Riggs supplied essential editorial suggestions as manuscripts achieved their final forms, and former and present students at Dartmouth have served critical roles in the essays' preparation and the book's production. These students include Michael Holmes, Adam Tapley, Kate Szilagyi, David Morse, Allan Klinge, Daren Simkin, January Moult, Annie Delehanty, Ben Young, Rosie Hughes, Nathan Raines, Kenneth Muigai, Pavel Bogdan, Licyau Wong, Erika Sogge, and Rafael Mendez. All have helped markedly to improve and edit the text. Our heartfelt thanks to Candace Akins and Katy Meigs for fine-tuning the text for publication.

The editors of *Balancing Two Worlds* particularly want to recognize *all* the students who worked with such industry, openness, and courage to bring their stories from the realm of the strictly private into more public view. Those who do not show up here have given no less generously of themselves. Finally, we salute the perseverance, insight, and honesty of all those whose essays make up this book.

Notes

1. Stacey J. Lee and Kevin K. Kumashiro, *A Report on the Status of Asian Americans and Pacific Islanders in Education: Beyond the "Model Minority" Stereotype* (Washington, D.C.: National Education Association, 2005), xi.
2. William Zinsser, ed., *Inventing the Truth: The Art and Craft of Memoir* (New York: Mariner, 1998), 6.

José Clemente Orozco, *The Epic of American Civilization: Migration* (Panel 1), 1932–1934. Hood Museum of Art, Commissioned by the Trustees of Dartmouth College, Hanover, New Hampshire

Introduction by Russell C. Leong   Asian Americans

"NOW BECOMING AWARE OF THEIR OWN PERSONALITY"

The American continental races are now becoming aware of their own personality, as it emerges from two cultural currents – the indigenous and the
European.

Prospectus for Dartmouth Mural, "Epic of American Civilization," José
Clemente Orozco, 1932

In 2004, when I first stumbled into the reserve room in the basement of
the Baker Library at Dartmouth College as a visiting speaker, I did not realize that it contained one of the greatest masterpieces of public art in the
United States: the Orozco frescoes. The intensity and passion of José
Clemente Orozco's vision of mankind,[1] culled from a New World sensibility that contained both Christ and Quetzalcoatl, made me ask myself,
how and when would Asians also be considered a part of these native and
migratory American cultural currents?

In the 1930s, when Orozco was painting these frescoes, discriminatory
alien land laws declared Asians not born in the United States ineligible for
naturalized citizenship; miscegenation laws prohibited marriages between
races; and legal and de facto discrimination kept many Asians in segregated
urban ghettos and schools.[2] A decade later, during World War II, 110,000
Japanese Americans were interned in bleak barbed-wired camps scattered
across the western United States.[3] During this period, the Koreans, East
Indians, Filipinos, and Chinese who had emigrated to Hawaii or to the
continental United States or to other parts of North, Central, or Latin
America were still seen as immigrants and settlers, rather than as true

Americans with any contributions to make, other than their labor. Under such circumstances, it is no wonder that Asian Americans were not seen as part of the broader vision of American civilization.[4]

Fifty years have passed since the "Epic of American Civilization" was brought to life on Dartmouth's plaster walls. The graphic magnitude, depth, and artistry of Orozco's societal and political concerns remain unrivaled. Today, however, we cannot imagine an America without two other major currents of our culture: the African and the Asian. While the black power, civil rights, and literary, cultural, and political movements of African Americans during the past fifty years have toned and shaped what we now call American culture, the Asian American influence has been perhaps more subtle but just as powerful, and today is increasingly transnational due to continued immigration from Asia.[5] And, for the record, we might also add a third cultural current: after 9/11, the United States and Americans became profoundly aware of the significance of Islam and the Middle East, both within and outside of our borders. Unfortunately, this latest current has been seen primarily in narrow and prejudicial terms, without the type of historical context that has occurred in the case of African and Asian Americans.[6]

Today, due to immigration and refugee resettlement, more than ten million Asians and Pacific Islanders live in the United States. Before the 1965 Immigration Act, Asians who entered the United States were severely restricted. With the end of the Vietnam War in 1975, Southeast Asian refugees, including Vietnamese, Cambodians, and Laotians, began to enter the United States.[7]

According to the National Education Association's report, "The Status of Asian Americans and Pacific Islanders in Education," the Asian American and Pacific Islander category "is very diverse with over 50 ethnic groups, 100 language groups. . . . Asian Indians, Chinese, Filipinos, Koreans, and Vietnamese make up 80% of the AAPI category. The other large AAPI groups are: Japanese, Hmong, Lao, Native Hawaiian, Pakistani, Samoan, and Thai."[8] Some are multiple-generation Americans, some are immigrants, and others are refugees. Mixed-race peoples and adopted children continue to break racial and ethnic barriers and stereotypes. Diversity in religion and sexual orientation also means that Asian Americans and Pacific Islanders must be seen as multidimensional peoples, rather than as models of either extraordinary economic and educational success or of dire poverty and hopelessness.[9]

Becoming Aware Now

Those who find themselves living in the Americas, no matter what their ethnic, educational, or economic background, must ultimately "become their own personalities," melding their point of view with their points of origin and their places of settlement. For immigrant or refugee families and their children, this "process of becoming" often means struggling with the contradictions of race, generation, economics, class, work, religion, gender, and sexuality within the family, workplace, or school.

Perhaps nowhere is the struggle more raw, poignant, and moving than in the words of the younger generation at the cusp of such becoming. What does becoming mean for the fourteen Dartmouth students whose essays are gathered in this book?

In asking questions, these students seek answers, however provisional or pragmatic. We readers can also find insights within the candid accounts of their personal lives and in the experiences of their family and friends. However, rather than dealing primarily with issues such as class, racial violence, political representation, the skewed economic status of Asian Americans (rich and poor), or gender inequalities, these students have elected to focus on their own identities and the process of discovering their own personalities. In so doing, they allow us intimate glimpses into the nature of the individual social and psychological development of some young Asian Americans in the first decade of the twenty-first century.

Despite their varied socioeconomic and ethnic backgrounds, these fourteen students all found themselves at an Ivy League school, having been nurtured, encouraged, and taught to reach their educational (and market) potential in a society in which an elite education is key to further social mobility. Nonetheless, these writings are as sensitive to issues of generation, gender, and race as they are to the varied class backgrounds of their mostly immigrant first-generation mothers and fathers. Although this book contains essays by students of Chinese, Japanese, Korean, Vietnamese, Burmese, South Asian, and mixed racial ancestry, it does not include the stories of Cambodian, Hmong, Laotian, Thai, Native Hawaiian, Samoan, or Filipino students. This fact perhaps reflects current class and educational realities and disparities in the United States: that is, the skewed educational and economic success of East and South Asian Americans as compared with Southeast Asians and Pacific Islanders, if measured by conventional indices including U.S. Census statistics, housing, and poverty levels.[10]

As Dean Krishna states in his essay, "American Pie," "In the end, it all comes full circle: for all the psychological progressions I make about my future place in this world, I am constantly mediating my historical identity." He joins others as he grapples with defining a social and cultural identity. Their questions are individual, but at the same time also collective and authentic in their quest to be a woman or a man, to be a citizen, to believe or not to believe, to reconcile race, religion, and generation, or to integrate gender and sexuality. Above all, these essays uncover the quest to be human in an epoch that tends to homogenize and dehumanize difference.

Generations of "Sticks and Salt"

In understanding and contextualizing the essays collected here, I have looked to scholars who currently do research on Asian Americans, especially on 1.5-generation (foreign-born but arriving in the United States between ages five and twelve) and second-generation youth identity. According to Pyong Gap Min and Kyeyoung Park, "The abolition in 1965 of the forty-year-old Asian exclusion act, close post-war political, military, and economic connections between the United States and several Asian countries, and the fall of South Vietnam in 1975 have resulted in a mass influx of Asian immigrants to the United States."[11] They state that many children of these post-1965 Asian immigrants and refugees have completed their college education, while others currently attend school. However, it was not until the mid-1980s that 1.5-generation and second-generation students became a significant part of the student body in schools, colleges, and universities in Los Angeles, San Francisco, New York, Honolulu—at community colleges as well as state colleges and universities and elite private universities. For these students, a major issue is ethnic attachment—to their family, community, and religion—or ethnic identity—with their country of origin. Such identities, according to Min and Park, are "multiple, fluid, and heterogeneous, as well as gendered, classed, racialized and ethnicized."[12] Although it is a truism that generational identities often involve familial and peer conflict, such struggles also can help to generate new identities within a dialectal process of becoming.

Patrick S. is 1.5 generation, born and raised in Korea. At the age of four he moved to the United States. In his essay "Distilling My Korean American Identity," Patrick states that "philosophy offered a middle ground between the 'stone-cold hardness' of science and the 'mushiness' of English."

He decides to pursue philosophy rather than his original major in biology. Patrick, in his quest toward self-actualization, discovers that "the real process of getting to know your identity involves as much an element of creation as it does of discovery. The very act of searching for one's identity may in fact unavoidably affect what one 'finds' and what one chooses to jettison."

Phuoc Nguyen's account is less sanguine. In "Sticks and Salt" he contrasts the experiences of his mother, a Vietnamese refugee, to his own upbringing in the United States. Not having a traditional father (his father left the family early on) and having a mother who encouraged and doggedly pushed her children toward higher education (which sometimes included physical beatings) sets up a pattern of conflict within Phuoc Nguyen. His essay attempts to reconcile his mother's expectations with his own process of becoming acculturated in the United States. As he states, "Bringing you into the world entitles them to your eternal deference, no matter how much pain they have caused you."

Coping with generational differences takes myriad forms that may involve the intellectual, psychological, and even the physical. Amy Lee, in "Turning against Myself," is a second-generation woman born and raised in New York's Chinatown. She candidly admits she is "yellow on the outside and white on the inside," having become estranged from her family and community by the time she entered college. In high school she was diagnosed with hystiocytic lymphoma—cancer of lymphatic system stem cells. After twelve weeks of intensive chemotherapy and five weeks of radiation she is in remission but has lost much of her hair and gained thirty pounds. The mental and physical scars from this experience remain with her. In learning how to cope and survive, Amy realizes that she is the one who is responsible for herself; not even friends, family, or intimate relationships can take away this responsibility for the self.

"Another shot of green tea and study some more"

As Nazli Kibria observes, it is often in the college setting that second-generation Asian Americans—including Chinese and Korean Americans—begin to revise and refine their identities, to articulate and negotiate issues of race, gender, and generation both within and outside of the classroom. She points out some common perceptions of Asian students that are useful in reading the other essays in this book. It is up to each reader to decide whether these provocative essays debunk or reinforce such perceptions, or whether they provide new ideas and images for our reflection.

Asian Americans, including students, have been positioned as a "model minority," a group that is, according to Kibria, "culturally predisposed to socioeconomic achievements. In educational settings, this stereotype is tied to the assumption that Asians are good students . . . a minority group that is successful through merit." This often excludes Asians from consideration as a minority or from affirmative action programs and creates tension and distance between Asians and other minority groups.[13]

To an extent, such positioning has led to racial hostility on college campuses and xenophobic fears of a "yellow invasion." Kibria points out, for example, that student culture uses such phrases as "Made in Taiwan" to refer to MIT and "University of Caucasians Living among Asians" to refer to UCLA—both universities with large Asian populations. Asian students are also resented for being "damned curve raisers." The reputation of Asian students as superachieving nerds is linked with the idea of foreignness. As Kibria suggests, "the deficient social skills, passivity, and orientation toward math and technical subjects . . . suggest a certain lack of comfort and familiarity with the norms and expectations of U.S. culture." She points out that another student image associated with students from Asia but that also affects Asian Americans is the image of the foreign student as a conspicuous consumer, clique-oriented around clothes, cars, and clubs. This is seen as culturally "not American," as well as gender-biased and male dominant.

Kenneth Lee, in "Receding Past, Advancing Future," presents himself as a "Burmese American who spoke neither Burmese nor practiced Buddhism. What kind of a person was I—a Burmese American in shell only?" As we learn more about Kenneth, we find that he is in fact a Sino-Burmese of Chinese descent. Kenneth gives us a vivid and moving picture both of his Chinese Burmese family and of the process of self-discovery he went through in his college years. Rather than being trapped by racial and ethnic duality, however, he learns to reconcile all the elements of his personhood: his gender and class status, his ethnic background, and the diversity of the students around him.

Fuyuki Hirashima is a second-generation Asian woman who was "raised by Japanese parents in New York City." Her life, though different from Kenneth's, is a process of "balancing on the hyphen"—also the title of her essay. Being in a college setting also challenges her—in terms of romantic relationships and the stereotypes of Asian females and around academic expectations "to excel in math and science." The stereotype, as she ironically puts it, is that "all Asians are nerds who lock themselves up in their rooms all day and study until the words become blurry. Then they take a shot of green tea and study some more."

Even names define person, gender, and one's relation to family, school, friends, and the world, according to Leah Lee, or ChungHee as her mother calls her. In her essay "Korea Is My Heart and Soul, America Is My Mind and Spirit," this second-generation Korean American woman writes that she often feels "stuck" as she tries to make sense of her femaleness and her Koreanness and accept the two as essentially who she is. "Being female is so closely tied into being Korean that at times rejecting (or accepting) one means doing the same with the other. . . . Can I hold on to the value of autonomy, of independence, of self-actualization that is so admired and sought after in American society while keeping the values of family, community, duty, and obligation that are the cornerstones of Korean society? Can I be happy with the same things that make my parents happy?" Her answer is that she remains split.

Origins and Ethnicities

One particular ethnic identity that has emerged over the past decade is the South Asian identity in the United States. Those who originate from East and Southeast Asia (China, Taiwan, Korea, Japan, Vietnam, Laos, Cambodia, Thailand, Malaysia, Indonesia, Burma, and the Philippines) have an identity in the United States that differs from those who are from South Asia (India, Pakistan, Nepal, Bhutan, Bangladesh, Sri Lanka, and the Maldives). As Rajiv Shankar points out in the foreword to *A Part, yet Apart: South Asians in Asian America*,[14] East and Southeast Asians "dominate the Asian American platform, in terms of their sheer number in this country, because of their shared sense of trauma with America, and their (by now) highly developed and motivated social and political structures within the American establishment." On the other hand, he adds, South Asians "are a significant and fast-growing branch within the Asian family, and are by themselves highly successful and self-conscious participants in the American idiom." For these reasons, we cannot merely lump the contributors to this book as Asian American without making such a differentiation in their self-recognized ethnic identity. An alternative, challenging look at contemporary South Asian American identity is presented in "Satyagraha in

America: The Political Culture of South Asian Americans," a special issue of *Amerasia Journal.* This issue offers articles that debunk the stereotype of "South Asians in the United States as a monolithic group with an essentialist culture that is offered as an exotic artifact." The editors instead see "South Asians as subjects of history, whose cultural terrain is seen as contradictory and active"—and often clashing.[15]

Asha Gupta, in "In Search of a *Sangam,*" writes about a trip to India with her mother on which they discover places that are known as *sangams,* points of confluence where bodies—geographical, physical, spiritual, or intellectual—meet. She travels to Allahabad, a village that "sits on the convergence of the rivers Ganga, Sarasvati, and Yamuna." Every twelve years, millions travel there for the Kumbh Mela, a Hindu bathing festival of rebirth. They then travel to Kanya Kumari at the southernmost tip of India. Asha states: "Breathing the air was intoxicating; all that water, all those different entities from different places that had seen different things coming together to create one being. I felt very connected to these *sangams.* The separate waters are akin to the mishmash of different origins I have felt within myself, never knowing where I fully belong, *if* I fully belong."

After this journey, Asha feels more comfortable with being both Indian and American. Despite her very Western experiences of American-style feminism, activism, sex, and drugs, she feels reconnected to her Indianness and channels it into activism and creative writing projects.

Aly Rahim grew up in Vancouver, British Columbia, as both a Muslim and a Canadian. It was not until the post-9/11 backlash that he felt "an uneasy amalgam of fear, anxiety, and apprehension, for I know my sense of identity was forever changed. . . . It is a sad truth that many members of our society will forever see my identity as an irreconcilable contradiction." Aly's family was part of the Shia Ismaili Muslim community, and his father had gone to Canada in 1972 as a political refugee from Uganda following Idi Amin's expulsion of South Asians. His father, on his return to Karachi, Pakistan, in 1979, was matched to a Pakistani bride. Now his family is part of the Ismaili success story in Canada, economically and educationally speaking. Even though Aly has not yet been the target of racial epithets or violence, in his essay he points to a more insidious challenge: "The university professor who uses authoritative scholarship to explain why Islam and Muslims are anathema to the West terrifies me far more than the evangelical pastor preaching from the pulpit."

As a child in West Des Moines, Iowa, Dean Krishna was always rubbing his dark-skinned knees to get the dirt off. However red they turned, he writes, "they would always go back to blackish brown." This is one of Dean's first experiences of difference based on racialized traits, which he describes in his essay "American Pie." His father epitomizes the American dream: he emigrated to this country with nothing and became rich by starting his own business. Yet Dean believes that was a foreigner's success and that the practical social philosophy his father had for making friends and making money does not apply to him. For Dean, the media's GI Joe image shaped his idea of what is "American." And yet Dean has always felt the American media failed him, "as it provided me with only two images of skin colors that could be an American—white or black."

Born and raised in Qatar, Sabeen Hassanali and her family settled in Houston. Her family is also part of the diaspora of Shia Ismaili Muslims who have settled throughout the world. On a visit home from college, Sabeen discovers that she is being "matched" to a young Pakistani suitor. For her, "growing up as a Pakistani American with traditional parents has meant constantly dealing with fundamentally divergent attitudes, including those toward education, love, and 'home'." She has made a conscious effort to remain "a Pakistani," grounding herself in her faith and culture while "asserting [her] autonomy." Despite her family's settling in the new land, however, she comes to the realization that her permanent home is meant to be the home of the husband whom she marries—and not necessarily by choice, but by custom. In the end, Sabeen must rely on her faith as a person, on her Pakistani American Ismaili Muslim self, to help her reach a decision about whom to marry.

What Are You?

Beyond issues of ethnic and generational identity but equally complex for these Asian American students are issues surrounding mixed-race ancestry, gender, and sexuality. According to the clinical psychologist Maria Root, multiracial persons are regularly asked such questions as, What are you? How did your parents meet? Are your parents married? Deeply entrenched stereotypes about slave masters cohabiting with black women, or of U.S. soldiers having affairs with Asian women during the Pacific Rim wars that affected China, Japan, Okinawa, Korea, the Philippines, Vietnam, Cambodia, and Laos, have led to misconceptions about race, ethnicity, and sexuality in relation to multiracial persons.[16]

Ki Mae Ponniah Heussner's mother was born in "Klang, Malaysia, to my Chinese grandmother and my Indian grandfather, and although she too grew up as a racially mixed child in a race-sensitive society, I often forget that this is an experience we share." Ki Mae's white father, from the Midwest, married her mother in graduate school, but the two divorced when Ki Mae was eighteen months old. "Most people receive their inheritance the day their parents die. I received mine the day I was born," Ki Mae states. She continues to search for herself in the medley of ethnicities and cultures that sometime leave one "dependent on them all—but alone, without any."

"I'm black and Korean, devoid of sympathy for culture vultures / that / circle over my head, a fateful halo reminds me that it's time to / be free / of the 38 parallels I've seen folks draw on me." These lines are part of his poem "On Being Asian," which begins Anthony Luckett's essay "Multi-hued." Anthony was born in Suwon, Korea, to a Korean mother and African American father. They moved to London and then settled in San Francisco. Anthony's mother and father eventually went their separate ways, and he became a foster child for a number of years. For a time he lived with a white family where he was a victim of sexual abuse. He later lived with a single Korean woman and finally with two Korean families. Despite his geographic and sexual ordeal, Anthony's most profound issue remains his biracial heritage: "To my Korean friends I always felt like the token black guy. To those two black men who passed me on 43rd Avenue one indelible night, I was a 'Chink.' The powerful feelings of contempt and racism are vivid and lasting." A moving moment in Anthony's account is when his mother asks him to change his last name (his African American father's) to his mother's Korean surname. In the end, Anthony retains his surname because "my name has been my basic identity since I was born." He concludes that "race matters. And it doesn't."

Emerging Diversities

For Asian Americans, gender and sexual roles have been tied up with the myth that they are a homogeneous, heterosexual, model minority who practice the values of hard work, discipline, filial piety, and assimilation into the American mainstream. This myth applies equally to East, Southeast, and South Asians in the United States, with various specific cultural manifestations. Such a narrow view of gender has to some degree hidden underlying issues involving domestic and household rights, immigrant rights, labor and workplace issues, women's rights, interracial relations, and anti-Asian violence. In terms of sexuality and Asians, the model minority view simply denies sexual diversity as a real issue. For Asian Americans, then, how to reconfigure personal, sexual, and racial identities takes both individual and collective forms. Most of the essays in this collection that touch on gender or sexual diversity issues focus on the personal and individual, rather than on the collective or institutional. However, as Dana Takagi, a sociologist argues, class, race, and gender cannot just be "disentangled into discrete additive parts." Marginalization is not as much about the quantity of experiences as it is about quality of experience. And, as many writers, most notably feminists, have argued, identities, whether associated with sexual preference, racial origins, language, gender, or class roots, are simply not additive.[17]

Johnny Lee's "No Such Thing . . ." probes issues of male sexual identity and homosexuality. He describes poignant scenes of his Korean mother confronting him with tears and a Bible about his sexuality, and the possibility that his own father might have had gay experiences. The essay is more complex than the usual coming-out account that tends to blame the conservative Asian culture. As Johnny concludes, "Korean society, as many will tell you, is generally not accepting of gays. It's a fact I have grown to understand and live with. However, I do not tell my story to have Korean culture criticized as backward and antiquated. Even through all the sadness, I never once damned my parents, nor my Koreanness."

Vincent Ng ("Farewell My *Tung-Tew*") is, in his own words, "an ambivalent twenty-one-year-old Chinese Canadian still exploring my sexual orientation." *Tung-Tew* is Cantonese for a Chinese feather duster often used for corporal punishment. In Vincent's essay, it is used as a metaphor for the type of punishment his father experienced from his own father. The harsh and ambivalent relationship between sons and fathers overlaps generations, as Vincent discovers when he attempts to reveal his sexual orientation to his father: "I longed for openness in our relationship, yet I instead received a very limited definition of masculinity that excluded vulnerability." Nonetheless, Vincent's college years provide him a way to break down the traditional "molds that my Chinese father had set down, exploring things in dramatic and even ostentatious ways."

Future Impulses: Practicing Faith

While reading these fourteen essays, I discovered a closer, though unforeseen, linkage between Orozco's earlier vision of "creating here an authentic New World civilization" and the early visions of these young Asian American students. Their essays, read as a whole, serve as an indicator of an American society that strives to be multiethnic and multicultural yet remains a flawed and ferocious civilization. Precisely because these essays are personal accounts of migration and settlement, of family and friends, they compel us as readers to face the mirror of history and time, to ask ourselves basic fragmented questions of identity once again: Who am I? Who are you? What do I desire? What do you desire? Am I a part of, or apart from, my family and community?

Within this dual impulse toward both belonging and transformation, family and religious practices take on new currency and meaning for a number of these writers. Whether from Korea, Pakistan, Japan, Singapore, Vietnam, Burma, or "born in the USA," the writers have seen the religion of their parents and communities tested by migration, assimilation, sexual orientation, and the fire of a post-9/11 American society.

Johnny Lee, for instance, recounts how "internal conflicts quickly arose as soon as I hit puberty, which was when I realized that I was more interested in penises than vaginas. Afraid of eternal damnation, I tried for years to repress any and all thoughts of sex as much as I could."

Yet for others, faith was a constant in the formation of family values and relations. As Aly Rahim notes, "Religion seemed to be an important part of many of my non-Muslim friends' families, so I did not think its role in mine was unusual." For Rahim and Sabeen Hassanali, who are both Pakistani Ismaili Muslims, their faith-based identity was sorely tested after 9/11, when being both Muslim and South Asian were conflated as "the foreign, terrorist other."

On the other hand, some Asian Americans tried to blend into the white world, like Kenneth Lee, of Burmese descent. For him and many others, language and faith were significant markers of ethnic identity—even if they were not spoken or practiced in daily life. After all, within the homogenizing impulses of American society, there were few things that made them different, and these differences included political beliefs, sexual orientation, faith and religious practices, and language.

As I first wrote this introduction, thousands were being rescued and hundreds had already died in the muddy quagmire of New Orleans and the surrounding Mississippi Delta. Whether in Biloxi, Beijing, Baghdad, or

Bangladesh, the world media cannot help but compare Hurricane Katrina and its aftermath with the recent Southeast Asian tsunami and the quagmire of the U.S. occupation in Iraq. As these global events unfold, they force us not only to look *within* ourselves but *beyond* ourselves. After all, we are citizens of a world that is in conflict yet connected through blood and water, guns and gold, desire and disease, spirit and body—and last but not least, by the written word.

Notes

1. See http://hoodmuseum.dartmouth.edu/collections/orozco/migration.html.
2. Sucheng Chan, *Asian Americans: An Interpretive History* (New York: Twayne, 1991).
3. Jerry Kang, "Thinking through Internment: 12/7 and 9/11," in *Asian Americans on War and Peace*, ed. Russell Leong and Don Nakanishi (Los Angeles: UCLA Asian American Studies Center Press, 2002), 55–62.
4. See "Asians in the Americas: Transculturations and Power," *Amerasia Journal* 28, no. 2 (2002), and "Across the Color Line, *Amerasia Journal* 26, no. 3 (2000–2001), with articles by Grace Lee Boggs, Vijay Prashad, Arif Dirlik, Mitchell Chang, and Claire Jean Kim.
5. Russell C. Leong, "To Our Readers," foreword to "Edward Said's Orientalism and Asian American Studies," *Amerasia Journal* 31, no. 1 (2005).
6. Leong and Nakanishi, *Asian Americans on War and Peace*.
7. "30 Years Afterward: Vietnam and U.S. Empire," *Amerasia Journal* 31, no. 2 (2005).
8. Stacey J. Lee and Keven K. Kumashiro, *A Report on the Status of Asian Americans and Pacific Islanders in Education: Beyond the "Model Minority" Stereotype* (Washington, D.C.: National Education Association, 2005).
9. Helen Zia, *Asian American Dreams: The Emergence of an American People* (New York: Farrar, Straus, Giroux, 2000).
10. Eric Lai and Dennis Arguelles, eds., *The New Face of Asian Pacific America: Numbers, Diversity, and Change in the 21st Century* (Los Angeles: UCLA Asian American Studies Press and *Asian Week*, 2003).
11. Pyong Gap Min and Kyeyoung Park, "Second Generation Asian Americans' Ethnic Identity," introduction to *Amerasia Journal* 25, no. 1 (1999), ix–xiii, and Min Zhou, "Coming of Age: The Current Situation of Asian American Children," *Amerasia Journal* 25, no. 1 (1999): 1–27. In the same issue of *Amerasia Journal*, see articles by Hung C. Thai on Vietnamese youth, Bangele D. Alsaybar on Filipino youth, Kyeyoung Park on Korean youth, Joann Hong and Pyong Gap Min on Korean adolescents, and Mia Tuan on multigenerational Asian ethnics.
12. Ibid.
13. Nazli Kibria, "College and Notions of 'Asian American': Second-Generation Chinese and Korean Americans Negotiate Race and Identity," *Amerasia Journal* 25, no. 1 (1999): 29–51.
14. See the foreword by Rajiv Shankar in Lavina Shankar and Rajini Srikanth, *A Part, yet Apart: South Asians in Asian America* (Philadelphia: Temple University Press, 1998), ix–xv.
15. See *Amerasia Journal* 25, no. 3 (2000).
16. See Maria Root, ed., *The Multiracial Experience: Racial Borders as the New Frontier* (Thousand Oaks, Calif.: Sage Publications, 1996), 3–34.
17. Dana Y. Takagi, "Maiden Voyage: Excursion into Sexuality and Identity Politics in Asian America," in *Asian American Sexualities: Dimensions of the Gay and Lesbian Experience*, ed. Russell Leong (New York: Routledge, 1995), 21–35.

GENERATING NEW IDENTITIES

Phuoc Nguyen Sticks and Salt

"*Con không biết mạ đã trở qua bao nhiêu là nội khổ để đem con qua nước Mỹ này*—You don't know how much I went through to bring you to this country," my mother said in a soft voice as she lay staring at the ceiling. A stream of tears flowed from the corner of her eyes and down past her ears and, finally, was absorbed by her pillow. At times like this, I would sit next to my mother on our torn carpet listening to her recount the tragedies that happened to her in her previous life—the life of misery she left behind in Vietnam. My older sister, Chau, on the other hand, could never stand to listen to our mother's repetitious stories. She would usually go to our other bedroom, close the door, and delve into the imaginary world of romance novels. I remember praying at the start of these episodes that I would not end up crying myself, because my mother instilled in me her native belief that *nam nhi đại trượng phu đổ máu không rơi lệ*—real heroes never show tears even if they are bleeding to death. No gods or spirits answered my prayers, however, and after each episode I would feel low and unmanly because I had let tears fall—even though I wasn't bleeding to death!

"*Dạ mạ*—Yes, mom," I respectfully responded. In Vietnamese culture a child must always acknowledge his parent with a polite "*Dạ*" (pronounced *ya*); any less respectful response could well lead to a beating. Soon after I learned how to talk I realized that being polite was much better than being hit.

"When I was your age, living in my village, I never had a full meal to eat. Most days we would only be given one small bowl of rice and a dab of fish paste for flavor. I wasn't as lucky as you are today. I could never eat meat every day like you can. No wonder you're so big and tall." As far back as I can remember, my mother always started her stories by establishing that her childhood was utterly bleak compared with my life of luxury. To this day I am not sure whether she wanted me to feel grateful that I had enough food to eat or was pitying herself as she realized the vast contrast between her younger years and mine.

"But Mom, you said before that your village was next to the sea. How come you didn't go fishing to get more food?" As a child I enjoyed asking my mother questions during her storytelling, not because I was curious about her life but because it allowed me to get a word in. I felt important and satisfied when I actually said more than just *dạ mạ*. In a Vietnamese family, when an adult is talking it is usually considered extremely rude for a youngster to interrupt or speak their mind about *anything*. This is especially true when adults are having a conversation and children *nói hốt*—cut in. I recall painful slaps in the face when I cut off my mother's sentences with simple questions such as, "When's dinner gonna be ready, Ma?" or "Can I go over to Son's house to play?" Considering that a burning red cheek was the normal result of asking my mother questions while she was talking, I felt ecstatic when my inquiries led to answers instead of pain.

"Well, son, it wasn't easy to catch fish in the terrible waters of the South China Sea. Sometimes, on bad days, entire fishing boats would sink with their crews aboard. So, the little fish that we *did* manage to catch we would make the most of. Now, where was I? . . . Oh, yes, about my childhood . . . *Trời ơi*," she said with a sigh. After a short, uncomfortable pause, she continued: "I was cruelly beaten daily by your grandmother, and often for no good reason. She had fourteen children, but I was the only one who ever got punished. I don't know why. She'd beat me if I didn't fetch enough firewood for cooking. Or if I didn't cut up enough food to feed the pigs. Or if I stopped fanning her during those scorching summer days because my hands felt like jelly. Or . . ." And on and on. At this point in her narrative I would have difficulty understanding her because her nose was stopped up from crying so much. Sometimes I tried to pay closer attention so that I could catch everything, but often I would not bother since I knew by heart all that she wanted to say.

"I remember one time I was playing jump rope with my friends near the Buddhist temple. Well, after only a little bit of jumping my mother came running toward me, very angry. She screamed, '*Ông cố nội mi*—Damn your great-grandfather, Huong! [a slang term used to scold severely]. I told you to watch *Gái* [my mother's younger sister] in case she wants to take a shit. Now she's shitting all over the floor inside the house and what are you doing here? *Playing?*'" My mother caught her breath as she stopped crying, then continued. "She was so mad her body was shaking. Then she picked up a huge stick and whacked me so hard on my head. I was bleeding everywhere. The cut left a lifelong scar." As always, my mother parted her hair in the center and leaned her body toward me to show me the remnant of that day. Whenever I saw it I would think of the irony; my older sister has a scar in exactly the same spot from when my mother smashed a glass bowl on her head because my sister did not finish her chore properly. I felt sad for both of them because their mothers had treated them with such violent cruelty, but I felt more sorry for Chau because her mother was perpetuating a custom that she abhorred: the custom of using the switch instead of words to teach your children. My mother never saw how ironic her actions were. She believed it was her duty to discipline her children so they would not end up as *bụi đời*—the dust of life, the wretched—joining gangs or getting pregnant before having a career.

"I never had a chance to go to school past kindergarten," my mother continued. "Grandmother didn't want to spend the money to send me to the village schoolhouse. She said that I'd be more useful at home tending the pigs and chickens. You're so lucky, you know that? To be able to go to school every day and not have hours of chores to do when you get home. That's why you have to do well in school, or else you'll be such a disappointment to me." For some reason I sensed that my mother deliberately added that last sentence just to get a message through to me.

"The worst period in my life was after I married your father. I had just given birth to Chau, when your father disappeared without a trace. I finally tracked him down in Hanoi. I found that he was living with his first wife, a woman that he had never told me about." The intermission was over and the stream of tears started flowing again. "I was devastated to discover that the man I loved and trusted had betrayed me."

After hearing my mother describe my father's deceit, I simultaneously felt resentment, sympathy, guilt, vengefulness, and incredible sadness. I resented and even hated my father for ruining my mother's life. The anger I felt was so overwhelming that I would tremble and have trouble breathing. Sometimes I sat there and just wished that he were standing right in front of me so that I could pick him up by the throat and slam him against the wall as hard as I could. I'd scream at him, "You damn asshole! How could you treat your wife like that? Don't you have a conscience? Is this the model that you want your children to follow? I am ashamed to be your son! But don't worry, I won't turn out to be like you, you piece of shit!" At the same time, I felt sympathy for the incredible pain my mother must have endured since that episode. She did nothing wrong; her only mistake was falling in love with a lying womanizer. Yet, oddly, mixed together with my pool of negative emotions was a slight ripple of joy. I felt happy that my mother was courageous enough to take her children away and leave her unfaithful husband behind in his poverty-stricken home in Vietnam. I was shamelessly content that he still had to live in filth with his first wife, while our family, although poor compared with others in America, at least had enough to eat every day.

Throughout my early childhood, scenes like the one described above were commonplace. Almost anything would set my mother to telling those stories: seeing happy couples walking together in the park, my sister and I not doing our chores, watching television shows that depicted any aspect of Vietnam, and especially if any of her children were not doing well in school (i.e., not getting straight A's). At night, after hearing her stories, I would cry myself to sleep thinking of how much I should hate my father and how much I should love and respect my mother. I could not comprehend how my father could have consciously treated my mother as inhumanely as he did. What confused and bothered me even more was how, after suffering so much because of him, she still treated him and his family with deference, as I eventually discovered.

My family life has been undeniably eventful for as long as I can remember. My first memories are of escaping from Vietnam and landing in Hong Kong, a stopping point on the way to our final destination, America. Though I only recall random scenes of our journey, my mother has filled in the rest so I have a fairly detailed knowledge of those few days that drastically altered our lives.

In the spring of 1981, my mother, then fairly wealthy thanks to a prospering business, decided that she wanted to give her two children educational opportunities that her country could not offer. She did not see a fruitful future for us because our father had abandoned us and because of our status as Southern Vietnamese. When the *Viet Cong*, the Communists, unified the country, they discriminated against those who associated themselves with the South during the war. I was only four years old, my sister just six, when on one ordinary night my mother told us to say good-bye forever to our homeland. . . .

A blinding flash of light snatched me from my restful sleep. Five seconds later the inevitable boom of thunder crashed around our little boat and sent everyone into a state of panic. By this time my uncle had turned on the motor, so the vessel moved swiftly. Unfortunately, the speed of our craft was not the only change in our condition; I could feel that the constant swaying motion had turned into erratic jerking. When I peered out into the darkness I saw an army of massive waves rushing toward us.

"*Mạ, con sợ qúa*—Mommy, I'm so scared!" I cried. But the raindrops on my face hid my tears and the booming thunder drowned out my attempts to communicate with my mother. I finally caught her attention by pulling on her sleeve as hard as I could.

"*Con đừng sợ nhé*—Don't be afraid, son," my mother comforted me. "It's just a little storm. It'll be over real soon." She covered my sister and me with a plastic bag, and we huddled so close to her that I could feel her heartbeat.

"*Chị Huồng ơi, Chị Huồng!*—Sister Huong, Sister Huong!" cried my Uncle Thuy, suddenly approaching us from out of nowhere. He continued in a disconcerting tone, "There's too much weight on this end of the boat. We need more people to move to the bow. If we don't do it fast then waves will flip us right over. Put Phuoc on your back and I'll put Chau on mine. Then we'll slowly walk up there."

"Phuoc," she said directly into my ear because at any other distance the thunder would drown out her voice. "We're moving to the front of the boat. I'm going to give you a piggyback ride, so you grab on as tight as you can, okay?"

"*Dạ*," I acknowledged, and quickly climbed onto her back while the storm pummeled my body with what felt like a thousand pebbles. Without thinking, I locked my arms around my mother's neck and grabbed each of my wrists with the opposite hand. Then, I wrapped my legs around her waist and held them tightly together. As we began inching toward our destination just a few meters away, my awareness of my surroundings increased tenfold. I saw every wave as it crashed into the side of the boat, I anticipated each boom of thunder, and I felt every drop of rain against my skin as if it were a needle piercing my body. I held tight to my mother and did not budge, and it seemed as though I became an extension of her body. When she lifted her left foot to take a step, I felt the left half of my frame move with her. Amazingly, I did not cry during our trip to the bow. I guess I just trusted my mother to keep me alive.

"*Gần tới rồi con à*—We're almost there son," my mother said. "Don't worry." When I looked up I saw the bow just a few steps away, but I did not yet feel that I could breathe a sigh of relief, and I kept my tight lock around my mother's neck and waist. It turned out that intuitive action saved my life, because a few seconds after her reassuring words, a huge wave slammed into the side of our boat with such force that it threw her off her feet and sent us plunging into the freezing, choppy waters of the South China Sea. I do not recall feeling scared. When I was under water my instinct told me to hold onto my mother as tightly as I could, to close my eyes to avoid the sting of the salty seawater, and to close my mouth so as not to swallow anything. I do not know why I didn't panic; I just didn't. Fortunately, my uncle, who was following closely behind with my sister, dove in after us when he saw our fall. We were quickly brought back aboard the boat.

Following our dramatic rescue, the heavens blessed us with sunshine and peaceful waters. The gods also bestowed another miracle on us. Several days after our departure, just when we were about to deplete our food supply, we came across a cargo ship headed toward the very destination we wished to reach: Hong Kong. A year later, in April 1982, my mother began to realize her dream of raising us in a land where opportunities, not obstacles, lay before us. What she did not realize was that she herself, by trying to instill in us her native culture, would become the major obstacle to her children's success in American society.

Throughout my early adolescence I wished I had a more understanding mother. I believe that most of my growing pains could have been avoided if my mother had experienced similar feelings when she was an adolescent. Mother did have growing pains but not the type characterized by self-consciousness and rebelliousness that is associated with adolescence in America. She spent her teenage years as a house servant in *Huế*, a large city in central Vietnam, so the problems she faced during her adolescence were obviously far different from the ones I faced during mine. She never had the opportunity to think about herself because she spent all of her waking hours doing chores for others. In contrast, my adolescent environment was relatively self-involved and self-absorbed; my concerns centered primarily on myself rather than on others. Thus, my mother tended to trivialize the difficulties I encountered because she thought—and logically so—they were far less serious than what she had experienced as a teenager. Because our adolescent worlds were as different as black and white, my mother had no idea how to deal with a son who was changing dramatically right before her eyes. She did not know how best to assist me through the tough times because she had no understanding of the cultural and social pressures facing teens growing up in America. She was often insensitive and apathetic when I came to her with adolescent issues that were serious to me, such as when schoolmates made fun of me or when I asked her to buy gel for my hair.

When puberty first began I did not think it was going to be the time of tremendous psychological change that the sex education videos at school had depicted. I felt like the same little kid that I had been before: going to class in the morning, coming home to do homework and watch television in the afternoon, talking to my mother before going to bed, repeating this same routine day after day. The only difference that was obvious to me was that my voice started cracking—but even that did not bother me because I understood it as a natural part of human development.

At the time I was only aware of my physical transformation, but I can now see that a mental change had begun in me as well. Starting in junior high, I remember gradually gaining an awkward self-consciousness and low self-esteem, a newfound interest in girls, and an awareness of my lack of peer relationships. In retrospect, I can see that my experience was nothing out of the ordinary for a child of that age. Yet, my life did have an additional, *extra*ordinary factor. Culturally, the conditions under which I interacted with others my own age were typically American, while at home I confronted a virtually traditional Vietnamese environment. On the one hand, my mother did not understand American culture and disapproved of the American beliefs—such as gender and racial equality or free speech in the family—that I had adopted. On the other hand, the children at school who were not Vietnamese did not accept the culturally Vietnamese side of me, probably because they saw it as strange, as not being "normal."

Before the sixth grade I never thought about how I looked. Yes, I knew that I was Vietnamese, but I never felt that I was an outsider in school because of my racial difference. With the onset of adolescence, however, I became acutely aware of my bodily characteristics. In grade school I was your stereotypical skinny, short, brainy Asian kid with a bowl haircut. In prior years, when kids made fun of me by calling me "Chink" or "nerd," I usually paid no attention to them. This was true until an incident in which I received a disciplinary referral and was sent home.

One day, during music class, a Caucasian classmate, Eugene, was getting upset because the teacher, Mr. Epstein, had told him he was out of tune. The entire class giggled as Eugene squeaked the words to "Yankee Doodle Went to Town." I, being a wiseguy, said loudly, "No more, Eugene, please!" With a frustrated look Eugene quickly turned to me and yelped, "Shut up, you damn *Chink*!" The old me would have just laughed it off without giving what he said a second thought, but that day something else came over me. A rush of anger swept through me, and I wanted to beat him up right there, on the spot. The only thing that restrained me from doing so was my music teacher; I did not want to disrespect him by disrupting the class. So, I decided to wait until later. When recess time came and we were all let out on the grass field to play kickball, I had only one thing on my mind. As soon as I caught sight of Eugene I ran over and tackled him to the ground with all the might that my eighty-pound body could muster. We wrestled around on the grass, throwing blind punches at each other until the recess supervisor pulled us apart and gave us both referrals. The principal sent me home because I was the one who started the fight. Eugene's words had somehow touched a highly sensitive area inside me, an area that told me that I was not the same as everyone else. His words had made me feel incredibly low.

When I came home that day, my mother saw my scrapes and bruises and immediately became concerned. Strangely, I did not feel any pain when she rubbed the eucalyptus oil (a Vietnamese cure-all) on my wounds. Instead I felt proud and confident, because this time, unlike previous times, I had stood up for myself when others might have thought I would be weak and passive. My raised spirits were short-lived, however, because in one sentence my mother demolished whatever strength I had gained at the time.

"What?" my mother asked. "You got in a fight because he said you were Asian? *Sau con ngu qúa vậy?*—Why are you so stupid, son?" She spoke as if she didn't believe that "Chink" was a derogatory word. Maybe if I told her again, I thought, she would understand.

"But, Mom, that word is racist! He wasn't just saying that I was *Asian*," I repeated. "It had a different meaning."

"Who cares what he meant," she responded. "It's just a word. Those white people are all racist anyway. Next time he says that to you, just ignore it." Ignore it? *What?* How could I do that when Eugene had insulted me? And how could my mother say that *all* Caucasians are racist? Didn't the fact that she uttered those words brand *her* a racist? "And they're bigger than you, you know. I don't want you to get hurt again. We're smaller than they are, so we just have to act our size. Next time he makes fun of you, just turn your head and laugh." I did not know how else to persuade her. My mother did not seem to understand that in America equality is cherished and sought after, while prejudice is not tolerated. Wasn't that why she decided to risk her life and the lives of her children to come here in the first place? My mother's words directly conflicted with what my teachers had taught me in school for years. How could I reconcile this? I could not believe what she said or do as she ordered because the morals that I had acquired from school were too strong.

This incident posed yet another problem for me: When should I listen to my mother and when should I not? In the past she had always taught me the dos and don'ts of life, the difference between right and wrong, and how to be a good person. It was simple—mother was always right, no matter what. Thus, I always listened and took her words to heart. Now that I recognized a flaw in her beliefs I did not know what to do or to whom to go. Incidents such as this were not unusual in the years before I entered high school.

Another example of the cultural clashes that plagued me is the traditional beatings I received from my mother throughout most of my childhood and early adolescence. In elementary school, all my teachers taught me that excessive spankings were not a productive or lawful form of discipline. They said that in the past Americans did spank their children, and even teachers were allowed to physically chastise naughty students. However, they said, American culture has progressed since then and few parents still beat their children. Now everyone considers physical punishment cruel, barbaric, and potentially traumatizing for the child. In contrast, in Vietnamese culture beatings were as normal and accepted as hugs and kisses and "I love yous" are in American culture.

Whenever I went to school after a beating I tried my hardest to hide any signs of having been punished. I felt embarrassed and ashamed that my mother still practiced this barbaric custom. When I learned about child abuse in the classroom I could not help but ask myself whether the pain my mother inflicted on me was abuse. Yet, the idea of reporting her to the authorities never entered my mind. I still do not know why I did not tell anyone. Maybe I thought that people would look down on my family if they found out the truth, or that my mother's reputation would be blemished. Maybe fear of my mother's wrath also played a role. Probably most important to me was the thought of what would happen if she were arrested. I feared I would end up in an orphanage, maybe a foster home if I were lucky. That possible outcome was not particularly appealing to me. Consequently, up until my high school years I passively accepted my punishment while being tormented by the knowledge that it was wrong. My mother, however, did not think that hitting me was anything out of the ordinary.

Vietnamese village tradition justifies, even promotes, beating children as a sign of concern and love for them. With this in mind, my mother must have loved us a great deal because she showed her concern and love for us time and time again. She spanked us primarily when we were disobedient: talking back, cutting in on adult conversations, speaking English inordinately at home, not completing chores, staying out too late, fighting with each another, and especially bringing home report cards with anything less than straight As.

A typical beating occurred in the fourth grade when I brought home a report card on which I received a B+ in handwriting (in *handwriting*, for goodness sake!). After glimpsing at my grades with anticipation, apprehension immediately set in; I knew the penalty that was waiting for me at home. And that day I walked home especially slowly in an attempt to prolong the period that I was *not* in physical pain. Alas, nothing can last forever. When I showed my mother my grades, tears were already flowing down my face, as if I wanted to get warmed up before the *real* crying began. As soon as my mother saw the B+ she instantly switched into her raging disciplinary mode.

"*Bé, lấy cây roi*—Chau, go get a switch," my mother said. My sister knew her responsibility and quickly fetched a fly swatter—one with a metal handle. I would perform the same duty when she was to be beaten. When our mother beat the two of us together, I was the designated switch-fetcher, since she always spanked the oldest first. My mother signaled for me to lie down on the carpet with my stomach flat against the floor. With the tool in hand, ready to inflict pain, she first started lecturing.

"Phuoc," she said in a calm voice. When she lectured her voice sounded supportive and encouraging, as if she thought that I would learn more effectively if she did not scream.

"*Dạ,*" I squeaked. *Da* was the only word I dared say, because any other words would not help reduce the punishment.

"Son, you know I brought you to America because I wanted to give you an opportunity," she continued. Out of all the ways she could hurt me, guilt was one of the most damaging because it made me feel unworthy and undeserving of the "luxurious" life I had in America. "I wanted to give you an opportunity that you could not have in Vietnam—that is, to get an education and become successful. If I had known that you would do badly in school, then why would I have risked my life and left my family and homeland just to bring you here?"

"*Dạ.*"

"Now I have to teach you that you can't disappoint me." She began raising her voice, which indicated that physical pain was approaching momentarily. "How can you get a B+ in *handwriting?*" I cried out as the thin metal handle left its mark on my bottom. My mother believed only in spanking the rear end, because it had cushioning, and wounding it would not hinder my ability to do schoolwork. She rarely hit us on the head because she thought that striking there would decrease our intellectual capacity. I lay submissive and well chastised until the punishment finally ended.

"*Thương con cho cây cho mui, ghét con cho ngọt cho đường*—Loving your child means giving them sticks and salt; hating your child means giving them sweetness and candy." In other words, hit 'em if you love 'em, spoil 'em if you hate 'em. My mother always told me this lovingly as she gave me a bath and then spread eucalyptus oil on my wounds. She probably thought that everything was over and we could continue living as if nothing had ever happened. She never considered that the physical pain she inflicted on us might be transformed into long-term emotional and psychological pain. Even now, when I ask her why she hit us so often, she responds, "You kids needed it. If I hadn't beaten you then you'd never have gotten to where you are today. You'd probably be in some Vietnamese gang somewhere. Probably robbing people's homes and killing them." Then, of course, she brings up examples of Vietnamese kids who are serving time in prison precisely because their parents gave them "sweetness and candy" rather than "sticks and salt." Apparently she sees our educational success and others' criminal behavior as a validation of her actions.

Another issue I had with my mother was her inability to empathize with my growing self-consciousness and low self-esteem. With just a few simple words or actions my mother could have raised my self-image by leaps and bounds. Instead, her insensitivity only exacerbated the effect of problems I had with my name, my hair, and my clothes.

One of the biggest causes of my low self-esteem when I started puberty was my name. For as long as I can remember almost everyone I have met has mispronounced my name at least twice. It was so embarrassing whenever I met anyone new that I wished I did not have to meet new people at all. But the worst aspect of my hard-to-pronounce Vietnamese name was the name-calling that resulted, which I endured all through school, and still endure now on occasion. From elementary school through and beyond high school my name was the subject of a laundry list of teasings. And it was not as if I had a name like "Jaime," which everyone harmlessly pronounced "Himee." People could easily turn my name into very vulgar words if they wanted to—and I believed that everyone around me wanted to. A few examples: "Fok," "Foo . . . ok," "Pook," "Fuck," "Phuoc you!" "What the Phuoc!" or "MotherPhuocer." For the extra-creative there was truly an infinite number of ways to distort my name. In my high school yearbook was a picture of me hitting a forehand—I was on the tennis team— carrying the caption, "Phuoc 'U' Nguyen kills a forehand." Those kids could not have realized that every time they poked fun at me I wanted to crawl into a cave and not come out until everyone was mature enough to accept my unique name.

Sometimes I wished I could change my name into something ordinary like John or Joe, but my mother would not have approved. She did not understand the pain and embarrassment that I was going through. When I told her about people making fun of my name she would usually laugh and say, "Fuck? Ha, ha . . . isn't that a bad word? Ha, ha . . . that's kinda funny." At those times I thought my mother was the most insensitive, uncaring person in the world. How could she laugh at me, her son, when I had just told her that everyone in school was already laughing at me? Did she think it would make me feel better if she laughed as well? Of course, I did not ask her those questions. Thinking about it now, I believe that my definitions of hurt and my mother's were completely different. The pain and hurt that she endured for most of her life in Vietnam was probably ten times more difficult than what I endured, which is why she could not see that I was in pain. She was probably thinking to herself, "You think people laughing at your name is painful? Think again, son. That's nothing compared with my pain. I'll give you an example. When I told your grandmother that your father had another wife, she was so ashamed of me that she kicked me out of her house. She said, 'You whore! How could you marry someone else's husband!' Now *that* was pain, son. I just can't see how your name could bring you that much pain." Needless to say, I never asked her if this was really what she was thinking at the time.

In junior high school, hair was of the ultimate importance to nearly everyone I knew. The pretty girls sculpted their hair to look perfect, while the cool boys slicked their dos back with gel. I, on the other hand, had a stereotypically Asian bowl haircut that was straight and flat. Everyone teased me about my hair because only "nerds" had bowl cuts. My obsession to fit in with the cool kids was so strong that I tried creative and unorthodox ways to give my hair a lift. My mother, unsurprisingly, did not care much when I mentioned that I needed gel to style my hair.

"We are not wasting money to buy useless things," she responded to my inquiry. "You're too young to be so vain. You're only a little kid."

"*Dạ mạ*," I responded as usual. However, even though my mother was unwilling to help me improve my self-esteem, I took measures to achieve this goal. My scheme was quite simple. Every morning I woke up extra early to take a shower and comb my hair back. Then, during the car ride from home to school, I rolled down the window and stuck my head outside. I found through trial and error that my hair would stay combed back the entire day if the wind blew on it long enough. When I got to school my hair looked as if I had used a blow dryer and gel. Compliments from friends and teachers made me leap for joy! The only down side to my method was that during the winter I arrived at school with a cold headache every morning. Eventually, my mother prohibited me from rolling down the window, and I unhappily went back to the nerdy bowl cut that everyone teased.

Ever since my family moved to America we have been poorer relative to most households in this country. My mother has no education and does not speak English, so one of the few jobs she could find was as a cook in Vietnamese restaurants. The little money she earned did not go very far after she paid the bills and bought food. The clothes I wore reflected our poverty. I remember that in junior high school a kid named Cody always made fun of my shoes. "Hey, how come you still wear Velcro shoes?" he ridiculed. "What, you can't tie shoelaces or something?" It was not that I could not tie shoelaces; I wore Velcro shoes because they were on clearance at the thrift store. When I asked my mother if she could buy me a new pair of shoes, she said, "What? Are your shoes torn? If they are then tape them back together. Don't act spoiled, Phuoc. You're lucky enough as it is, you know."

"I know, Mom, but these shoes are so old and they're hurting my feet," I said with a puppy-dog face, hoping she would pity me. "Can't you just get me something cheap that has laces?"

"Phuoc, Mother did not raise you to be spoiled," she said in a strict voice. I nodded and tilted my head toward the ground. "Now you know that we aren't rich. And the money that I *do* save every month I want to send to Vietnam. You know Grandpa and Grandma are much poorer than we are. So we have to tighten our belts a little so that they can enjoy their old age."

"Mother, I thought you said that you resented Grandmother. Why are you still sending money over there?" I asked in a quiet, submissive voice.

"Yes, many things she did to me were very cruel, but that doesn't give me the right to be *bất hiếu*." *Bất hiếu* means to neglect your filial piety. Filial piety and duty are as much a part of Vietnamese culture as racial equality is of American culture. This Confucian ideal dictates that you must respect and pay homage to your parents both while they are alive and after they pass. You must support them in their old age even if it means not supporting yourself first. If you are *bất hiếu* to your parents, then your children will inevitably be *bất hiếu* to you when you grow old. Bringing you into the world entitles them to your eternal deference, no matter how much pain they have caused you.

"You know what I always tell you, son," my mother continued. "The eighty-year-old emperor must still kowtow before his mother of one hundred. No matter how old or far away I am, I must always support my parents. As for you, you're not starving, you're not naked, you're not homeless. What do you have to complain about?"

I convinced myself that I *was* lucky and should not ask for too much. At nights I fought with the vanity demon inside me, who always told me I deserved a new pair of shoes. The demon's opponent was a grateful angel who constantly persuaded me, "Phuoc, be content with what you have because there are so many less fortunate ones out there." These internal clashes kept me up far past my bedtime. In the end, I still wished I had a pair of shoes with laces.

Not until college did I discover the full extent to which my family diverged from mainstream American culture. This discovery was a years-long process, during which my understanding was augmented by such factors as acting in an Asian American drama group, taking courses on East Asian philosophy, and numerous interactions with other Asian American students at my college. What I found was that Confucianism played a tremendous role in creating this disparity. Besides the tenet of filial piety, several other precepts in this ancient ideology shaped the manner in which our family lived throughout my adolescent years and, to some extent, lives to this day.

There is a widely known Chinese proverb, originating from Confucianism, that states, "A woman who marries a rooster will follow that rooster, and a woman who marries a dog will follow that dog." In essence, this proverb expresses the idea that no matter whom a woman marries, she will forever be his wife, for better or for worse. I did not realize it at the time, but many of my mother's actions that infuriated me during high school stemmed from her subconscious conformity to this antiquated belief.

Our family had lost contact with my father even before our arrival in America in April of 1982. It was not until six years later, when I was in junior high school, that we received a photograph from him. Apparently he had learned of our whereabouts from a relative who had returned to Vietnam for a visit. The next news of my father came after my mother took a trip back to her homeland during December of 1993, my senior year in high school. I listened intently as she recalled her encounters with him, as if I were getting word of the fate of a father who went off to the Vietnam War. She also described his dozen or so children from his two other wives. As if the pain of hearing of his commitments to *other* families was not enough, my mother followed this news by showing me a disturbing video of her month-long trip. There was a scene in which she went to a worship temple in my father's home village near *Quảng Trị*, in central Vietnam, to pray for the souls of my ancestors on his side of the family. My mother's culture stresses the importance of a woman honoring and worshiping her husband's forefathers. Watching this ceremony, I felt uneasy, although I understood her motives for taking part in it. In the past she had taught me the Vietnamese belief that the spirits of your ancestors are always watching over and protecting you. If you pray for them and burn incense to feed them, they will bring you good fortune wherever you go. That was what my mother intended to achieve by her visit. This part of the video did not bother me. What did distress me was that she had invited my father to pray alongside her. She paid his way from *Cà Mau* all the way to *Quảng Trị* (about 600 miles) just to light incense! No, no, I can't believe it, I thought. She must've brought him there to shoot him in the head, right? She wanted to expose all his sins in front of his entire village before guillotining him. Most likely no one would object to his execution, after all. He has to pay for the lives he wrecked, and my mother would play the role of the grim reaper. I'm convinced of it . . . I quickly snapped back to reality when my mother started speaking again.

"Don't you think your father is still as handsome as ever?" she asked. My eyes widened and my jaw hung as I considered whether or not my ears had actually heard the words she had uttered. "You look just like him." I dreaded those words more than anything. I did not want my mother or anyone else to compare me with my father, the father who had abandoned us and left us destitute. By this time I was breathing heavily and trying my best to suppress my fury.

"Mom, why did you talk to him and invite him to come see you?" I asked in a calm, controlled voice. "I thought that you resented him for all the horrible things he did to you."

"Well, yes. But, in the end we are still husband and wife and he is still your father," she replied casually, as if all those stories she had told me all my life were lies or gross exaggerations. "And besides, I asked him up there to pray so that your ancestors will protect you and bring you happiness. I didn't do it for myself, you know."

That night I went to sleep wondering what kind of woman my mother was. In my early years—up until high school—she was the figure to whom I looked for strength and perseverance; she was the figure who controlled my daily life, who gave me my emotions. The only times that I can remember experiencing intense feelings were when she told me the stories of her sad life. However, having seen on the video how her face lit up when she looked into my father's eyes, how she laughed out loud at his nonsensical jokes, and how she referred to him by the traditional word *Anh*, used by wives to beckon their husbands, I didn't know what to think about my mother. Although by that point in my life I had broken away from her emotional control, I still had a great deal of respect for my mother's courage and endurance. This episode forced me to reconsider my judgment of her.

Initially I thought she was weak for her inability to say, "Hey, jerk! I don't need you! I have lived alone and raised my children without your help in the past, and I can *still* do so. I came back to Vietnam to see the rest of my family, not *you!*" Instead of doing what I thought was the honorable thing, she gave in to her misogynist traditional culture that says the man you marry is your husband for life, under any circumstances. This is especially true if the wife bears children with the husband. I have heard a great number of stories in which husbands left their wives for other women, and when their extramarital affairs did not work out their wives welcomed them back home with open arms. This happened to two of my mother's sisters, Hương and Gái Chị. With hindsight and a deeper understanding of Vietnamese culture, I can see the reasons for my mother's behavior.

A second example of Confucian ideals shaping our family dynamics again reveals the inherent gender discrimination in Confucian philosophy. The principle of *trọng nam khinh nữ*—privileging males and marginalizing females—expresses the notion of unequal treatment of genders by parents, as well as by society as a whole. In the home, girls must assist with chores, while the boys, after studying the day's lesson, can go outside and play with other boys in the village. Although my mother never said directly that she thought I was more important than my older sister, there were many examples of subtle—and not so subtle—preferential treatment.

As a child, Chị Châu was probably my closest friend. Because our mother rarely approved of our associating with other kids, Chau and I did everything together. She was only one grade ahead of me, so our age difference did not put us at a disadvantage in terms of understanding one another's interests and feelings. Back then, we always shared intimate secrets, like which of the boys in her sixth-grade class liked her, or my crush on a girl named Jessica Theodore in fourth grade. I suppose our family situation made our relationship stronger than average brother-sister relationships. For instance, when our mother spanked us we would take a bath together and comfort each other while we cried. No one understood how we felt but us; this made us depend on each other for support.

However, the situation changed greatly when we both started high school, primarily because of Chau's growing resentment of the preferential treatment our mother gave me. For example, my mother assigned more chores to Chau (although this did not mean she let me go have fun, as I also performed duties in our home). This was another case where my mother's culture and American culture clashed, this time resulting in a severed relationship between brother and sister. In fact, I think the real reason for Chau's resentment was that she felt our mother loved me more than her, and that she was accordingly neglected. This inequality strained my relationship with Chau so greatly that she decided to run away from home in her senior year of high school. It would be a long two years before Chau and I were able to speak to each other again and develop a new relationship.

A few years ago, when I had just returned from a study trip to China, my sister invited me to spend the night in her dorm room on campus. That night she and I had a long conversation about our relationship with each other and with our mother. In our talk she revealed that she felt isolated and victimized by both our mother and me because she thought that we deliberately wanted to, in so many words, make her life a living hell. "Do you remember the summer after the sixth grade?" she asked, as she lay in her bed staring directly at the ceiling. "I had to go to summer school at Einstein Middle School, but Mom didn't have a car so she couldn't drive me." This would be the first of many examples she would cite that evening.

"Yeah, I know," I answered. Chau and I communicated mainly in English when my mother wasn't around, because we felt more comfortable with it.

"Well, do you remember how I got to school and back every day? I had to skate for three miles just to get there in the morning. Then for another three miles to get back home. Do you know how tired and hot I was?"

"Yeah, I remember," I sighed after a short pause, "I felt bad for you. Why didn't you ask Mom to buy you a bus pass? They're not nearly as expensive as a buying a new car."

"You think she would buy *me* anything?" she asked. My sister started crying quietly, as if she didn't want me to hear it. "Maybe if *you* were the one skating she would."

"You shouldn't say that; you never asked her," I argued.

"What was the use of asking? I knew her answer would be no." I knew what Chau said was true. After an uncomfortable silence she started again: "So, what happened the next summer when *you* had to go to Einstein?" I had hoped she wouldn't bring this point up because I knew I could not argue with her. The following year, when *I* needed to get to summer school, my mother bought a car just in time to drive me. I had always thought it had been a coincidence, but lately I had entertained the idea that my mother had bought the car just to make sure *I* didn't have to skate to school.

"I know," I said quietly, dropping my head and sighing again. "Mom bought a car."

"Why didn't Mom buy a car when I needed a ride?" she demanded. I had no answer. "She only bought the car because she didn't want *you* to have to skate to school! And you know it. Phuoc, why don't you just admit it? Mom loves you more than me," Chau cried. I guess the reason I felt reluctant to admit that our mother preferred me was because I felt guilty for not doing anything about it. I felt responsible for not saying to my mom, "I don't think you should give me fewer chores than Chị Châu," or "Why don't you buy Chị Châu a bus pass?" I felt special being the more important one, or the better one, in my mom's eyes. But after talking with Chau, I could no longer overlook the outright discrimination behind so many of my mother's actions.

A final example of the Confucian culture in which I grew up was the significance my mother placed on academic achievement. Before starting college I never found academics a challenge. I cannot recall ever studying excessively or having trouble understanding concepts in school; I usually prepared only enough to make the top marks on tests. I made insubstantial efforts and yet never received less than an A in any of my high school courses. To be honest, this situation left me with only mediocre feelings of achievement. Yet, although *I* had little pride or elevated self-esteem due to my grades, my mother radiated more than enough pride and self-esteem for the both of us.

My mother might be what the Japanese call an "education mama," which means a mother who experiences feelings of accomplishment vicariously through the successes of her children. These women usually have not had the same opportunity their children have to get an education, and so they concentrate all their efforts to make sure their kids achieve what they themselves always wanted to achieve. I think the only difference between an education mama and my mother is that my mother found my actual academic work uninteresting and dull. Seeing the A's on my report card alone made her excited, and she proceeded to take all the credit for those grades because, as she always said, without her sacrifices and virtues those grades would have certainly been F's.

In my senior year in high school I happily gave my mother many reasons to show off to our neighbors what an intelligent son she had raised and why everyone should respect her for her incredible skills as a mother. I myself rarely felt comfortable telling others—especially family members—about my accomplishments because I did not put that much effort into attaining them, and thus did not think that I deserved them. I took satisfaction instead in witnessing my mother's aura of pride, which often lasted for weeks after my report cards came home.

My years in college have allowed me to develop a new, more equal relationship with my mother. I think the time I spent at school three thousand miles away from her has made us both appreciate and respect each other—although she would never *admit* that she respects or appreciates me. She now sees me as an independent individual, and I see her as both a mother and a friend. I know that she takes much pride in seeing me succeed in my academic life, but even though I want to make her proud of me and hope that she gains the proper admiration she deserves from those in Vietnam, I do not base my goals and aspirations on a desire to please her. If in the process of attaining my goals I also make her happy, then I will have lived up to both my American and Vietnamese ideals: doing things for myself and doing things to show respect for my parents. I praise my mother when I see improvement in the way she is raising my younger half-siblings, Tai and Carol, over how she raised Chau and me. I think she realizes that she cannot force every aspect of Vietnamese culture on children whom she is raising in America. When I go home for vacations I function as the man of the house, taking care of the bills, fixing doorknobs, and attending parent-teacher conferences. I am the sole male family figure my brother has to look up to, which puts pressure on me to be the best role model I can be. I play the parts of parent and role model willingly and with satisfaction.

As for my search for the culture that best suits me, I have come to the decision that neither Vietnamese nor American culture alone can satisfy my needs. Thus, I consciously pick out the best aspects of each culture and synthesize them into one. For instance, while I believe in the American ideal that every person is equal, I disapprove of children not treating their elders with respect and proper manners. On the other hand, while I accept the Vietnamese value of taking care of your parents in old age, I reject the tenet that only by beating your children will they succeed in life. I do not consider myself a product of either Americanization or Vietnamization; rather, I am enjoying the best of both worlds.

From the academic success of my sister and me, it may seem that our family is living out the American dream. We escaped from a war-scarred country that offered us few opportunities and arrived in a land that my mother knew nothing about. She worked hard all her life to provide her children with a home that was conducive to learning. My mother created such an atmosphere by using the whip, along with guilt-provoking stories, to encourage us to learn. Now that two of her children are excelling in their respective post-secondary institutions, my mother feels she has done an admirable job of raising us. However, her feelings of pride came at a high cost to our family, the price for our success being her severed relationship with Chau. Of course, maybe my mother did not know any other way to raise us than by the rules of her native culture. She did not realize that most families bring up successful children without using the switch. In my family, at least, the practice of Confucian ideals led to decreased communication and, ultimately, to feelings of isolation similar to what Chau and I felt then and are still experiencing. Fortunately, my mother, after seeing her family structure crumble because of her, realized that her child-rearing methods needed improvement. She knows now that her children will inevitably become Americanized to some degree. Accordingly, she allows more freedoms to Tai and Carol; I hope that, with a little less pain, they will also live up to her ideals.

Since graduating from Dartmouth College, Phuoc Nguyen has earned graduate degrees in public health and medicine. Now married, he is in residency training on the East Coast.

Patrick S.   Distilling My Korean American Identity

I am a Korean American. More accurately, I am an American with a limited Korean background. I lived in Korea until I was four years old. I don't remember anything of the Korea I experienced before moving to the States, apart from some vague images. Perhaps that is why I don't speak the language well anymore. All my childhood memories of Korea were presumably encoded in the Korean language, which I spoke exclusively until I was close to six years old. Those memories now seem inaccessible to my thoroughly Americanized consciousness. The several times I have returned to Korea, I felt completely the foreigner, and Korea seemed for the most part unfamiliar to me.

This is not to say that being of Korean heritage meant nothing to me in my childhood or during my adolescence, or that it means nothing to me now. Being Korean has always been significant to me. But the nature of that significance has varied across periods of my life. As an adolescent, being Korean meant being different. I attended a small private school in the Midwest. I was not the only Asian in the school, but Asians constituted only a small minority of the student body. I never encountered or perceived any racist attitudes at the school. The real effect being Korean had on me was less a product of others' attitudes toward me than of my own perception of how others perceived me.

Everyone knows that no adolescent wants to stick out in a crowd. The desire to be "normal" may just be the sine qua non of adolescence. Being a member of a minority group made it hard for me, as a teenager, to avoid feeling like I "stuck out." Being Korean was a liability I felt I had to overcome; I thought that others were constantly conscious of the fact that I was

Korean and therefore different in some way. And although being "different" isn't bad per se, being "different" is not usually desirable to self-conscious teens, and it certainly was not desirable to me. I didn't want to be different, but because I couldn't do anything about it I avoided calling attention to myself. If people didn't notice me, then maybe they wouldn't notice my differentness. If people didn't notice my differentness, then maybe I wouldn't feel it, either. I suppose that is how I explain to myself how I got to be a "quiet" person.

But, I did wish that more people *knew* me somehow. For all my desire not to be noticed, I still resented the fact that people saw me as "quiet"— and not much else. I wasn't a "nobody" in my high school class—that would have been hard in a class of twenty. I did well academically, and people seemed to know that. But being labeled "smart" was never much satisfaction to me. Being the one to get the highest score on the calculus test did not seem to me to reap many benefits. It was just another label. So I was quiet—but smart, too. And that's how people would talk about me. If only people really knew me, I thought to myself, they would see me not just as a quiet (but smart) person but as a regular three-dimensional individual. The paradox, though, was that although I didn't want to be known only for being unnoticeable, I did not want to be different from everybody else.

Today, being Korean has a significance to me that differs greatly from the significance it had when I was younger. As a teenager, I felt that I was first and foremost an American, and that my Korean background was of marginal importance in my personal makeup. I tended to believe that the impact on me of being Korean extended only as far as my physical characteristics. My parents often exhorted me to recognize that I should not and could not ever deny my Koreanness. My parents wanted me, I think, not to just accept the fact that I was Korean but to embrace it. But I always thought they had it all wrong. As an adolescent, I simply wasn't interested in my ethnic roots. I wanted to ignore them. Besides, I rationalized, race was something to be downplayed and minimized, not highlighted and brought to the surface. After all, wasn't the ethos of the late '60s, the age into which I was born, that each of us should celebrate the bonds that tie us all together and not the differences that distinguish us? And perhaps most important, I asked myself, how could we expect others (i.e., non-Koreans) to ignore our racial differences if we ourselves did not? My adolescent preoccupation with, or quest for, inconspicuousness blinded me to any satisfactory answer to this last question. I could not reconcile my almost fetishistic desire to be "just an American teenager" with any sort of conscious, positive recognition or affirmation of my cultural and ethnic roots.

By the time I was in college, I was beginning the long hike up and out of the murky depths of adolescence, facing concerns that I had never before confronted. During my first month at school, I met new people almost every day. I marveled at the excitement I felt in suddenly finding myself surrounded by a thousand people, my classmates, whom I had never seen before, and who had never seen me. The primary task everyone seemed to be undertaking was to get to know everyone else, to find out as much as possible about as many people as possible—mainly by attending as many parties as possible. It was not too long before I realized that while I was trying to find out about others, all those others were trying to find out about me, too. But, my God, what *was* there to find out about me?

At the threshold between adolescence and whatever comes afterward, I found myself knowing my new friends virtually better than I knew myself. I sometimes felt as if I were a completely uninteresting person. Not uninteresting in the sense of inducing ennui in the people I interacted with but uninteresting in a broader and vaguer sense, in the sense that I had a hard time identifying those features about me that *defined* me as *me*. On reflection, I guess I could say that I had been altogether too successful in my earlier struggle and quest for qualified anonymity. I saw that it was time, then, for me to undo much of what I had done during my adolescence. I started engaging in a process of discovery, which finally allowed me to leave adolescence behind, a process I refer to as the "personal identity distillation."

The way I conceive of it, the process involves the boiling off of the "solvent" of one's personality, that is, all the "stuff" that coexists with a persons' individuality but that doesn't constitute it. As more and more of the "stuff" boils away, the "solute," or residue, that remains becomes more and more salient and knowable. It is this residue that defines and constitutes a person's identity. It is the material that allows individuals to be distinguished from one other in some substantive way. The residue, the end product of the distillation process, is a person's identity in its pure form. Before the distillation, identity is "dissolved" and therefore hidden, secret, invisible. Before distillation, it's hard to really know how one person is different from the next, just as it's hard to tell the difference between water containing dissolved salt and water containing dissolved sugar. But after the distillation, the residue becomes tangible and directly viewable.

The point of the process is not to find out that "everyone is different." In identifying the residue of your personal distillation, you may consider important, that, in fact, your "residue" has much in common with someone else's "residue." Paradoxical as it sounds, that commonality may help you conceptualize your personal identity. Thus, for example, Koreanness might be a constituent of my identity, although obviously, I'm not the only one who's going to have that constituent. In the context of the rest of the factors that make up my identity, though, the single factor of Koreanness might mean one thing to me and quite another to someone else.

An interesting weakness of the distillation metaphor is that the idea of a substance being distilled out of some solvent suggests strongly that the substance was "there" all along. The metaphor of distillation suggests that the residue of the process—identity—is simply *discovered*. But, in fact, one doesn't just discover one's identity. I would suspect that the real process of getting to know your identity involves as much an element of creation as it does of discovery. The very act of searching for one's identity may unavoidably affect what one "finds" and what one chooses to jettison.

In essence, what happened after I got to college was simply that my quest for "sameness" (qualified anonymity) was replaced by a new quest—a quest for individuality and identity. While I stubbornly denied my Koreanness throughout adolescence, I felt almost compelled to examine it once I reached college. I needed to know whether being Korean really was an essential part of my own being, or whether that part of me could just be boiled off. I traveled to Korea for a summer to find out, participating in an intensive language program at Yonsei University in Seoul that was geared primarily toward Korean Americans like me. That summer, aside from learning to speak Korean a lot better, I learned a great deal about what being Korean meant to me. I learned that it certainly was not the center of my being, but neither was it at the outer fringe. But the important point for me was that I had finally stopped contending that being Korean meant *nothing* to me.

As an adolescent, it was impossible for me to give a satisfactory answer to the question I brought up earlier: How could I expect others to overlook my Korean attributes if I myself did not? Implicit in the question was a fear of being set apart from everyone else for my Koreanness. The interesting thing, which I can only now see, is that by ignoring my own Koreanness, I may have made it difficult for others to look upon my Korean heritage as anything more than a matter of *race*, a classification under which I could not but be regarded as different. If I had been more willing to recognize Koreanness as part of my identity, then maybe that would have pushed others to similarly perceive my Koreanness as a part of my personality, a part of me to be confronted and accepted—or rejected—like any of the other aspects of my personality, and not as a mark of categorical difference.

Part of my identity in high school was as a "brain." The "brains" were the students who did well in science and math. If you happened to be a superb student in English, or history, or French—well, then, that was that. You were just good in English, or history, or French. Unless you were also highly proficient in one of the sciences or maths, you did not merit characterization as a "brain."

My high school classmates tended to impute "brain" status to me. Perhaps that's partly why I thought of myself as a "science" person when I entered college. I was good in the sciences; I was interested in the sciences generally; and I took it for granted that I would go to medical school and become a doctor, following in the footsteps of both my parents. In fact, before I went to college, I tended to think of it as nothing but a necessary stepping-stone on the path to medical school, and medical school a similar step on the final path to my preordained profession. But on reflection, I don't think my interest in becoming a physician really explains why I thought of myself as a science person. I knew even back in high school that one didn't have to be a science person to become a physician, and I did as well in English and French as I did in any of the sciences. Moreover, in terms of my actual interest in the subject matter, I found myself more engaged in English than in my science classes. So, why, I've asked myself, didn't I think of myself as an English person, or more generally, a humanities person?

I think it's fair to say that most people want to have as rosy and flattering a conception of themselves as possible. In high school, it was flattering to me to be able to think of myself as an intellectually competent person. And, naturally, the best way to maintain that self-conception was to think of myself as a science person. Well, at least it was natural back in high school.

By the time I reached high school, I had been strongly ingrained to believe that to be intellectually competent—smart, a "brain"—meant largely one thing: to know "The Answers." If you were smart, you were privy to a relative abundance of answers. The sciences and maths—at least at the high school and perhaps even at the early undergraduate level—were subjects well suited to the quest for answers and tended to provide confirmation for the notion that being smart and having the answers meant one and the same thing. Being proficient in English provided no marker of intellectual competence insofar as it didn't imply having lots of answers. So how could being good in English establish intellectual distinction? I resisted thinking of myself as an "English" person as opposed to a science person largely because that would have been hard to square with a self-conception and sense of self-worth centered on intellectual proficiency and academic commitment. It seemed to me that to conceive of myself as an English person would have been to abandon any claim to intellectual accomplishment. I might have even thought that English types were people who couldn't hack it as science persons—"wimps."

When I first arrived at college, I intended to become a biology major. Biology, after all, seemed the subject logically prior to medicine. Then I went to a meeting for prospective premeds. At this meeting, all of us would-be doctors heard about the myriad courses prerequisite to taking the MCATs and being admitted to medical school. What surprised me, though, was that one did not have to major in the sciences to go to medical school. What's more, I learned that well-rounded medical students were very much in vogue among medical school admissions committees. By all reports, medical schools tended to look *favorably* on candidates who majored in the liberal arts. This came as a revelation to me. I had been given the perfect excuse, I thought. I could major in something other than a science and have a perfectly valid reason for doing so; it would be instrumentally useful. Yes—I would become an English major, but only because majoring in English would make it easier to get into a top medical school.

Armed with this strategic bent of mind, I groomed myself to become an English major. But then I encountered a significant obstacle. I found out that I didn't like the subject. Somehow, English classes just didn't seem to be all that I had cracked them up to be. I enjoyed the lectures, and I enjoyed most of the reading, but I found myself intellectually disengaged from the subject matter. It's not so much that the subject bored me, it just seemed that everything was "made up." The primary texts of English—the poems, novels, and such—seemed to me chronically indeterminate in meaning and significance. One literary critic's interpretation of Yeats or Woolf seemed to me just as appealing as another's, and I personally could see no objective way of even comparing one against the other.

Freshman spring term, I took an introductory course in philosophy. From the first day of lecture, I was hooked. That was the first college course I took that genuinely excited me. In fact, I think it was in that course that I felt for the first time the thrill of being stirred up by *ideas*. I remember actually feeling my heart race as the professor in the first or second class meeting began to schematize the questions that would provide the themes of the course. What is knowledge? Is moral knowledge possible? Are there defensible arguments for the existence of a god? How do we know that anything exists? What does it mean to be moral? Why should people act morally? What is a "mind?" What is the relation between mind and body? And so on. As the professor presented the class with these questions—the kinds of questions that form the broader basis of general philosophical inquiry—I felt overwhelmed. The questions startled me. It had never occurred to me during my eighteen years of existence that those kinds of questions could or should be asked. I was astonished to think that for eighteen years I had never thought to grapple with a single one of those questions. Now, as I listened to those questions, I wondered why I never had. And I wondered how one could in any sensible way go about answering them.

I stayed with philosophy and chose to major in it. (Now that I look back, I think maybe I concentrated on philosophy too much—to the detriment of a more diverse learning experience.) But, for me, philosophy offered a middle ground between the "stone-cold hardness" of science and the "mushiness" of English. At least in a simplistic sense, argumentation in philosophy bowed to more or less objective (but not formulaic) standards of justification. I found that it was possible for an argument in philosophy to be just flat-out wrong (e.g., in virtue of being badly reasoned) in a way that an interpretation of or an argument about a literary text never could be. On the other hand, I discovered that in philosophy, unlike the sciences, even as a novice one could carefully read a classic piece of writing like Descartes' *Meditations* and, at least on a simplistic level, be able to find flaws and formulate substantively meaningful critiques of the author's arguments. I found that to be enormously empowering. How exciting it was to engage in debate with, rather than just learn about, the philosophers who had laid down some of the foundational bedrock of contemporary Western thought!

In the end, I became a "philosophy" person through and through. English? I abandoned it. Science? I abandoned it, too, at least as an academic pursuit. I used to think that perhaps the real reason I was attracted to philosophy was that I seemed to be good at it, or at least much better at it than I was in English or the sciences. But I now think that the better explanation is that philosophy was the one intellectual activity that I found to be intrinsically satisfying. I never felt the need to justify the study of philosophy to myself in instrumental terms. I just loved doing it, and doing it made me feel somehow genuine. I experienced the philosopher's sensibility as something that seemed authentic to me from the beginning. It quickly became part of the core of my crystallizing identity.

I've been talking at length about finding my identity, but I haven't yet mentioned the single most important event in my development as a person. At college, early in my junior year, I met the woman with whom I would promise to spend the rest of my life. Until I met Laura, I had never shared any significant part of my life with anyone.

I come from a pretty good-sized family. I have a brother and two sisters, all younger. My parents emigrated from Korea when I was four. Although they were brought up in Korea, my parents are quite liberal (culturally) and have become more Americanized than most other immigrant Korean parents I know. Our family is quite close, by most people's standards. Although my family is united in love and mutual care for one another's well-being, I don't think we have ever shared a deep understanding of what goes on in each other's inner lives. I shared countless experiences with my brother and sisters as we grew up together, but I don't think I really comprehended what it means to share one's life with another until I met Laura.

You would think that, never having done so before, I would have had tremendous difficulty expressing myself in a personally revealing way to Laura. But just the opposite was true. After our relationship became serious, I was never afraid to divulge practically anything I felt to her, and I found myself divulging quite a lot, including most of what I've been writing about in this essay. As our relationship developed, events unfolded such that, finally, I felt the need to tell Laura something I had never told anyone, aside from my parents: that I loved her.

I believed that by telling her, I would be making myself vulnerable to complete emotional destruction. But I had to tell her, even though I was unsure whether she would tell me the same. On Valentine's Day, the moment came. I revealed to Laura that I had come to depend on her for my happiness, and that I would be left immeasurably lonely by her absence. I told her that I loved her. Without hesitation, she responded in kind. What a breakthrough that was! At that moment, I should have realized that I had radically departed from my life as I had known it and had entered a life in which I was no longer alone. For me, that moment of reciprocal communication of love between Laura and me represented the moment at which my identity intersected with hers. Each of us became a part of the other. For me, that meant that from that point on, I would never be able to understand my identity without considering what Laura means to me, and what I mean to her. Sometimes I think the only part of my identity that really matters to me today is the part that encompasses what Laura means to me. Sometimes, I think my entire life revolves around her, and that everything I do is for the benefit of our life together.

I can't begin adequately to describe the empowering effect my relationship with Laura has had on me. I don't think that my outward personality has changed all that much, but I have come to believe that my life has significance. I mean something to somebody. I am irreplaceable in the eyes of somebody. Whereas before my relationship with Laura, my activities in life seemed somehow lacking in thematic integration, now they seem endowed with an undeniably unifying purpose.

Even my relationship with my family has changed because of my love for Laura. Because Laura has redefined who I am, she has also redefined who I am in relation to my family. First of all, Laura was able to describe my family to me in ways that I could not have seen myself. I realized that my family was indeed a close-knit one, albeit one that is reserved in its display of sensitive emotions. I think the most important thing I realized about my family through Laura is that, although in some respects we do not explicitly share our lives with each other, we unhesitatingly make sacrifices in our own lives for the benefit of one another's lives; we share our physical and practical burdens, if not our emotional inner sancta.

My family accepted Laura about as readily as a family could be expected to. That fact is, to me, especially significant because Laura is not Korean. She is Italian. The topic of interracial marriage seems to be a major issue for my generation of Korean Americans. But for the interracial couples I know, race tends to be a nonissue. This was certainly true for Laura and me, and that is partly why I've neglected to mention our difference in race up until now. But I consider myself lucky, because my parents never so much as hinted at disapproval of my plans with Laura. They repeatedly tell me that they find it easy to see Laura as one of their own daughters. Laura's own parents also seemed to be more than agreeable to our relationship. They expressed happiness at the fact that Laura had found "the right person," and for them, that was enough.

It's ironic. The aspect of my adolescent life that was singularly the *most* affected by being Korean, or more accurately, by my attitude toward being Korean, was my social life, or rather its absence from my teen years. It wasn't *because* of my Korean qualities that I never really dated anyone. It was only because of my insecurity about being Korean that being Korean was an issue at all. Part of the problem was that I feared rejection. But everyone fears rejection to some degree. The *real* obstacle for me was a feeling of inappropriateness. I somehow felt that it was inappropriately presumptuous for me to even ask someone who was not Korean out on a date. It was impossible for me to imagine that my race would not be an issue, and I felt uncomfortable putting anyone in a position in which she had to pretend that it wasn't.

I never really stopped thinking these sorts of thoughts until I became involved with Laura. The depth of our relationship has completely dissolved all of those feelings for me. Laura has helped me to see that being Korean is part of who I am, but that it need not define my relationships with others. Her love for me erased all the insecurities I have ever had with my Koreanness. Without that love, I would never have been able to understand much of what I have tried to express in this essay. My personal identity may have been formed before I met Laura, but not until after I met her did I have the strength to face it.

After graduating from college, Patrick S. went to law school and then obtained his PhD in philosophy. He now teaches on a law faculty at a large law school in the Northeast. He remains happily married to his college sweetheart, Laura.

Amy Lee   Turning against Myself

As I am writing this story about my life, I am a senior in college and am considering a career in clinical psychology. I was born and raised in New York's Chinatown. I am a second-generation Chinese American woman and the first in my immediate family to go to college. My parents have only high school educations, and yet, they have managed to spoil me with all the riches any woman my age, coming from a very cosmopolitan and materialistic city, could ask for. As I get older I am only now beginning to realize the sacrifices my parents have made for me.

When I was living at home I had an extended family that was very involved in my upbringing. Unfortunately, it appears the longer I am away at school the further apart we become. I suppose the drifting apart is a very natural occurrence; it's just that right now is such a major transitional period in my life. I have reached that age when I am supposed to be an adult, make my own decisions, be independent (financially and psychologically), live on my own, and so forth. As graduation approaches, parts of me want to stay in this in-between stage where I am independent enough to make decisions on my own and pretty much do my own thing, yet at the same time know that I always have my family to fall back on whenever the "going gets tough," especially financially. It is only now occurring to me that as soon as I graduate I am going to be out in the "real world." I will live on my own, actually earn a salary, and take care of myself . . . how scary!

My family is quite complicated. My father and I do not get along very well. He is always working. When I was growing up he was never around. When I was home he was at work, and when he was home I was asleep. At times I have been very resentful of him, particularly since he seems to favor my younger brother over me. In fact, as his first child, I think my father had wanted me to be a boy. I have heard that it is a Chinese cultural preference to want one's firstborn to be a boy in order to carry on the family name.

I would not say that I am lacking because of the absence of my father during my growing up. In fact, my uncles have treated me like their own daughter. I know that I am their favorite. As a result, my cousins have become somewhat resentful of me, and as they are getting older we all have tried to show no favoritisms. I do sense though that there is a great deal of competition between me and Uncle Wang's oldest daughter. When I was growing up my family had no one to compare me with since I was the first female to go to college. But now that my cousin is in high school, I have a feeling that her parents are putting a great deal of pressure on her to do as well, if not better, than I have done. And as I am the first to tread a path for my other cousins and brother to follow, I have sensed a great deal of pressure to be the "perfect" role model for them.

I have a great deal of respect for my mother, and yet we have never been very close. She has basically supported me and my brother both financially and emotionally the whole time we have been home. She claims that my father provides her with assistance, but I am somewhat skeptical. He used to be a compulsive gambler. Now he is compulsively playing the stock market. My father has recently opened up a new restaurant in Connecticut. He now lives up there and comes home in the middle of the week and then leaves again. I have never talked to my mother about this new arrangement. She must be quite lonely with her husband away from home so often. I am not quite sure why they are still together. I sense no love, communication, or friendship in their relationship, and yet they are still married.

I see so much of myself in my mother that it scares me. The sad part is that I see in myself what I perceive to be the reason for my mother's unhappiness—always giving and never asking for anything in return. In the past I used to convince myself that this self-sacrificing is okay because it validates my very existence. I now realize there is a time and a place for me to give to others, but in the process there must be plenty of times and places for myself. I am presently trying to work this out. I see how my inability to say "no" to other people and always wanting to make everyone happy have the potential to destroy me. As I have come to understand this I have come to understand my mother.

Growing up in such a small, close-knit community as Chinatown has sometimes been very stifling for me. Everyone knows everything about what everybody else is doing. In a way, it is nice to see how everyone is watching out for one another, at least when you want to be looked after. However, it has been difficult for me to come to terms with my own roots. When I was young I used to hang out in Chinatown with various Chinatown gang members. At the time there were two gangs, one consisting mostly of American-born Chinese youths and another of those born in China. Throughout my upbringing there were constant gang wars between the two. When I was twelve years old I started to hang out with these people. As one can imagine, it was a pretty rough environment to grow up in.

Just before I broke away from that group, which consisted mainly of high school graduates (interestingly, most of them are now cops!), a friend of mine was stabbed to death in an alleyway. I was not allowed to attend the funeral because undercover detectives would be there taking pictures of all those who attended with the intention of questioning them about the murder. The people in Chinatown never talk, so no one ever found out who stabbed him. It was definitely a gang-related incident with lots of rumors going around as to who was the possible murderer. Anyway, I stopped hanging around with them and started to become good friends with people in my high school.

In high school I did not associate with any of the other Chinese students because, at the time, I thought most of them were geeks who followed the stereotype that most Westerners have of Chinese kids: exceptionally bright in math and sciences, greasy hair and thick glasses, and of course, always spoke with that strange Chinese accent. I was the complete opposite. I hated math and sciences, and I was one of those vain adolescents always concerned about my appearance, and I still am. I was pretty much accepted as being a "cool" exception (this sounds so juvenile to me now). To prove that I was not like "them," I made it a point never to associate with the other Chinese kids in school. As a result, I gained a reputation in high school and in Chinatown as being "white-washed" and a "banana"—yellow on the outside but all white on the inside.

Starting in the sixth grade and going on into my high school years I prided myself on those stupid labels. With each year, I further and further disassociated myself from most Asians. I had done such a good job of denying my own culture that oftentimes my friends would forget that I was Chinese. I remember a couple of times at swim team practice people would make racist jokes about gooks and Chinks, and I laughed along with them. What an idiot! The fact that these people felt comfortable saying these jokes in front of me was proof that I had done a good job of denying the color of my skin and the slant of my eyes. One time this fellow swim team member had just finished telling a racist joke when she realized my presence. She later apologized but added that it was so weird, "You really are not like them. You're different. I mean, you don't look like them and you don't talk with an accent the way they do. I don't consider you like any of 'them.' I guess that's why I said the joke in front of you." The scary thing, now that I look back, is that was the type of remark I wanted to hear. I was so desperately trying to fit in that I was willing to deny my very essence for it.

Unfortunately, things have not changed all that much since I have gone to college. Most of my friends from Chinatown have gone back to school and are doing pretty well for themselves. I still feel as though I do not belong to them because for so long I had tried to distance myself from them. Now that I am older and less intimidated by people because of my race, I have learned the importance of one's culture. I have discovered the need for Asian role models and a sense of connectedness with my own roots.

Last winter when I was home I became attracted to a Chinese guy. I was really excited. I had not dated an Asian man since my sophomore year in high school. We dated a couple of times but it ended up being a total catastrophe. After our second date he asked around about me. The scary thing is that he knew my whole life story from the few people he had asked. He had been told all sorts of things, including: "Well, Andy, you don't have a chance, she only dates white guys." I was disgusted by everyone in Chinatown. Didn't they have anything better to do than to keep tabs on me? Here I was trying to reconnect with my roots and go against my reputation. Unfortunately, I guess a reputation is hard to overcome. I was really hurt when he stopped calling. I thought I liked him, and I thought he was interested in me, too. My friends told me that I intimidated him. I do not know how I did, but they said that it was because he had never finished college and that since I appear to have so much more going for me, he felt inferior. What a crock! Anyway, I was greatly disappointed. To this day, I do not know why he stopped calling; maybe he just was not interested or maybe my friends were right . . . who knows. I had hoped that during the term I would get closer to my own community. Instead, my attempts to come back into the Chinese community only distanced me further from Chinatown. In fact, after that incident I stopped calling my friends from Chinatown, and I started to hang around with my non-Asian friends again. Rather than try to prove those who believed in my reputation to be wrong,

I only further confirmed their beliefs, and my own, for that matter. I guess I am yellow on the outside and white on the inside.

I still sense that many of my former friends from Chinatown are resentful of me because there was a time when I thought I was better than them. Now I see that I am no better and no worse. If anything, I am so much the worse for feeling the need to deny what is inherently mine. I am no longer embarrassed to be Chinese. I no longer try to disguise my Asianness by dyeing my hair a lighter shade of brown. I am just beginning to be proud of my roots and realize the importance of them. Someday, I would like to be able to go back and reclaim what used to be mine—my culture. However, I guess I really don't deserve to be taken back into their arms. Why should they? I had rejected them, so why should they let me back in? I am sure they must think that since I wanted so badly to be like white people, they are just fine without me. The problem is that I need them. I need to know what it is like to be Chinese. It would have been great to feel connected to those students protesting in Beijing. Instead, I was very far removed from it, and I used my being in college as an excuse to be uninvolved. I even suspect that my own family feels as though I look down upon them.

At college, I definitely have more non-Asian friends than I do Asian friends. I seem to have connected myself with the black minority population rather than the Asian community, maybe because many of them come from either New York City or Boston. We therefore have many inner-city experiences in common. Many of the Asian women I have met here are from the suburbs and appear to be better-off financially than I am, and I find that rather intimidating. My junior fall semester I lived in a residence that is affinity housing for black students, and I have considered many times becoming a member of the Afro-American Society. Once, I even considered joining a black sorority. I don't yet understand why I have tried so hard to be accepted among the black community here at my college, and yet, I have no desire to form any affiliations whatsoever with any Asian organizations.

Perhaps as I get older I will want to do something that would get me in touch with more Asians. Maybe my friends from home will forgive me and realize that I was just going through a phase. Or, perhaps my graduate school plans will take me to a part of the United States where there are more Asians. Or maybe things will stay the same. For some reason I cannot find a happy balance between my Asian friends and my non-Asian friends. There seem to be two factions, which I cannot bring together.

Strangely enough, despite the fact that I would like to come to terms with my culture, I still become embarrassed by the stereotypes. Even now when I am with a group of non-Asian friends, I feel a degree of uneasiness because of my race. As I did in high school, I still want so badly to conform to a non-Asian culture, and yet intellectually I know that denial (or abandonment) of my own heritage is not the answer. Intellectually, I understand the need to be with my own, and personally I sense that is what I want. The problem is that socially, I have not gone much further than when I was in high school.

For me, the issues of race and being a woman are two separate aspects of my life. When I look back over my adolescence, being female was far more important to me than being Chinese. Thus, in order to understand me as a woman, one has to understand how one particular event in my life has shaped me into who I am now. In the middle of my senior year in high school I was diagnosed as having hystiocytic lymphoma—cancer of the lymphatic system. As a result of this illness, I had to miss most of my senior year. Prior to the diagnosis I had missed the first three months of school because of an infection that would not go away. It was not until after it was determined that I had cancer that those three months in the hospital made sense.

When I think back to the time when I was sick, I really cannot recall much about the illness. I can tell you what I have and a summary of what happened: I was diagnosed as having hystiocytic lymphoma (T-cell type) cancer almost three years ago. I underwent twelve weeks of intensive chemotherapy (receiving next-to-lethal dosages of some drugs) and five weeks of radiation (one zap five days a week for five weeks). I was one of the twenty-one reported in the United States to have this type of cancer, and I was the seventh person to try this new drug treatment. I lost all of my hair, and I gained thirty pounds from the steroid medication.

I missed all but four months of my senior year in high school. I became sick right before the school year was to begin and had to spend a month in the hospital. No one knew what was wrong with me at the time. I had an ulceration on my left breast and a high fever that persisted for a whole month and suddenly disappeared. I was sent home as being "non-diagnostic." I returned to school, made up my work, applied early to college and was accepted, and completed my senior paper (the only requirement I needed to complete in order to graduate).

I became sick again in March. This time it was the real thing. The ulceration came back, but this time in the form of a big blood blister. I went into the hospital thinking that it was simply a recurrence of what had happened the previous summer. I was concerned about what another major surgery would do to my breast, so a plastic surgeon performed the operation. I was told that the worst it could be was cancer. I figured they were talking about breast cancer, seeing that the ulceration site was on my left breast. "That's no big deal, I could get a mastectomy and everything would be fine. Flat-chested women are sexier anyway." Or so I rationalized. But the worst did happen. What was supposed to be a simple surgical operation in plastics turned out to be six months of pure hell. The tissue that had been removed was malignant. However, it wasn't breast cancer the way I had thought. It turned out to be some rare form of lymphoma. Lucky me!

Actually, I do remember there being a big commotion when the diagnosis was made. Many of my family members and friends were furious that the diagnosis was missed the first time around. Many people were advising us to sue my doctors. A friend of my family who was chief of cardiology at a major hospital had a top oncologist look over the results for a second opinion and "to watch over your doctors' shoulders so they won't goof up again. Now they'll know you're someone important and you're not to be messed around with," this friend of the family said. I resented all of this fuss that was being made over my case. I trusted my doctor and that was all that counted as far as I was concerned.

So much of that period of my illness, before I entered college, is a blur to me now. I remember crying a lot. Crying because of all the pain I was causing my family and friends, crying for them and for me, crying from the pain caused by the tumor and by the nausea, crying out of fear and frustration, crying out to the world for someone to help me. Unfortunately, no one heard my crying. I had to go through all the fighting by myself. Yes, I did have the wonderful support of family and friends, however, being hit with a disease such as cancer, for which there is no known one-hundred-percent cure, taught me how to rely upon myself. The cancer-ridding drugs destroyed all the malignant cells, but it was I who went through the treatments, the throwing up, the weight gain, the hair loss, and the aftereffects of the disease. No matter how much people loved me, they could not take my place and go through all the suffering I went through. I was the one who had the cancer, therefore only I could go through it. Cancer has shown me that when it comes down to a serious crisis, I am the only one I have. I have fought for my life and have fortunately come out a winner.

As I have said, the malignancy occurred on the side of my left breast. It was such a humiliating time for me. Not only did I have to separate my body, which was constantly being exposed to those ever scrutinizing doctors and residents, from the rest of my self, but I also gained thirty pounds and lost all of my hair. I refused to look at myself in the mirror because when I did, I saw someone I did not know. How could something so cruel happen to someone so young? It could not have possibly been happening to me. I had too many things to do, too many dreams to fulfill, so much of life to live.

At the time, I hated myself. In fact, remnants of all the anger, hate, and feelings of hopelessness that I have suppressed while I was sick are still present. The scars both physically and mentally remain. It is only now, four years later, that I am beginning to accept that I was the one who went through all of that hell. The very act of describing that time of my life, which I have tried so hard to blot out of my memory, is my own attempt to become closer to when I was sick, with the hope of better understanding how it has shaped me. In my journal, the August before beginning my freshman year at college, I wrote:

August 26

I finished my last radiation treatment on Tuesday. Supposedly now it's all over. I'm done with my twelve weeks of chemotherapy and my five weeks of radiation, yet I'm still not relieved. The doctors haven't even mentioned whether my tumor is cleared or what. I don't know. In fact, I don't know many things. I don't know whether I'm healed, whether my cancer will ever come back again, or what will happen tomorrow. Nobody ever knows what will happen the next day, but for me it's different. All I know is that I have to wait. If two years go by with nothing happening, I'm considered in remission; in five years, I'm considered cured. I'll have to wait five years with the fear of this hell coming back again. I won't let this prevent me from living life to its fullest while I can, but it's so unfair! Why has all of this happened to me? Everyone keeps on telling me that this is a test, a time to build character. Well, I'm so tired of being tested—of facing what appears to be numerous obstacles, one after another. I've had it up to here with character! When are they going to stop? I have so many dreams. But I'm not going to make another wish because it seems as if every time I do the extreme opposite happens. Earlier, I wanted only two things: to have my hair back before school started and to be my normal weight again for college. Instead, it's three weeks before school and all I have is a whiffle crew cut and I'm only 4 pounds lighter than I was at the peak of my fatness. And I can remember when I was at the hospital I didn't mind having breast cancer—my only fear was losing all of my hair. As luck would have it, I did not have breast cancer and I lost all of my hair. So now, I'm not going to wish for anything because at the rate I'm going, I'll only be disappointed again. . . .

(Later on that night) My goddaughter just told me I was fat and ugly. My cousin Amanda and my brother are always making cracks about my fat and my bald head. I'm trying so hard to be strong, but it's so hard!!!! I need someone to talk to. Someone with whom I can share my fears, angers, and dreams. I've been strong for so long and I did it all by myself, but everyone has their limitations. I long for the time when I can truly love myself and say, "I'm beautiful." If little kids see me this way, can you imagine what grown-ups must think . . . after all, they're looking at the same person. I feel so alone. Boy does it hurt to think of what I've become. I really have no friends, friends I can talk to. I've been suppressing all my feelings and I fear in the long run it will be detrimental to my health. But those are the breaks. I don't feel like I need a therapist, all I need is a caring and understanding ear—I shouldn't have to pay for that.

Now that I look back, I realize all the support I had. My friend Andrea would come over every day after school and do her homework with me. Two of my former teachers would come over every once in a while to have their lunch with me (the hospital I was staying in was just around the corner from my high school). My mother, aunts, uncles, and cousins came to see me almost every day. Everyone was there for me. I truly do not know if I would have been so faithful to any of my friends if one of them had been in a similar predicament.

Starting college was extremely difficult. I began the fall term wearing a wig. Meeting people with it on and not having my real hair made me such a paranoid person. As it turned out, no one noticed. I did tell one of my friends, Susan, about it toward the end of the term. I cannot remember her reactions anymore, and I cannot recall why I had chosen her over all the others to share such an intimate secret with. I even studied in her room at times without my wig on. It must have been a shock for her to see me whip off this wig and to appear in front of her with only short stubbles on the top of my head. The wig was so annoying. It was so uncomfortable. At times, I felt as though my brains were being squeezed together. Whenever I was in my room by myself or with Susan, I would walk around without the wig, always remembering to lock the door.

The most complicated aspect for me was the shower room, which we all shared. I had a single room but there was no way the college could provide me with my own shower. Obviously, I had to take the wig off when I was in the shower. Each time that I wanted to take a shower, it was such a traumatic experience for me. I did not know whether I should leave the wig on and take a shower wearing a shower cap over my head, or what. Anyway, what I had to do was try to sneak showers at times when I least expected people to be using them. Because I was so paranoid, however, I did not want the people on my floor to think I was strange because I never showered, so I would wear a towel over my head in the hallway. Once I was in the shower I would quickly whip on this opaque shower cap, just in case someone unexpectedly peaked in. I would save the hair washing, what little of it that I had, to last, which I did very quickly and with great stress the whole time. Fortunately, no one ever walked in on me. Thinking back about it now, I really was paranoid. If people happened to be in the hallway talking when I had gotten out of the shower, I remember that I would sit in my room with a blow dryer blowing into the air, just so that people would hear a blow dryer coming from my room. What a pain!

Fortunately for me, no one ever found out. The fall term ended, and I came back winter term with a drastically different and very short hairstyle. Everyone was puzzled by me. No one could understand why I would cut my long hair so short. I remember wanting to just laugh in people's faces when they were trying to decide which hairstyle they liked better. Most concluded that they liked my hair short. I wanted so badly to say: "You moron, of course you're going to like my hair short. What you had seen before wasn't my real hair, you idiot!" It still amazes me that no one ever suspected anything. I have since then told some of my friends about my hair, and to my surprise all of them have been shocked. I cannot believe no one knew. It seemed so obvious to me. There is one picture of our whole dorm in which I am dead center of the picture with my wig looking as if it is about to fall right off my head. How could they not know?! I suppose that it is natural for people to generally not go around wondering if someone is wearing a wig. Perhaps because I have spent a short time with a wig, I am more sensitive to things like that.

It seems so juvenile to see how drastically my hair loss affected me. However, this all happened at a time when physical appearances meant more than anything else. I was just starting school and was meeting all these people. Most people would want to make a good impression. I believed I had to be outgoing, upbeat, and always present myself with a smile.

Little did anyone know that I was petrified. Even little things, such as giving hugs, were a trauma for me. If someone's arm accidentally grabbed or got caught on the hair, good-bye wig, hello humiliation. I remember always feeling tense at parties, especially when we all got together and did goofy adolescent-type things like shaving-cream fights or play-fighting. Instead of feelings of excitement, I experienced feelings of dread, anxiety, and overall low self-esteem.

Throughout the whole illness I elected not to see a therapist. I had seen one the first time that I was in the hospital, and I was not pleased with him. I think that because the therapist was a man and would never say anything during our sessions, I was uncomfortable around him. As a result, when I was actually diagnosed with cancer, I felt that I needed to handle it on my own. This therapist's inability to reach out to me when I was in dire need of a listening and understanding ear has fueled my passion for wanting to be a therapist for the terminally ill. Even though I thought I knew what I was doing by deciding not to see anyone during treatments, I have learned in hindsight that having someone with whom I could share all of my frustrations and feelings of anger and anxiety is the most helpful resource anyone could ask for. Despite my present understanding of the benefits of releasing boiled-up emotions, this wisdom comes only years later. When I was sick, I was determined to help myself psychologically.

The spring of my sophomore year I became very depressed and decided that I needed to see a psychiatrist. I remember at one point a thought had occurred to me of how much better it would be for me to end my own life before those little cancer cells could come back to get the best of me. What a thought! Needless to say, that thought really scared me, and I knew then that I needed help.

It was hard for me to see a therapist since I had refused to see someone earlier. I went to see one against my family's wishes, being a typical Chinese family whose members always keep things to themselves and are very reserved. Within my culture it is unheard of to go to someone outside of your family, particularly a person not of your own culture, for help. Their philosophy is that as a family we can get through anything. My philosophy is that if they are part of why I have some of the problems I do, how can they possibly help me? So, there was a huge debate about whether I should see a therapist. I became upset because everyone seemed against my wanting to finally do something to help myself. I was so proud of the fact that I was actually doing something only for me and not for other people. My family members, on the other hand, are so set in their ways. I still do not think they can understand why I needed to talk with someone. I remember a conversation I had with my youngest aunt. We had been talking about my seeing a therapist and I remember her saying, "Why do you need to see a shrink? You have problems, well, you're no different, we all have problems. Do you want to hear my problems?" After her, my uncle got on the phone and the gist of his attitude was: "You want to talk about your problems, why don't you give me the one hundred dollars an hour you pay that therapist and I'll tell you about yourself. Better yet, I'll charge you fifty. . . . I'll give you a discount since you're family." My mother did not say much about the whole thing. Her thinking was that as long as my oncologist thought it was the right thing to do, then I should do it.

Despite my family's wishes, I saw a therapist for my entire sophomore summer and all of my junior year. I remember my first session with her. I was afraid to start talking about my feelings because I was embarrassed to cry in front of her. Somehow, I got this strange notion in my head that as soon as I started to cry, I would not be able to stop. At the time, I felt like a walking bottle of emotions that were just waiting to burst out. If I were to let even a little bit of it out, I thought I would never be able to stop them—all my emotions and tears would just ooze on out. Needless to say, it took me a long time to open up to her. In fact, it took me the whole summer. That summer, however, was the greatest of my life. I used that whole time to focus on myself and not on academics, not on other people, not on other projects, just me. I became very close to all of my friends, and I think that is only because I learned to feel more comfortable about myself.

During the very same sophomore summer, something else happened that proved to me I have indeed been suppressing all these unsettled emotions and thoughts about my illness. I was taking a course entitled "The Biological Woman." I had been pissed-off by this woman who was giving a presentation on breast cancer. From my point of view, she knew nothing about breast cancer. All she could tell the class was what she knew from having read about it. The closest she had ever been to breast cancer was through her mother who had had a mastectomy. She admitted her ignorance of not actually knowing what it was like to have cancer. That's not what got me angry. What infuriated me was her insensitivity and ignorance. She had no clue that someone in her audience might actually be suffering from cancer.

That lecturer got me so angry that later that night I started to tell my friend Susan about it over dinner. I was fine at dinner. We talked about my cancer, and she asked me about lymphoma. Strangely enough, despite the fact that she was the only woman on campus who had seen me without my wig, which would indicate that we must have been pretty close, she never knew what type of cancer I had until that night. It is strange. Outwardly, I am a friendly and outgoing person, and I will let people know a lot about me on the surface. But when it comes to intimate personal details, it is hard for me to open up and expose my vulnerabilities to other people. Even though I claim to want someone to listen to me and feel sorry for me, it is so hard for me to ask for help from other people. I hate to impose on people, and I guess a great deal of this type of attitude has to do with my up-bringing. As I described earlier, my family is very private and they keep family problems within the family only. Telling outsiders about one's problems is just not done in my family. Despite knowing that keeping things in can lead to a great deal of psychological maladjustment, I cannot erase how I have been brought up.

After dinner, I went back to my room, and I started to think about having a recurrence. A friend stopped by to visit, and we started to talk about what was making me so upset. I tried to explain but the tears came pouring out. I was crying over everything—crying for having been sick and all the pain I must have put everyone through. I also started to think about how much worse a recurrence would be at this point in my life. I have made many more close friends and acquaintances. If I were to get sick again I would be putting twice as many people through the same misery as I did the first time. I did not want to cause them any pain. I seemed fixated on this notion that while I was at school I was going to get sick again and die and leave all these great people I have met here. I was a basket case that night. My friend tried to calm me down and put things back in perspective for me. Eventually, I calmed down, I think more out of exhaustion than anything else.

It seems so strange that I have this constant worry of hurting other people. I do not quite understand why I am so obsessed with not hurting other people. It seems that whenever I am hit with something I react to the initial impact with concerns for others. It is only when and if I have the time that I start to worry for myself. I think it is because it is so much easier to worry about other people's problems than to admit to my own vulnerabilities. It has been a couple of years since I underwent treatment, and I find it easier to talk about the type of things that happened to me when I was sick than to talk about a recurrence.

Thoughts of a cancer coming back are always present in my mind somewhere. Even though I appear to be healthy, my risks of recurrence are higher than for an occurrence in the general population. So, unlike most people my age, whose biggest fears are being alone, no job postgraduation, no graduate school, and so forth, I worry about dying. This is not to say that I spend all of my waking hours worrying about getting cancer again. In fact, I avoid thinking about it as much as possible. I would be such a morbid person to be around if I were obsessed with dying. Occasionally, however, I do think about it, and the thought scares me. I do not know what I would do if I ever got sick again. I don't know if I would have the energy to fight back as fiercely as I did the first time around. I do not mean to sound negative, because I am sure that if push came to shove I would gather all my resources and never give up. But, one never knows. . . .

Now that I have been given a second chance to live, my outlook on life has changed somewhat. So much of one's everyday existence is taken for granted in the hustle and bustle of living. Interestingly, before I was sick, in my attempts to keep up with the typical way of living for many adolescents (going to school and stressing about grades, dating and worrying about boys, hanging around with all my girlfriends, being obsessed with my weight, etc.), I was, in fact, not living. I was merely going through the motions. I was not experiencing and feeling, rather, I was simply glossing over life. How sad! It was not until I was forced to function in what I thought was a state of pseudo-existence that I discovered how simple the act of living can be. Though I was struggling to overcome a fatal disease, so much was going on all around me, and I was noticing all of it.

I remember one time looking out of the car window while I was being driven to the hospital and being so jealous of all those people on the outside who were so much healthier than I was. All these people were rushing about doing their own things, taking no notice of me watching them, but I saw them. At the time, I thought I was not living. It is only in hindsight that I realize I actually was. I felt the wind blowing, heard the cars moving, saw the people walking and sweating from the heat—*living*. What does all this mean? Well, now when I catch myself worrying about things that really will not matter in the grand scheme of things (e.g., grades, postgraduation plans, or relationships), I step back for a second and remind myself that I should be grateful that I am alive to experience the aggravation in the first place. I must admit that only some of the time does this reasoning work. I am still a worrywart.

It took me a while to understand that having had cancer not only brought me closer to myself as a human being but also to myself as a woman. Having the tumor located on my breast was such a trauma for me. I remember wishing so often that I were a man. I selfishly thought that it would have been easier for a man to expose his chest to every person who wore all white or blue than it would be for a woman. Why couldn't I have gotten a tumor on my arm or something? Why my breast? I truly think that with each time I had to disrobe myself in front of curious eyes, and with each time someone's unfamiliar hands probed my breast, I lost more of myself as a woman capable of feeling sexually attractive. I also thought that it would have been less humiliating for a man to lose all his hair. I don't know how I could have thought such a thing! Cancer is a disease that would have been trying for anyone to experience, regardless of sex, and it is not something I should have been wishing on others. The experience would have been just as painful for me if I had been a man. What I should be celebrating is the fact that I, as a woman, whose body has been mutilated with scars and violated by countless nameless faces and probing fingers, have overcome this deadly disease and can now look at myself in the mirror. No longer do I loathe what I see in the reflection, which is not to say that I like what I see either. I still have a long way to go before I can look at my body in the mirror and hug that person who is looking back at me. I long to be able to respect myself again.

Since I have been sick, my relationships with people, especially with men, have been strained. Because there was a time in my life when I was fat, ugly, and bald, and because remnants of this low self-esteem still remain, I have had a warped sense of sexual identity. When I think back to that part of my life, everything is intentionally dark and vague. There was a great deal of sleeping around with people who knew nothing of me nor I of them. There were a few one-night stands, all of them meaningless, all of them centered around lots of alcohol and sex. I remember carrying on a relationship, if you can call it that, with this man who thought I was in medical school. Despite my lies and the fact that I knew nothing about him except his name, address, and phone number (all of which could have been as fake as mine), the relationship lasted for a couple of months. I would call him whenever I was in town. We would go to dinner, go out on the town, and then have sex. As I think back on it now, it almost seems as if his wining and dining me were done in exchange for sexual favors I would render later. He and the others knew nothing of me. In fact, I did not even know myself in these futile attempts at connecting with men. With each penetration, I grew deeper and deeper into myself, to the point in which each sexual act was simply that, a sexual act between some man picked up at a bar and some woman who had lost all respect for herself.

That part of my life took place during my first two years in college. My existence at that time was almost a nonexistence based on lies and deceit, both to others and to myself. When I looked into a mirror I saw a disgusting body. I used that unwanted body to further devalue myself. I had one-night stands with men who did not know me because, at the time, I thought they were the only ones who would be attracted to me. Throughout my first two years in college I sincerely thought that if any man were to see me for whom I really was—a person infected by a disease that had scarred her physically and mentally for life—they wouldn't want to have anything to do with me. Who, in their right mind, would want to become romantically involved with someone who had just been treated for cancer and may potentially not be around long enough to provide any hope of a long-term relationship? Why would someone want me with all my problems? Life is complicated enough with just the daily hassles of living, who would want to bother with someone like me? How could anyone be aroused by a woman whose breasts are deformed? I always have to have the lights out when I have sex. I am using the term "sex," and not "making love," intentionally, because what I was doing with these one-night stands was not out of love but out of hopelessness.

Fortunately, that deadly game of love I was playing has ended. But it has taken an acquaintance rape, thoughts of suicide, and lots of psychotherapy to get me to where I am now. Through the help of my therapist, I have come to see that I am not such an abnormal and horrible person after all. I have stopped looking for love in all the wrong places, and I have come to realize that the love I search for is within me and not at some bar. I am probably making this happy ending sound quite easy, but it is not. I am still searching to find out more about myself. The older I become, the more I learn that there are a lot of gray areas in the world. With each answer I think I find, I have more questions.

I have come a long way from those days of one-night stands. I have since met someone who has been attracted to me for me personally and not as someone who could provide a service. He has shown me that love is not something one gets in exchange for something else. We have been together monogamously for more than a year and are still going strong. He is ten years my senior, and I often wonder if he is something like a father figure to me. Oftentimes, when I am with him, I feel like a child who is comforted by his love and attention—something I never got from my real father. Yet, even he does not understand me fully. I still long for someone who will truly feel what I have felt.

I realize that it is close to impossible for me to expect to meet someone who will understand what I have felt—the fact that it is hard for me to open up to people does not help matters. I see my family members, who are not demonstrably emotional people, and how they react to stress—usually by sticking together as a family to fight back, only to drift back into themselves again. Then I see myself, and I hope that I can be different. I hope my present boyfriend will be patient with me as I continue to search for who I am in the midst of my Chinese heritage and my fear of a recurrence of cancer.

Amy Lee is happily married. She works as a psychotherapist helping those living with chronic medical illnesses and personal growth issues. She herself continues to live with cancer.

CHALLENGING THE
"MODEL MINORITY" LABEL

Kenneth Lee   Receding Past, Advancing Future

Sitting on the brick porch of the college student center and sharing French fries with my friend Jim, I spent one afternoon watching other students tromp back and forth with bags of new books in each hand. I smiled, reflecting on all the people I had met in the first week of college and looking at the fall foliage in the distance. The maple and oak trees hanging overhead had begun to shed; brown and orange leaves slowly swept past me in the gentle winds. As I breathed in the clean New England air, thinking how at ease I felt at my college, a group of ten Asian American students wearing black trench coats walked past us.

"There goes the Asian invasion," Jim said without turning his head. I snapped my head toward him and looked at him incredulously.

"What?!" I gasped.

"There," he responded, pointing to the Asian American throng. "The Asian invasion." He turned to me and grinned. "Don't worry, man, you're different. . . ."

As those five words rolled off his tongue during my freshman orientation at college, I realized that I had accomplished something seemingly incredible. All my life, I wanted people to judge me for who I was, not just as another Asian American. I wanted people to see past my black hair and almond eyes, to make my Asianness transparent so that everyone could see the *real* me. By labeling me as "different," Jim validated the one thing that I desired most: individuality.

And yet, as an Asian American, I was shocked by the ignorance of his remark, the racist overtones that overwhelmed the compliment. As I repeated Jim's phrase over in my head, I began to question both his statement as well as myself. Was I really different? Did I belong to that cluster of Asian Americans when the only thing we shared appeared to be the features on our faces? Or did I belong in the American mainstream, even though my Asian features would always set me apart? Where did I belong?

Coming into college, I had been certain of my place in the world, where I fit into the melting pot of America. I believed that race did not matter and that people could, and should, look past differences in skin color. I believed in the merits of assimilation, conforming to the characteristics of the majority while still preserving individuality of the self. But at college, I found myself surrounded by a large Asian American community for the first time in my life, a community that challenged my notions of identity and questioned the quixotic world I had constructed. What did it mean to be Asian American? Was it just the black hair, the dark brown and narrow eyes? Was it dressing in black, associating primarily with other Asian Americans, and taking every opportunity to rail against "The White Man"? Or was it something much more than that, something deeper than skin . . . as thick as blood and older than America?

For years I had ignored my own heritage, trying to blend into the white world that surrounded me. I was a Burmese American who spoke neither Burmese nor practiced Buddhism. What kind of person was I—a Burmese American in shell only? Indeed, I questioned if I was hollow, an empty vessel of endless prime time sitcoms, Big Macs, Air Jordans, shopping malls, and French fries. I was Asian on the outside and American on the inside, living in two worlds, simultaneously belonging to both and neither. With Asian and white communities existing side by side at my college, I began to wonder which group I fit into. Did I even have to choose? Could I be like my older brother, who chose not to choose and instead mixed with whites, Asians, and other minorities throughout both high school and college? For the longest time I believed this was the ideal path, the way all Americans should think, outside of skin and class and judgment. And yet, how could I deny that I looked different from most of the Caucasians in the world? Every person whom I have ever met identifies me as an Asian American. Do they secretly chime "ching-chong" every time I pass by? Or do they perceive me as an American? Is it something in between? Although this is my native country, people always ask where am I from *originally*. How many worlds can I possibly fit into? These are the questions and the issues that I have wrestled with. These are the demons of race and ethnicity that I have ignored for so long, demons that emerged in college and threatened to torment me. Only recently have I realized the need to acknowledge and fight them, or else be trapped in the tides of ignorance.

Questions of race and identity were much simpler in Needham, a pre-dominantly wealthy, white suburb of Boston, Massachusetts, where I was born and raised. I grew up in a household of six—my parents, my grand-parents, my brother, and me—three generations living under one roof. In 1975, my mother and father emigrated from Burma (currently known as Myanmar), a Southeast Asian country located between India and China (while "Burma" is an anachronistic, British colonial term, I will use it throughout my piece since this was the term my parents used). The so-cialist military of Burma had seized control of the government in 1961, na-tionalizing all private enterprise and throwing the once prosperous "Jewel of Asia" into economic turmoil. My parents, who met and married in med-ical school, decided upon graduation to leave Burma for a better life in America. They arrived in New York with only seven U.S. dollars between them but with a drive to succeed in America. They eventually found jobs as doctors in Boston: my father worked in obstetrics and my mother in pe-diatrics. In 1980, my father brought his mother and father, whom I would call Paw-Paw and Kong-Kong (Burmese for grandmother and grandfa-ther, respectively), to live with the family. My brother, Arthur, and I were born two years apart, first-generation Americans.

From an early age I realized that I did not physically look like the Cau-casians who lived in the neighborhood. My straight black hair and almond eyes appeared radically different from the brown hair and blue eyes of the people whom I saw as I walked down tree-lined streets holding my mother's hand. On television, I never saw any characters who looked like me. "Your father and I grew up in Burma," my mother told me when I was very young, signaling from the start that our family was *different.* "Al-though you are Burmese, you look Chinese like your father. I do not look very Burmese either because my skin is light. Your Uncle Lha Kaba, he is tall and dark-skinned, *he* looks Burmese." Throughout my childhood, my mother told me stories of her life in Burma, constructing an elaborate world in my imagination. She told me how she grew up with eight broth-ers and sisters at 48 Latha Street, how she waited for the *muhinga* vendor to come by in the mornings with his vat of famous broth, how the fish in America was okay but not as good as the fresh fish found in the Rangoon marketplace. My home was built upon story and tradition.

One might have thought that in a home where Hakka Chinese, Bur-mese, and English were spoken, I would have grown up multilingual. This was hardly the case. I began speaking very late for a child—at age three. When I did begin to speak though, I spoke both English and Burmese. Yet, from the very beginning, I was exposed to far more English. Watching television and seeing newspapers on the table, I increasingly encountered English speakers and words. At night, I cuddled in my mother's bed as she read books such as *Curious George* and the *Berenstain Bears* to me. Immersed in an English-speaking environment, my Burmese skills inevitably deteriorated. By age four and the start of kindergarten, I began using English primarily to communicate with my parents; I called my mother "Mom" instead of the Burmese term "Mei-Mei." Tragically, as I see it know, by age five my Burmese skills had fallen to the point at which I could not recall simple words and phrases that I had used only a few years earlier. I began to speak even more English to make up the deficit.

While other Asian parents may have been shocked to see their children lose their mother tongue, my parents hardly voiced any disappointment. After all, they themselves never taught either my brother or me to read or write in Burmese. Perhaps they saw my decline in Burmese skills and my rise in English skills as a natural part of growing up in America. But even more important, my parents did not bring a wealth of "culture" into the household. They never celebrated any Burmese festivals or holidays to remind me of their homeland, nor did they force any traditions on me. The one holiday we did celebrate, Chinese New Year, was celebrated by eating noodles. I barely had any sense of what it meant to be Burmese. Rather, the culture I was born into was a distinctly American one, a consumer experience that had me clamoring for pizza, Chips Ahoy! cookies, and Transformer figurines.

My father seemed deeply ambivalent about my Americanization. On one hand, he approved of my growing English skills, an American voice without any trace of foreign accent. "People respect you because you can talk good," he once said. But on the other hand, he despised the increasing grip of American life over his children.

"You Americans!" my father often screamed when he saw Arthur and me eating pizza at the dinner table. "You Americans don't eat *our* food because you . . . you . . . you've been brainwashed by all that television!" This was my father's version of parenting: screaming and complaining about our Americanisms.

I hardly knew my father growing up, but I inherited his blood. . . . stoic, measured, willful. During childhood, my father was a distant, almost solitary figure. In many ways, he was a typical Chinese father, where his only major role in the family was to place food on the table. Working double shifts at the hospital to save every penny for my college tuition, he usually came home tired and grumbling. He flopped in front of TV or listened to talk radio, preferring to scream at the weatherman or the first-time caller than speak to Arthur or me. In fact, he seemed to spend more time arguing with his parents than talking to his own children.

When I was five years old, I spilled a cup of water on the table. My father leapt up, threw down his chopsticks, and glowered over me. "Ai ya!!!! You're spilling! You are *always* spilling things! You *always* do this!!" I shrunk into my seat, unable to look at him. If I ever spilled a drop of chicken curry onto the table, he would point and grunt in disapproval. When he complained, my face usually flushed and I bit my lip; it came to the point where I feared making mistakes around him. In order not to provoke him, I gradually stopped talking or doing anything around him. My father's short temper was not a cultural phenomenon, just a personal one. So was his thriftiness.

The first time he took me to a Toys"R"Us, I asked him to buy a water gun for me. Looking at the price and scowling, he said, "You want *this*? No, you don't need this." The gun was only five dollars. "I never had toys growing up. I only had a tin can and chopsticks; it was my drum. That was my only toy. You Americans . . . you are all so spoiled." After that, I learned not to ask my father to buy anything for me unless I wanted to hear him complain. By the time I reached high school, I stopped responding to his perpetual complaints, answering him with "Yeah, whatever."

My mother and I, on the other hand, have always been close. When I was very young, my mother cooked fried rice and noodles for the whole family on Saturday mornings. I always stood behind her, clutching her red *longhi* (a sarong) with my tiny fist, looking up at her back as she tilted the wok back and forth over the gas stove with her left hand, her right hand darting back and forth over the counter for a bottle of soy sauce or a bowl of bean sprouts. Cooking was always a loud affair, the pans hissing and crackling, the air vent roaring overhead, the spatula scraping the speckled black and silver surface of the worn iron wok. The kitchen smelled like onions, the walls and cupboards habitually covered with a thin film of grease. The scent of fish sauce, curry, garlic, and turmeric permeated the kitchen air, hung in the corners for days. The kitchen was alive. I loved those mornings clinging to my mother's thigh, sniffing the scent of peanut oil from her *longhi*, standing by her side just to be with her.

My mother was the center of the household. She fulfilled the role of the typical Asian mother by taking care of all household duties, such as cooking and cleaning. But she also worked full-time as a pediatrician. As a young boy, I saw the differences between my mother, who came home from work, gave me a hug, and then started to prepare dinner, and my father, who came home from work and complained about his day. Although my mother and father both played into traditional gender roles, my mother's tireless efforts at work and at home made me respect her far more than I did my father.

My mother helped me with my homework, prepared cupcakes for school bake sales, occasionally bought me toys, and did everything a mother could possible do. She once told me, "Your father's parents wanted to help raise you when you were younger, but I told them that I could handle it by myself. I don't want you to turn out like your father." I realized early on that I was my mother's creation, a boy shielded as much as possible from the influence of my father's side of the family.

And yet, my mother could not shield me from the outside world, which was seeping into everyday life. I could not hide in the world of the *longhi* forever when the world of McDonald's French fries, Super Mario Brothers, and Jell-O pudding snacks were calling. Television and the start of elementary school provided outlets into the white world. At the time, I never felt that the Burmese and white worlds existed in isolation of the other, but instead blended into a happy, seamless existence.

I embraced the white world through my friendships with classmates and neighbors. My best friend in elementary school was Matt, whose parents were first generation Italian Americans. I owe a large chunk of my "Americanization" to Matt, whose family embodied the ideal American family in my mind. At Matt's house, I learned how to play baseball and tasted my first spaghetti and meatballs. At the age of seven, I also witnessed my first "proper" Friday night family dinner. Knives and forks were arranged around a wooden table with napkins and clean, dry plates. The kitchen smelled like freshly baked bread and oregano, the way a home should smell. Matt, his parents, and his siblings sat and asked, "How did your day go?" When I told my parents that I was going to eat at Matt's house, they cautioned me to chew with my mouth shut, keep my elbows off the table, and be courteous. But Matt's family acted so casually that dinner was always fun and loud; it felt more natural than dinners at my own house.

I often came back from Matt's house, belly fat with chicken Parmesan and rigatoni, telling my mother how Mrs. Capriotti's food was superior to ours. I pointed out how their kitchen didn't smell like grease and how all their dinner plates had matching blue designs on the edge. My mom usually nodded and smiled as I went on and on about the Capriotti household.

In contrast, my family rarely ate together. After returning from school, my brother and I would usually eat chicken curry or fried rice in front of the TV set. When my father returned home at 9 p.m., my mother stewed noodles and vegetables for the two of them. While my brother and I did homework at the dinner table, writing out multiplication tables and vocabulary words, my father would sit in his chair in a "Beijing squat," slurp soup, and whine to my mother how some patient had disrespected him that day. There was rarely any dialogue between my father and me that mirrored the conversations between Matt and his father, who high-fived as they talked about the most recent New York Yankees victory.

My friendship with Matt solidified my comfort around Caucasians at an early age, as did my friendships with other white neighborhood kids in Needham. With tree-lined streets and churches on every other corner, Needham was once labeled by a major metropolitan newspaper as "one of the last white enclaves in Boston." While my family was one of a handful of Asian families in the area, I was rarely treated any differently from other children in Needham. People never stared as I walked down the street, nor did they follow me around in stores or beat me up. This was a major benefit of living near Boston; even though Needham was not highly populated by minorities, everyone had seen Asian faces before. I was hardly a novelty.

Nevertheless, I did face moments of discrimination in my neighborhood. The first racial incident of my life that I can recall took place in front of my house when I was six years old. My brother had recently taught me how to ride a bike, and I was practicing riding back and forth on the sidewalk. As I focused on the rotation of the front tire, I inadvertently veered off the sidewalk and ran right into the path of another bicyclist. As my front tire ground along the tire of the other bike, the cyclist braked to a halt. I gazed up to see the scowling eyes of a blond teenager.

"Don't you know how to ride, you fucking Chink?" he snarled. He reached out for my handlebars and thrust my bike away, riding off and muttering to himself. It was the first time I had ever been called a Chink. I had no idea what it meant. But it hurt. I quickly peddled to my backyard where my brother and his friends were playing. I said nothing to them. I never told anyone what happened. Although this episode frightened me, I did not develop negative feelings about Caucasians; after all, Matt was white and we were best friends. I believed that one person could not represent a group.

My cultural assimilation began in the streets of Needham, but they solidified as I progressed though elementary school. I attended a public school where there was a diverse mix of whites, Asians, and Latinos. At such early ages, racial boundaries did not exist; there were no cliques or ethnic divisions. I knew my friends looked different from me, but I did not care. No one cared.

In second grade, when my teacher told the class to depict "America: The Melting Pot," I drew children in sixty-four Crayola colors falling into a big gray frying pan, where inside everyone was a smiling, happy American. I liked that drawing a lot. It was how I envisioned America to be, a place where different people came together to become something unified, something better.

As I melted into the hodgepodge of elementary school, I ignored my Asian attributes and focused my energies on becoming as American as possible. Like all the other children, I ate pizza, drank milk, and talked about Thundercats cartoons. I stopped speaking Burmese at home as English became my primary language. I wanted to fit in—to be like everyone else. For the most part, I succeeded. I had many white friends who treated me like their brother. In fact, I was more popular than many Caucasian boys because I was a good athlete. My English was flawless, and I watched so much TV that I knew more about TV programs than the other kids. I was "cool."

And yet, there were always signs that I would never be truly considered American. When I was ten years old, I played a game of pick-up basketball at the park with my friends and a fifty-year-old man who was a park regular. Unlike most of my friends, I had never played much basketball before. I missed most of my shots badly and kept dribbling the ball out of bounds. The older man, who was on my team, began to mutter and avoid passing me the ball. The next time I got the ball, I shot it and actually scored.

"Hwaaaaaa!"

The man whooped like Bruce Lee in his action films and began to move his fists in a kung fu pattern. He looked right at me and laughed. I gritted my teeth and grew hot in the face. The man saw this and laughed harder. As soon as the game was over, I steamed off the court, trying to unlock my bike from the chain-link fence.

The man scoffed to one of my white friends, "These Chinese kids don't know how to play."

I tried to ignore his words. I wanted to run away.

"Kenneth is really fast," my friend said, "He can play."

"Nah," I heard the man say as I peddled away, "none of these Chinks can play." I peddled even harder to get as far away from him as possible. What had I done to provoke this man? I did not play basketball well, but was this grounds for him to ridicule me? Did I fit into the stereotype of the uncoordinated, unathletic Asian? The worst thing about the entire incident was that I did not say a single thing back to him. In his eyes, I was a poor athlete who ran away when confronted. This only confirmed the Asian stereotype in his eyes.

Whenever incidents like this occur, I pass through several stages of emotional response. My immediate reaction is often one of bitterness and anger. The slurs change from time to time, sometimes it is Ching-Chong and other times it is Chink, but they always hurt. They hurt because the words are representative of a greater hate and ignorance in the world. I realize that for all my Americanization, I may never be considered an American. But since these incidents were few and far between, I tried not to let them affect my worldview, my belief that people could see past my skin and realize I was just as American as anyone else.

I carried this attitude to my high school, Adelphi Prep, one of the best private schools in Boston. On my first day of sixth grade, I sat next to a black student, Luke, who turned to me and asked, "Are you Chinese?" "No," I answered, "I am Burmese." I developed this line into my standard answer whenever people wanted to know "what I was." People knew little about Burma and rarely ever asked further questions. My obscure nationality became convenient because it provided a means to neutralize the race issue. People knew I was Burmese, but in giving them little else to judge my Asianness, I made them judge me for my personality instead. By being Burmese, I also avoided the broad categorizations of "Chinese" or "Japanese" that people often use to generalize Asian ethnicities. I used my Burmese background in name only because it differentiated me. It made me distinct, as my brother and I were the only Burmese students in Adelphi Prep.

Throughout high school, I downplayed my Asian culture and heritage as much as possible. I believed that people should be judged for who they were on the inside, not for the color of their skin, the shape of their eyes, or the type of clothes they wore. To this extent, I tried my best to make my Asian attributes transparent, an invisible shell that people could look past in order to see the "real" me. I never spoke Burmese in front of my friends, nor did I declare that my favorite food was *Ohnokowswear*, a coconut chicken broth famous in Rangoon. When friends asked if I knew how to speak Chinese, I emphatically proclaimed, "No!"

The homogeneity of high school culture contributed further to my overall assimilation into the mainstream. While Adelphi had a large minority population of blacks, Latinos, and Asians integrated into the social framework, true understanding of diversity did not exist within the school boundaries. I had an extremely diverse group of friends in high school, but we never talked about racism, as if it did not exist within our borders. To me, Adelphi was a melting pot, where all differences and all races amalgamated into something cohesive—something better. Even the school stressed over and over the importance of belonging to the Adelphi community, a type of conformism in itself. I believed in that philosophy, that people should put aside differences and come together as a tight community.

For this reason, I rarely attended the meetings of the Asian Caucus, a small group of Asian students who played mah-jongg and watched Hong Kong action films together. I believed they were an Asian support group: unpopular Asian Americans at Adelphi who needed to associate with each other, their ethnicity a crutch. The Asian Caucus, to me, represented the worst type of organization because it promoted isolationism. I felt students who joined ethnic-based clubs banded together for no reason other than their ethnicity.

I attended only one Asian Caucus meeting during my Adelphi career. My friend Phil was giving a speech on the lack of an Asian American presence at Adelphi Prep. As I walked into the classroom late and strutted to a seat in the back of the room, I felt superior to many of the kids in the room because I did not *need* to be there.

Phil posed the question, "How can we raise Asian awareness around Adelphi?" No one spoke for thirty seconds. I thought the moment ironic . . . *this* was why there was a lack of Asian awareness at Adelphi: the silence of the Asian community, the inability to speak up.

"I think we can start by being more vocal," I snidely quipped.

Everyone in the room stared at me. "Who *are* you?" they must have thought. No one said anything for the next few seconds. During that time, I felt more out of place in that room of Asians than I did at any other time in my Adelphi career.

My brother, Arthur, never cared much for the Asian Caucus either. Like me, he believed such ethnic-based organizations created more discord than unity in the Adelphi community. While both of us integrated well into the Adelphi mainstream, my brother was even more at ease than I was. Whereas I wanted to *believe* that race was a nonissue, Arthur *made* it a nonissue. During his junior year, he began dating a Caucasian girl named Stephanie. Although this relationship only lasted a month, I took this as a symbol of Arthur's supreme confidence of his place within the white-dominated culture. While Arthur made headway into the mainstream through charisma and confidence, I achieved a degree of social acceptance through high school athletics.

The stereotypical perception of Asians is often a book nerd who is physically inept and uncoordinated; I took pride in smashing that stereotype. I was the only Asian American football player in the school. I started on the junior varsity team as running back and cornerback. On the varsity, I started at corner and then moved to starting outside linebacker. During the winter and spring seasons for all four years, I ran track and pole-vaulted. I was captain of both track teams in my senior year.

I benefited enormously from being a good high school athlete. The stereotype of the "weak Asian" never followed me at any point at Adelphi Prep. In fact, my Asianness played no role as far as athletics were concerned. Within the football team, I was just another "one of the guys." Outside the team, I earned respect from other students because of my participation in high school sports. On an internal level, I was proud that I was an *Asian American* athlete. I was "cooler" than most of my nonathletic Asian American peers. I lifted weights to gain a "ripped" body, taking pride that I was probably the only Asian American at school to have one.

Although being an athlete helped me gain a measure of respect, I was far from being socially adept. Unlike my brother, I never had a girlfriend in my seven years at Adelphi. Part of the problem was my lack of social skills. I always felt nervous around girls—to me, they were another species. Fearing I might say something stupid or offensive in front of them, I chose to say nothing at all. Even in my junior year, I became anxious whenever a girl sat next to me in history class. Additionally, all my friends through childhood had been boys—I never had much practice talking to girls.

The other part of the problem was my perception. The vast majority of girls at Adelphi were white; I was not. There were no Asian American girls in my grade, so I consequently focused my high school crushes on Caucasian girls. I never let anyone know whom I was attracted to because I was sure my feelings would never be returned. Caucasian girls would never find me attractive because, after all, I was Asian. Walking through the halls of Adelphi Prep, I often watched the eyes of white girls as we walked past each other. Their eyes passed right through me; I was not even there. Were Asian males not masculine enough? Even though I was strong, tall, and fit, was I still not good enough in their eyes?

I often said to myself, "I wish I were white." During free periods, I watched white boys and girls casually flirt in the library, sometimes kissing in public. I longed to be those white kids, who did not have to worry about racial boundaries. Even though I wanted to believe that race was truly a nonissue, the problems stared me right in the face. I tried to ignore the problem, the reality of it all, and worked harder to be more American than ever before. I shopped at the Gap, ate at Burger King, anything to make me fit in.

And yet, there were constant reminders that I was not white. My brother and I were once walking home from school when we passed three white men on the corner. One of them turned to the others, smirked and said, "Want to mess with the noodles?" I did not realize what the men meant, but one block later my brother whispered to me that the men were talking about starting a fight with us "noodles." I flew into a rage and almost turned back toward the men. Who did they think they were?

"Kenneth, calm down!" my brother sternly said. We stopped walking and he looked me in the eyes. "What are you going to do if you go back over there? What is that going to accomplish? Think about it." I could not think; I was too mad.

"But we can't let them go on saying shit like that!" I shouted.

"Yes, you can. Just walk away."

I have always hated the passivity that Asian Americans are said to display . . . that we don't complain, we work silently, we're not political. I hate it. And I told myself that I would never be one to fall into that stereotype. And yet, here my brother was telling me not to act, playing the voice of reason. And the more I thought about it, the more I realized he was right. What could I have done to change those men in any way? Would walking up to them and telling them off have changed anything? It's a helpless feeling when people you do not even know say things meant to hurt.

At Adelphi, I worked hard at my studies and did well in school, but my father seemed apathetic about my education. However, he surprised me junior year when he offered to drive me along the East Coast to look at colleges. When we arrived on the Yale campus, I stepped out in front of the admissions office.

"Dad, are you coming? The tour starts in five minutes."

"No. I don't feel like walking around. I'm going to park the car over there and sleep." He gestured to a shady spot under some maple trees in the distance.

"But . . . aren't you coming on the tour?"

"No."

"But . . . what do I do? Should I just come back here when it's finished?" "You can look around. Just wake me up when you get back." I felt bitter that he took so little interest in a process as important as college selection. As I walked by myself on the campus tour, I noticed every other teenager had their parents walking with them, asking questions, pointing to different buildings, and laughing. I felt alone.

And yet, I often did not give my dad enough credit. While he could never say that he loved me, he showed it through actions. I often woke on Sunday mornings and found sesame bagels and Philadelphia cream cheese sitting on the breakfast table. "Eat the bagels," my father would say without looking up from the Sunday *New York Times* Week in Review. "I got them cheap . . . twelve for three dollars." "That's great, Dad," I would laugh as I sat across from him. My father kept his head down, engrossed in some international event or financial crisis. We read and ate in silence on those mornings, the only sound being turning pages, never talking too much but never having to.

I seldom thought much about *why* he bought the Sunday *New York Times* and the bagels. He did not like either the *Times* or bagels; he much preferred the *Boston Herald* and steamed pork buns. But thinking back, he bought the *Times* and the bagels for me. While bitter that my father was not a great parent, I always knew that he loved me. He only expressed that love through complaints and naggings, but at least he cared. The day before I left for college, he asked me how to use the word processor on the Macintosh. I showed him and then went upstairs to watch TV. When I went to the basement later that night, I found a white, 8.5- by 11-inch piece of paper on the table. On the page he had typed the words *I love you.*

The start of college was an eye-opening experience. For the first time in my life I was on my own, without parental or high school teacher supervision. Unlike Needham, my college had a large minority population, unregulated and immense. For someone accustomed to wearing a tie and blazer and having an ethnically diverse group of friends, just the experience of watching other Asian Americans dress in black and self-congregate was new and awkward, almost frightening. Unlike the "melting pot" homogeneity of Adelphi Prep, my college offered an infinitely more diverse and complex social order to negotiate. Race was no longer an issue I could avoid.

However, I tried my best to ignore it as long as possible. During my first week, I received an e-mail from the College Asian Organization (CAO) inviting me to attend their first meeting. Knowing nothing about the group, I assumed it served a similar purpose as Adelphi's Asian Caucus: a social group for Asians who could not fit into the mainstream. I deleted the e-mail. In that first week, Arthur, who was at my college as well, asked me if I had attended any CAO meetings yet.

"I haven't gone to any meetings so far," I responded.

"I didn't think you would. You really limit the people you meet on campus if you join organizations like that."

"You think so?"

"Look around you, man. Why do you think all the Asians hang out together? Because that's who they know." My brother's conviction that race should not be a limiting factor when integrating into the mainstream made a lot of sense. Just as in high school, I did not want to be confined to knowing only Asians; joining CAO would seemingly contribute to that effect. Without realizing it, my own interactions with Asians and non-Asians during freshman year mirrored my brother's behavior. While I did not consciously or subconsciously imitate him, I believe Arthur and I came to college with such similar outlooks that our social decisions were nearly identical.

I also opted not to join either the Korean American Student Association (KASA) or the Asian Christian Fellowship, two strong Asian American institutions on the campus. As I was neither Korean nor Christian, I never felt the impetus to attend their meetings. By not joining any of these three groups, I closed the door to places that many other Asian Americans on campus would call home. But I was absolute in my determination not to limit the types of friends I made early on. Students at my college are quick to label Asian Americans who self-associate as "one of those" Asian Americans. I refused to be categorized.

One day, as I passed through the dining hall, a Korean friend, Sarah, invited me to sit with her and her group of friends. I did, but I was keenly aware that ours was clearly an "Asian table" with eight other Asian Americans already seated. By sitting down, I essentially "joined" a group that could be easily stereotyped. When a white acquaintance passed by our table and said "hi" to me, I looked up, and gestured with my hand but said nothing. I did not want her to see me with a large conglomerate of Asians. I chatted quickly with Sarah's friends and then bolted from the table. I was not ashamed to associate with other Asians, but to be grouped as "one of them" in my first week of school was out of the question. I would not let that happen. This was a situation that other Asian Americans may have undergone years ago in high school, but one that I now experienced for the first time. In the face of a sea of Asian Americans, I needed to maintain my individuality by asserting my Americanness.

During my first two weeks at college, I hung out mostly with my hall mates. Since they were all white, many of the friends I met through them were also white. I also met many Asians, not through CAO, but through regular means. I was so immersed in making new friends that I did not think of home until I received an abrupt call from my father on a Sunday morning two weeks into the term.

"Kenneth, is that you?" His voice was soft and calm. He cleared his throat. "Paw-Paw died Saturday morning." My mouth fell. I could not believe it. I knew that she had been growing sicker over the past year, but it was shocking to hear. "Arthur and you should drive down on Thursday. There will be a wake on Friday." He hung up the phone.

She was gone. As I sat on my bed and stared at the ceiling, I realized that she had been a ghost to me for a long time. When I was very young, she watched over me after school by making sure I stayed out of trouble. But as I grew older, increasingly speaking only English and embracing the fast-paced world of America, Paw-Paw faded into the background of the household. Since she spoke only Hakka Chinese and rudimentary Burmese, she had no means to communicate with me except through garbled phrases that I rarely understood. I nearly stopped talking to her altogether because communication became too difficult. She became symbolic of a past that I never knew and practically ignored.

At my grandmother's wake, all I could think of was *Zay twama*. *Zay twama* was one of the few phrases I said to my grandmother in the last few months of her life. We seldom talked. She woke up early in the mornings and steamed hard-boiled eggs in the kitchen, then sat in her usual seat by the window that faced the rear of the house, tapping the eggshells with a spoon. She never smiled, the bags of her wrinkled skin sketching a perpetual frown onto her cheeks. Every day she looked out the windows into those cool, gray mornings, staring at the concrete walls and the apartment complexes looming two blocks over. In Rangoon, my mother told me how Paw-Paw walked to market every morning, purchasing fresh fish and scallions, fearlessly bargaining with the outdoor merchants. In America, she seldom left the house. She traveled to Chinatown and church on weekends but returned home right afterward. Usually, she just sat by the window and watched her children and her grandchildren walk into the wide open spaces of America.

Zay twama means "going to the market." Whenever I wanted to leave the house, she asked *"Bae twama?"* wanting to know where I was going. Where was I going? I was a senior in high school: I was going to school, to the movies, to friends' houses, to Landsdowne Street. Every single time I left the house, she asked where I was going. It was incredibly irritating. Even if I only wanted to head up the block to buy the *New York Times*, she asked over and over again as I put on my sneakers when I was coming back. She was afraid of being alone; she was afraid intruders would enter the house and take her away. I ignored her endless questions, simply saying *Zay twama* as I headed out the door. This to the woman who saw me grow up from a baby into a man over twenty years.

The last time I saw her alive was the day I left for college. I had just finished packing the car with all my bags and clothes. Walking to her room upstairs, I saw her sitting on the side of the bed, waiting for me to come to her. She weighed less than a hundred pounds, her skin hung loosely off her frame like plastic bags. She saw me and smiled. Her eyes were filled with tears, which streamed down her cheeks. I hugged her. Walking back down the stairs, I realized how little I knew about my grandmother, and yet how much she loved me. It occurred to me that we never had a real discussion.

Few people came to Paw-Paw's wake, mostly friends of my parents to offer condolences. Only three elderly friends from her Chinese church came; Paw-Paw did not know many people in America. The room was sparsely filled with more ostentatious flower arrangements than people.

She lay inside the casket in the dark lavender suit she always wore to church, her face caked with powder, her body like a wax figurine. As I stood over her for the last time, memories from early childhood flooded back, times when she helped me to use the toilet, when she brought home Rabbit-brand candies from Chinatown for me. I wanted to cry, to release my thoughts and my regrets. But I could not. Instead of sadness, I felt empty and hollow. . . . that I hardly knew this tiny woman lying before me, that I could not force myself to cry, that I neglected her presence through nineteen years of childhood, that I was a heartless grandson.

My father stood quietly in the corner of the room, thanking people for coming. I wanted to see him cry, to tear, anything to demonstrate some emotion for the first time. Nothing. He did not cry once. While my brother, my mother, and everyone else in the room cried, my father and I stared at the dimly lit walls of the funeral home. So we stood side-by-side as the caretakers closed the casket, father and son, stoic and quiet in our matching black suits.

I returned to Hanover dedicated to reconnecting with my past. I selected Mandarin Chinese for my foreign language requirement with the sole intent of speaking to my grandfather and father in their native tongue. I dreamed of returning to Needham after freshman year and having long discourses with my grandfather about World War II, his childhood, why he decided to immigrate to Burma. I wanted to see the pride in my father's face when I could greet him with "Ni hao ma?" and maybe, just maybe, connect with him now that I knew his primary language. Perhaps this might bring us closer. I wanted all these things so badly that I eagerly plunged into Chinese class to master Mandarin and to realize my dream.

First-year Chinese was a disaster. On the first day of class, the teacher began to speak in Mandarin and didn't stop for five minutes straight. Finally, she said something in English that I could understand.

"This is a rare instance when I will speak to you in English this term. We will learn Mandarin by speaking Mandarin."

My head spun. During the first two weeks of classes, I did not understand a single thing in class. Chinese characters did not make sense to me. Unlike the English alphabet, which has phonetic sounds associated with letters that can be strung together to form words, Chinese characters consisted of multiple strokes, each character a different word with different meanings and sounds attached. I spent hours every night memorizing stroke after stroke, forgetting the characters only ten minutes later. In order to practice our Chinese verbal ability, considered the most important aspect of the language, we were expected to memorize and recite Mandarin dialogues in front of the class every Wednesday. I never gained the ability to string the characters into sentences, and so instead of memorizing grammar patterns and complete sentences, I spent long Tuesday nights memorizing the correct order of a thousand syllables. To worsen the situation, more than half the class consisted of Chinese Americans who already spoke Chinese at home and wanted an easy A. The Chinese professor often shook her head in disappointment when I struggled through simple readings. I began to hate attending class, to loathe everything about the Chinese language.

When I returned home for Thanksgiving break, I tried some of the Chinese I had learned on my grandfather. He could hardly understand me. My tones were wrong, and my words came out too slowly. When he spoke, it was too quick for me to understand. My father laughed at my pathetic attempts at conversation; he told me to study harder. But studying harder did not help me understand anything better. My dream of communicating with my father and connecting with my Chinese heritage seemed to slip away with every character that spilled from my mouth. I was too far removed from my Chinese past, too far away to ever capture its essence.

My separation from my Chinese past became all the more apparent when I traveled to Beijing on a college foreign study program. Strangely, for the first time in my life, I was in the majority. It was an amazing sight, to walk in streets where *everyone* had black hair and narrow eyes, where no one gave a second thought about me. I blended in totally and completely, at least physically. As soon as I opened my mouth, however, I fell back into the minority. When native speakers heard my slow speech and erroneous tones, they assumed that I was an *erbenren*, a Japanese person, most likely a tourist. Most were shocked when I told them I was a *meiguoren*, an American. What was certain was that I was not one of them. I did not truly belong in China any more than I did in the streets of Needham.

Back at college, though, I was fitting in better than at any other time in my life. I never doubted that I had made the right decisions because I made numerous acquaintances from all parts of campus during freshman year. Although I had been a bit of a social recluse in high school, I took every opportunity to meet new people at college. I still stood outside the majority of the existing Asian American population, but my interactions with other Asian Americans, especially girls, helped me socially. Since I was tall and athletic, a lot of Asian American girls thought I was handsome, which naturally boosted my ego. For the first time, I stopped feeling inferior about my own body, confident there were people who liked me as I was.

I began seeing a Korean American girl named Tina during my freshman fall semester. Previously intimidated in the presence of women, I felt at ease whenever talking to her. Tina was a peppy, outgoing girl from New Jersey who actually seemed interested in things I had to say. Like me, she was from a predominantly white neighborhood and considered herself Americanized. Our discussions seemed so natural that I wondered why I had not talked to girls before. We hit it off immediately and saw each other for three months. Although it did not work out in the end, our relationship meant a lot to me because it played such an integral role in my social development. For the first time, I knew that I could act naturally around a girl without being self-conscious. I came to the realization that girls were people too, and I need not worry about embarrassing myself all the time. Furthermore, simply knowing that someone thought I was attractive made me that much more confident in other social interactions.

Overall, freshman year was one of the best periods of my life. But this made the sobering reality of sophomore year feel much worse. Many sophomores began joining my college's Greek fraternities and sororities; many Asian males in particular joined Tri-Kap, which was known as the Asian frat. Since I did not drink alcohol and generally disapproved of diluting my individuality in the name of brotherhood, I declined to pledge into the Greek system. As many of my friends found homes in the Greek system or in other cliques, I found myself alone. While I had many good individual relationships, I had no coherent group or place to fall back on. It dawned on me how polarized the college campus was, how Greek sisters and brothers associated mostly with their houses, how African Americans tended to cluster with African Americans, how Asians tended to cluster with other Asians. The happy mirage of freshman year was over. Perhaps the reality was always there, and I had just neglected to see it.

The Greek system challenged and ultimately severed several of my friendships in the first months of sophomore year. Some of my male friends began to associate primarily with their fraternity brothers. Likewise, most of my female friends joined sororities; I began to see them less and less on weekdays and weekends. During this difficult period, I realized that many of my friends were finding new homes on this campus, highlighting the fact that I did not have one. I began to reevaluate many of my relationships, questioning if my large number of acquaintances was worth supporting in contrast to establishing a close group of friends.

As I began to question many of my past relationships, I also began to question myself. How did I put myself into this situation? Where was my home? Who were my true friends? The college mainstream seemed to have gone Greek, and I, who had always wanted to be in the mainstream, was anti-Greek. I also observed how many acquaintances of mine who attended CAO meetings during freshman year were still great friends with other Asian Americans during sophomore year. Perhaps I had missed out on something great as a freshman. I started to ponder my identity as an Asian American during this time of self-reflection. At college, people seemed more willing to celebrate their differences than to gloss over them as I had done. People were proud of their Asian history, not ignorant of it. How this differed from the mentality I had taken with me throughout high school and freshman year! I had always attempted to be accepted as an American and let my individuality stand on its own. At the expense of my Asian heritage, which I hardly thought about growing up, I had fully adopted an American persona, which I used to integrate into my college's campus culture. I had thus far ignored the entire Asian American social scene, never attended a CAO culture night, never gone to a China Society meeting. I realized that I was disconnected from the rest of the Asian community, that I was alone and hurting badly.

I also realized that my college was hardly the social nirvana I thought it was during my freshman year. My college is a white college. The vast majority of students are white, the faculty is white, and the residents of Hanover are white. And even though this is an Ivy League college, there will always be traces of racism. During the winter of my junior year, I attended a dinner with five sorority sisters and their dates at Panda House, a Chinese restaurant in Hanover. Although the dinner consisted mostly of small talk, much of the conversation revolved around who-hooked-up-with-whom and novel drinking games, inane conversation that only solidified my view that the Greek system contributed little to my college's intellectual life. I was the only Asian American at the table, but I was out of my element because of the discussion, not because of my race. As the evening drew to a close, one of the sisters looked around for our waiter so that we could pay the check.

"Which one of these guys is our waiter?" she asked the table.

"I don't know. They all look the same," one of her sisters blurted. When I heard her, I shot a glance over to her, my face tightened and fists clenched. She turned in my direction, met my glare, then turned to one of her friends. She put her hand over her mouth and comically mouthed "Oops!" with an innocent shrug of the shoulders. She was not even apologizing to me; she was "oops-ing" because I, an Asian American, had heard her comment. I burned on the inside, wanting to say something to her, but knowing this was neither the time nor the place to do so.

My social interactions with women at college expanded during sophomore and junior year, but never to the extent I would have liked. I was comfortable talking to women of all ethnicities, yet on a romantic level I never expanded beyond the Asian American realm. Despite the fact that I had a diverse group of friends, the two women I dated after Tina were both Asian Americans. One of my best friends, Kristina, once asked me if I only dated Asian women.

"No, I would date other girls, too," I said. "But . . . I don't know . . . it seems like only Asian girls are interested in me."

"Why don't you ask out white girls then?" Kristina responded. "You can't expect them to ask you out, you know." I shrugged my shoulders. I understood her point, but the solution was not that easy. Many white males on campus had Asian American girlfriends; there were few, if any, white women with Asian American boyfriends. This indicated to me that Asian males were not desired on a white-dominated campus. I had many white female friends, but I never considered asking any of them out. In my mind, to ask out a white girl was asking for rejection.

"I'm sure there are plenty of girls who would like to go out with you," Kristina said in an attempt to cheer me up. I smiled but doubted the verity of her statement.

Over the years I came to the realization that race *did* matter. There was no single epiphany, just a steady evolution borne of time and reflection. Furthermore, I recognized that I was not just American, but Asian American. I could no longer deny this. And in order to find true friends, I needed to let people see the real me; not the "me" who denied his Asian heritage, but the "me" who understood I was an Americanized Burmese American. While I maintained contact with my Caucasian friends, I made a concentrated effort to meet more Asian Americans.

Two of the most important friends I made during this time were Julie and Victor. Julie was a Taiwanese American who had also attended a private high school in the Northeast. Like me, she did not belong to any of the large Asian American cliques on campus and enjoyed a wide mix of friends. Victor was a Korean American with a strong sense of Korean tradition but likewise was not a member of a Greek house or an Asian American organization. After befriending Julie and Victor, I realized that I was not alone on the campus, there were other people like me who chose not to belong to the mainstream cultures. In addition, Julie and Victor provided the intellectual outlets I had previously and unsuccessfully sought. As Asian Americans, we shared common experiences growing up and living on margins of the larger Asian community. We discussed our different backgrounds and compared the ways our parents raised us. And yet that was not the reason why we associated with one another; we associated because we challenged each other in thought and argument. These two helped me build a foundation of tight-knit friends with whom I could share my thoughts and feelings. I no longer needed to hide my Asianness; I could be myself and true.

Although it took two years of difficult self-reflection, my college experience helped me realize much about myself. I came in believing in the melting pot, a noble concept no doubt, but one that was flawed and naïve. The presence of other Asians, the gain and loss of friends, and encounters with racism made me come to grips with my past and my identity. College taught me to think.

I recently asked my mother why she did not teach me Burmese growing up.

"Well . . . I think it's partly because of my experience with Arthur. He had a very difficult time understanding English in preschool. Paw-Paw and Kong-Kong spoke to him in Chinese, your dad and I talked to him in Burmese and English. He was not using enough English to understand it well. So when you started learning English in preschool, I thought it would be best for you to focus on that. I wasn't going to force you to learn Burmese at the same time."

"Did you think it was more important for us to learn English than Burmese?" There was a long pause before she spoke.

"Yes . . . it was important for you to fit in, to get a good education. Everyone here speaks English, I thought it was more important for you to learn English."

I asked her why she, unlike many Chinese and Korean parents, did not force us to speak Burmese at home. Many of my friends said their parents wanted to keep their culture and language intact.

"Most Burmese, like me, are Buddhist. We do not stress attachment—nothing is permanent, everything changes. We do not even own our bodies, how can we own the language? In Burma, we don't try to stop natural progress."

Her answer was simple, but it answered so much. I wondered if I would have been better off if she had forced me to speak Burmese against my will, so that I would have that link to the past as an adult. But my mother did what she thought was best for me. That is not something to regret.

During winter break of my senior year, as I sent out Christmas cards, I noticed that roughly half of them were addressed to Asian American friends. I scratched my head and thought about it for a second, unsure if I was happy or disappointed in that fact. My mind raced back to the five words spoken the first week of college: "Don't worry, man, you're different . . . ," the confusion I felt back then, the ambiguity of shock and pride. Three years later, the complexity of the issues has not faded. I cherish having a diverse group of friends. Still, I have made inroads into the Asian American realm, fully aware that I am Sino-Burmese and fully aware that I am quite Americanized. Although there were no particular incidents that crystallized the changes occurring inside of me, the important thing is that they *did* occur over time. I needed that time to realize that people *do* look at the color of my skin, they do see the features of my face. When people see me, they see an Asian American, not an American. But that's okay, I have come to accept that. By not acknowledging these facts, I was closing myself off, deluding myself, lost in a melting pot that had no meaning. I was shutting myself off from a people with whom I shared a bond thicker than blood and older than America. In the end, I have chosen not to choose. I choose to be me. I am both American and Asian American. This is the reality of the world I live in. This is the real me, what I present to others. No more masks, no more shells, no denial.

I often wonder what I will pass on to my children. I am certain that I can give them the love that my parents gave me. From my mother I learned of generosity, understanding, and warmth. I picture myself playing an active role in their childhood—reading *The Cat in the Hat* to my children at night, helping them with homework, taking them out to eat sushi on the spur of the moment. And despite our differences, I have learned much from my father. He has taught me to work hard, to value money, to be independent. I'd like to pass those values on to my children as well. But will they know anything of Burma and China? Will they learn another language? Will they be Asian in appearance only? I can give them love, support, and my thirst for knowledge, but is it enough? My mother would say yes. After all, life is about evolution. How can we hold on to what we do not own?

Still, I am constantly forced to reassess the past that has receded before me. My parents never gave me the culture that was their birthright. My own children will be even one step further from Burma and Burmese culture. What memories of the past can I deliver into their future? My mother's stories? The acceptance of inevitable change? But I refuse to look back at my abridged heritage with regret. After all, looking back is not in my nature. Like my father who came to America with seven dollars in his pocket and never looked back, I also look forward. I am constantly reminded of a quote in my favorite book, *The Great Gatsby:* "Gatsby believed in the green light, the orgiastic future that year by year recedes before us. It eluded us then, but that's no matter—tomorrow we will run faster, stretch out our arms farther." I am Gatsby in that respect—the American dreamer. I dream that someday I will be able to wholly and completely reconcile my identity, an identity that exists day by day, protean as the winds. I will never let go of my past, but my future lies somewhere out in the vast unknown of America. I will seize it.

After writing this essay in his senior year of college, Kenneth Lee went to New York City to work in publishing. Since then he has gone on to receive a graduate degree in English.

Fuyuki Hirashima   Balancing on the Hyphen

"All right, now here's a map of Japan." *Zip*, out flies a map of the world from the top of the chalkboard. "Let's discuss the cultural differences between America and Japan." Down, keep your eyes down. Same rules apply for staring at the sun—never look directly into the teacher's face. With my *samurai* (sixth sense), I can feel her eyes scanning, scanning the room, searching for the one. "Ah, Fuyuki, perhaps you can explain to the class what it's like to celebrate the Japanese festival of *obon*."

Through the fault of the eager teacher, I'm placed in a bind. I've never lived in Japan; I don't know what it's like to celebrate *obon*. But what's worse? Have your classmates think you're ignorant of your own culture, or rewrite just a teeny-tiny bit of Japanese history? It doesn't matter that I've never even heard of this holiday. It doesn't matter that I was born and raised in the United States. My face makes me the Japanese expert.

Like my face, my name sends up a red flag. Necessity forced me to ask my parents what my name meant. Throw out a foreign-sounding name with too many vowels, and people inevitably need to know what it means. *Fuyuki* translates into "winter treasure" in English. When naming me, my parents looked to a well-respected astrologer in the Japanese community, Minomi-san, for advice. The date, time, and place of my birth, the number of strokes in each of the characters of my potential name, and the alignment of the stars all were taken into account when choosing the perfect luck-filled word that would accompany me for the rest of my life. Even though it's actually a boy's name, the number of strokes in the name *Fuyuki* was perfect, so my parents decided to go with it. Minomi-san informed them that I was born under an extraordinarily lucky star, and that I would lead a successful and fruitful life.

My entry into this world was so effortless, so clear-cut. As I said, even the stars aligned themselves to favor my arrival. So, why does it feel as though all my life I've been carrying a load on my back—a load so heavy that my legs threaten to collapse from weariness, though thankfully light enough to leave me with hope? At birth, life is so simple. It is free from judgments, desires, expectations, and disappointments. But as the years go by, the clean slate becomes unrecognizable for some Asian Americans as they are partitioned and divided into groups. I am a second-generation Japanese American woman. I was raised by Japanese parents in New York City. And my life has been a constant struggle to maintain my balance on the implied hyphen in the term *Japanese[-]American.*

I've often wondered if it was possible for other people to understand what it's like to grow up as a Japanese American—to be asked by your parents, only half jokingly, "If the U.S. and Japan went to war, which side would you fight for?" Of course I cannot claim to comprehend Caucasian male experiences. *Who* I am depends so much on *where* I am. The fluctuating landscape reflects directly into my soul and leaves a pulsating imprint. In fact, I needed to travel halfway around the world before I learned that a person's experiences are subject to the whims of relation. *Majority* and *minority* are transient, relative terms that can be projected onto anyone, dependent only on location. Not until I traveled to India—where I interviewed several children as part of a research team during three weeks of my junior winter term—did I have the chance to understand and watch from the majority's perspective.

A swarm of children surrounds me as I hand out the little trinkets I've brought with me from the United States: pencils, beads, stickers, small spinning tops, and a few erasers. Things that I throw out on a regular basis at home are cause for fights here among the children in Jaipur, Rajasthan. One boy offers to jump off a bridge into the dark water below if I'll give him fifty cents. The price lowers to twenty-five cents when I shake my head no.

It was the first time I had ever been to such an impoverished region, and never would I have imagined what kind of world I would be stepping into. Yellow and black rickshaws bumping over the potholed streets of Bangalore and mud-caked cows roaming the cracked sidewalks replaced the subways and tight-lipped businessmen that I was used to seeing in New York. Children walked barefoot through cow dung, and men sat on the side of the road selling screws, used batteries, and bits of an alarm clock.

What I will never forget about the trip were the staring eyes, the quiet gazes that watched us as we ate, relentless in their pursuit. But most of the time these stares were not directed at me. They were focused on my white companions. The people in India have seen East Asians before, so I was nothing new. The white skin of my colleagues, however, was an anomaly. Crowds of people would stop, point, and watch as we crossed the street. Strangers followed us around for hours. I know this sounds mean, but I couldn't help but think, Ha! Now they know what it's like to look "different" from everyone else—to be judged because of the color of their skin.

Obviously the uncomfortable differences that my travel companions felt were greater than what I experience every day at college. But the basic concept is the same. When I walk into the dining hall with a large group of Asians, I feel the eyes following me, judging. What do they see when they watch me? Do they see a woman struggling to find her place between two worlds? Do they see the choices she has to make every day? White versus Yellow. American versus Japanese. Liberal versus Traditional. The way race and culture affected my life and identity were concerns for me even during elementary school years, when the most that should have been cluttering my fifth-grade mind was whether or not my mom packed enough cookies in my lunch box.

"Oni wa soto! Fuku wa utchi!" A hundred children with black hair and almond-shaped eyes screamed in unison as they chased a demon that had somehow found its way into the schoolyard. The weapon of choice: small green peas. Thousands of peas flew in every direction, turning the once white concrete ground into a lime-green sea. The children all knew that this pathetic looking demon would buckle soon under such a fierce attack. The demon was, after all, only our fifth-grade teacher wearing a cheap plastic mask.

In Japanese folklore, there is one day every year when a demon enters the household. It is vital that the family members expel this demon immediately; otherwise, bad luck will fall upon the house and those who live in it. So, everyone drives the demon out with dried hard peas while loudly chanting, *"Oni wa soto! Fuku wa utchi!"* Demons dwell outside! Good fortune enter in! My mother explained this to me, conveniently enough, *after* I had returned from Japanese school that day.

Two schools, two languages, two of me. One was a reserved little girl who was a bit too quiet, had big black eyes, and sat with her hands folded. People thought she was bright and called her Few-key as the vowels slid across one another indiscriminately. The other, Fu-Yu-Ki, was a loud little girl, who talked too much and spoke when she wasn't spoken to. People called her a "slow learner." The girl who went to American school on weekdays was told by teachers that she needed to speak up more in class and be more assertive. Instead, she faded into the background. The girl who went to Japanese school on the weekends, on the other hand—she was *too* assertive. She needed to learn to control her tongue.

In American school, aside from my quietness, which teachers did their best to correct, I had very few problems. When I took tests in class, the answers seemed to fly off my pencil. But more than anything, I loved to read. Whenever the librarian spotted me, she would bend over to rummage under her desk and dig out a few books that she had saved for me to read: *Charlie and the Chocolate Factory, Ramona Quimby, Old Yeller.* I would pack my book bag to the brim, and at times, the weight of it on my shoulders would literally tip me over backward. I would walk home with a book in my hand and my waist at a 90-degree angle, struggling to make it up the hill. Reading while walking became my specialty.

There was a secret place of which only I knew that provided a sanctuary for me and my books. Carefully, I would survey the area around me to make sure that no one was nearby. Then up I went. Up into a beautiful tree filled with so many pink blossoms that it was impossible to see that there was a little girl clinging to its branches. One branch curved out perfectly so that it cupped the small of my back and let me stretch out my legs. Blossoms drifted around me like pink raindrops and occasionally dropped onto the pages as though they were kissing the words. Hours would go by without notice until the sun dipped too far down for me to make out the letters.

In American school I always earned good grades and had glowing report cards to bring home to my parents. But place a Japanese book in my hands, and the words and I became fast enemies. They betrayed me so quickly that all I could do was stutter the syllables out slowly in bewilderment.

Report card day for Japanese school was always a dark one. I would open up the dreaded page and scan down the sheet. How many below average marks this time? Japanese didn't make sense. Next year I was going to be sent to the remedial class, but I didn't mind; I actually wanted to go. I was tired of always being at the bottom of the class—the one that got the 30 on the test. I knew that I was too dumb to stay in the "regular" class. I couldn't keep up with the other more "Japanese" kids who had just moved from Japan, or who were planning on moving back there sometime soon.

There was no incentive for me to learn Japanese. Why learn such a complicated language when Japan, or my "mother country," was nothing more than an estranged relative whom even now I've visited only twice in my life? All I really remember from my visit to Japan during elementary school was that my grandparents had Buddhist shrines built in their homes and that the incense candles smelled funny. My grandmother would chant weird monotonous phrases, words I couldn't understand, over and over again. Bowls of rice and water were offered to a picture of my deceased grandfather. I knew I had done something terribly wrong when my parents' eyes opened in horror after I asked if I could have some of the rice. Although I couldn't understand my grandmother's words, I remember being lulled to sleep by their beautiful melody—a slow, pulsing rhythm that seemed to capture the beat of life. But, sadly perhaps, it seemed my knowledge of Japanese went no further than an instinctive aesthetic appreciation for the cadence of my grandmother's native tongue.

Back in America, Friday night would slither out of its murky depths and snatch me from my warm bed—the night I finally consigned myself to stay up and do the Japanese homework I so abhorred. I spent hours laboring over a one-page essay. Let's see, how can I express in words what I felt when I saw Halley's Comet for the first time through a telescope? The sight of this heavenly body hurtling across the sky forced me to realize with startling clarity that our lives are just minute scratches on the universe as a whole. What ended up on the page in choppy, childish strokes was, "I saw Halley's Comet. It was nice. It was round and had a tail." I hated that I couldn't write. I hated that I had to simplify my thoughts and that, as soon as my hand touched the paper, they were transformed into awkward sentences devoid of emotion and intelligence.

Fear was in the air during my time in Japanese school. Fear of my friends finding out how stupid I was. Fear of being called on. Fear of the teachers. Talking back to a male authority figure was a suicidal act.

I vividly remember one occasion when a seven-year-old boy was harshly punished and humiliated for failing to do his homework. It was the fourth time he had missed an assignment: a month's worth of work. Our teacher, Takayama-sensei, who was usually jolly and joked around with us a lot— he told one funny story about how he farted at a dinner party—was very angry. The boy looked incredibly small as he shuffled up to the five-foot three-inch man to meet his fate.

Takayama-sensei's arm swung back, way back, and his hand came screaming toward the boy's face. The motion was quick, but it is burned in my memory as a slow, deliberate movement, frozen through time. I will also never forget the red handprint, or the tears, on the boy's cheek as he walked back to his seat.

All of the mean teachers were short men. I've come to the conclusion that there must be some correlation between height and temper. Perhaps when a short man becomes irritated, there just isn't enough room in the body to contain the anger, so it breaks out of its too-tight seams in an uncontrollable violent eruption.

My father, at five feet three inches himself, has also learned to compensate for his short stature through anger. I am the same height as he. My sister is the tallest of us, at a whopping five feet four inches. He has an explosive temper that breaks like a thundercloud over our heads without warning. My mother used to tell me that his temper had improved greatly in comparison with when they were first married. He used to get so angry that he would start throwing things at her. My mother would give him tomatoes as ammunition so that if she were hit, she wouldn't be injured. I remember wondering why she would hand things over to my father knowing that he was going to just fire them back at her. But that dynamic was the basis of their entire relationship. She was just making the best out of the situation. Although the worst my father ever did to me was administer spankings, his booming voice was enough to strike fear into my heart.

My father has a bad habit of calling my sister and me "*aho*," or "stupid." Being dumb in his eyes covers a range of issues. We're stupid if we come home late, raise our voices, leave the living room messy, or refuse to clear the table for him. Even though my sister and I both attended prestigious colleges, he does not hesitate to remind us of our lack of intelligence.

I recall one momentous occasion (at least it was in our family) when my sister challenged my father. She had missed curfew and my father was yelling at her and, of course, calling her stupid. During his barrage, my sister quietly interrupted and said, "Yes, what I did may have been wrong, but I'm not stupid." There was a short silence—one of those intensely electric silences—in which my father stopped to comprehend what had just occurred. He slowly became redder and redder and his eyes widened enormously. "YOU'RE STUPID!! What you did was stupid, and that's why you're stupid!!" His face was a few inches from my sister's face. Again, but this time with her eyes downcast, my sister quietly said, "Yes, what I did was wrong, but I'm not stupid." My father's face turned beet red, and he screamed, "YES YOU ARE!! *YOU ARE STUPID!!*" Battles are never won in my family. Everyone loses.

So, I learned how to melt into the background when the dark clouds began to appear. Better yet, I knew how to prevent them from coming. Don't disagree with him, and don't ever, *ever* disrespect him. Respect was an important word in our house. I had to respect my elders, parents, older sister, teachers, and strangers. This meant that I was never supposed to raise my voice or even speak in a "bad tone." I remember listening to my American friend fight with her mother once, and I was shocked that she actually yelled. She even cursed at her mother, which was unthinkable for me. What I learned from my father was to stay quiet, to keep my eyes down, and not to make too much noise when the tears slowly stained my cheek. Only then would the storm pass. Yes, bamboo will survive the monsoon because it bends and gives when the wind lashes against it. But I resent my father because I never learned how to stand tall like the powerful oak.

Dad was the one who had to be strong—he was the head of the household. He sat and waited to be served. If he wanted a drink of water, he told my mother or whomever was nearby to get it for him. Of course, my sister and I complied as well. We were afraid that if we said no, or, God forbid, told him "get it yourself," the thundercloud would appear and leave the room in ruins. Mom explained that he's an artist; he was supposed to have mood swings. That's how artists are.

Perhaps my father's position as the oldest son in his family has forced him to maintain this illusion of strength. As the male son, he is supposed to carry on the family name. But how can he if he has two daughters? He is expected to take care of his parents in their old age, but it just wasn't feasible to bring them to the United States. As an immigrant who barely spoke English, he was counted on to support his family on an unreliable artist's income. The majority of his life was manipulated by the whims of fate—at least he could control his household.

My mother has taught me what a good wife should be like. A good wife knows how to cook Japanese meals. She serves her husband a hot meal timed perfectly so that it is steaming when he sits down. She docilely listens to his conversation at night even if she's tired and has had a long day as well. She clears the plates and washes the dishes as he nods off in front of the television. She helps the children do their homework and remembers to tell her boss that she needs to take half a day off to go to a parent-teacher conference.

Although I respect my mother's quiet strength, her lifestyle doesn't suit my personality. I'm not the typical Japanese woman that my mother wants me to be, and I don't think I will ever be the stereotypical Asian female. When I first attended college, my mother spoke to me about how I should dress. She explained, "You need to wear more skirts." But I don't like wearing skirts. "But you'll look more feminine and more attractive." I don't care what other people think. "You'll get more guys and more opportunities."

But if those guys are only interested in me because of the way I look, then those aren't the types of men that I would want as boyfriends anyway. My mother's concept of relationships differs fundamentally from mine because she doesn't place reciprocity as a priority. In her mind, if a man is a good provider, then there's no reason why I shouldn't marry him. I tried to explain to her that I would rather remain unmarried for the rest of my life than spend it with a man I didn't love, but she didn't—or refused to—understand. I have this awful fear that my own parents do not love each other, and maybe never loved one another.

This fear first struck me, quite unexpectedly, in the fourth grade. Our assignment was to interview someone on his life. We asked questions like, "What's your greatest accomplishment?" "Describe the best/worst moments you can recall." My first interview was with Mr. Edwards, the funny old man who cracks jokes about hiding buffalo in the garage and who lives below us on the fourth floor. Greatest accomplishment? Meeting his wife of forty-six years. Best moment of his life? When he watched his children being born.

What a nice couple, I thought. But his story can't compare with my parents'. My mother and father met in Japan. They met through mutual friends, and they only spent time with each other on two occasions. Only two times, but they knew that they were meant for each other. They decided then and there to take the vows of marriage. My father's instincts as an entrepreneur advised him that America would be more accommodating to starving artists, so they swept off to the United States to build a life together. They were in a foreign land that they barely understood, but they gained their strength from their marriage and were able to pull through. I thought that was the most romantic story ever.

Expecting this fairy tale, I went to interview my dad. His greatest accomplishment was an art exhibition that he had had ten years ago. The best moment of his life was reserved for the grand opening of his new business. What? Those aren't the right answers. How could he say that his business was more important than his family? I pushed him. I kept asking him the same questions so that he would admit that his life wouldn't be complete without Mom. Or that he would cease to exist if it weren't for my sister and me. Finally I asked him straight out, "What about Mom? Wasn't marrying her one of the best moments of your life?" Without those laugh creases around his eyes that always give away his jokes, he answered, "I married her out of convenience because I needed a wife to bring with me to the U.S."

When I heard this statement, a dagger was thrust right through my heart. The facts of my fairy tale were true, but my parents' marriage was not based on a bedrock of love as I had imagined. Its foundation was financial security and "convenience." Convenience. What a horrid word. So that's why my mother pushes me to date as many guys as possible. "Don't just settle down with the first guy you meet." She's just warning me not to make the same mistakes she made. Sometimes I forget that arranged marriages still occur in Japan. A man with a smart Armani suit and a practical head was all a woman really needed in a husband. But not me. I want more.

Turning to my other Japanese American friends, I scrutinized what their family lives were like. Do their parents shower each other with words of love and contentment? Have I ever embarrassed them by stumbling upon an unexpected tender moment? Sadly, I've never personally witnessed any such displays of affection. Perhaps they have a quieter, subtler method of expressing their love for one another that I don't understand yet. At least I hope so.

Of course, before I even considered dating, marriage, and true love, my teenage mind was occupied with classmates, friends, and cliques. The public high school that I went to in New York City only accepted those who passed a test similar to the SATs. More than 50 percent of the three thousand students admitted were Asian. And within this mass of Asians, I found my niche in a large clique that consisted mostly of Koreans. In the springtime, you could always find a bunch of us sitting in the park behind the school, wasting time. We would befriend the security guards so they would turn their backs when we cut class.

For the most part, my Asianness was not especially apparent to me during high school. I felt as though I had a place in this world, surrounded by my Asian friends. I did have several African American friends whom I had met through track, and with whom I felt comfortable, but I had very few white friends. People might think there would be some kind of void left inside of me because of my lack of interaction with the Caucasian race. Not at all. When I explained my frustrations at my father's traditional ways, my Asian friends would nod and give me examples of how they dealt with their own fathers. We would talk about what a joke parent-teacher conferences were since our parents could barely understand the teacher. We helped each other when we didn't understand a particular English assignment because, unlike our white counterparts, we couldn't go home and have our papers cross-checked by our parents. It wasn't about speaking the same language, since I was Japanese and most of my friends were Korean. This bond that I felt arose from our common background. I never made a conscious decision to associate with Asians—it just happened. There were times I would feel uncomfortable and almost embarrassed that all of my friends were Asian. If I were white, would that even be an issue? Traveling with a large group of white friends, would I feel the same way? Would people look at me strangely?

It's comforting to blend among a mass of Asians. A deep sense of belonging characterized my time in high school as I walked among my second-generation Asian friends. It isn't the real world, though. In the real world, I'll have to make friends with white people and work with them. For that reason, my mission when I came to college was not to fall into the "Asian trap" again. I consciously pushed myself away from my natural tendency to associate with Asians.

The college I chose offers a freshman outing trip for its incoming class. We're supposed to meet and bond with the other freshmen in our group as we go hiking over the green mountains while singing our alma mater. Perhaps the start of my new non-Asian life at college will begin with these eight random students I spent four days in the woods with, I thought. The first week at school, we all got together and I went to my first (and last) football game. I had absolutely no interest in football, but I figured I'd try it out. What a waste of time. The home team's score could have been thirty-five or zero, it made no difference to me. But, of course, I pretended that I cared. Yelling and screaming for the football players dressed in green, I thought I was bonding.

I went to this football game because I didn't know where to start. How do I go about making white friends? There's an obvious plentitude here, but I couldn't seem to click with any of them. The pull into the Asian vortex was strong, but every time I was drawn back to them, I pushed myself away twice as hard. Plans that were made with an Asian friend would be cancelled if a white friend asked me to go watch a movie. I remember literally counting the number of white friends I had in comparison with the number of Asian friends I had.

My freshman roommate, Karen, was the epitome of whiteness. A recruited athlete from California, her blond hair and cute dimpled face seemed completely alien to me. She represented the white race, and if I could befriend her, it meant that I would be able to assimilate into this white college world. We got along very well. Our easygoing personalities helped us go through the entire year without an argument. But I don't think I was ever completely natural around her. My words were measured and weighed because I wanted her to like me. Even my jokes felt like they were processed and canned before I delivered them to her.

I was torn. I felt as though I was being pulled in two different directions. But why was there this division in the first place? Why was I even being forced to choose? I didn't want to become one of those "twinkies"—Asians who were completely assimilated into the white culture. Yellow on the outside, white on the inside. Late in the winter of that first year at college I came to a decision after talking over my problems with a white male friend. I was expecting optimistic words like, "Don't give up yet!" or "You just haven't met the right people." Instead, he said, "Why should you deliberately have to put yourself in uncomfortable situations? If you enjoy spending time with your Asian friends, then why look further?" What a shock! This white male was encouraging me to segregate myself from the white culture. But he made sense. Not everyone finds such good friends so early in their college careers. Why did I have this urge to push them away to search for something that may not even exist?

So, I stopped struggling. Rolling over onto my back, I let the river take me where the current flowed strongest. But it wasn't as simple as I wanted it to be. There is a definite division among Asians—apparent to few and rarely referred to directly—between those who are "real" Christians and those who are "Christian" but aren't really practicing. The "real" Christians go to church regularly and often attend meetings that focus on God; Christianity is a large part of their lives, and their beliefs frequently influence their decisions. Those who aren't really practicing, on the other hand, drink, party, smoke, and fail their classes. I am not Christian—there are only a handful of Asian Americans who aren't—and again, I found myself trying to balance between two different worlds.

This division among Asians, in both high school and college, was reflected in the lines that were drawn between acquaintances. Although no one said, "You're Christian, therefore we can't become good friends," the members of each group tended to stick together. Yes, there were breaks in the rules, and the groups intermingled frequently, but these crossovers were not permanent. So, where did I fit in?

I never received any answers from my parents, and I suppose it's partly because they—like me—are not sure what they believe. We celebrate Christmas, but more as a time to share with the family than as a celebration of Christ's birth. They never speak of Buddhism, although it was a prominent part of their lives when they were growing up. The slow chants of prayer uttered by my grandmother as the beads in her hands rolled back and forth, back and forth, provided me with only the most superficial understanding of the Buddhist faith.

In high school, since I didn't find guidance from my parents, I turned to my friends. They gave me poems, copies of Bibles, and verses because they cared about me and didn't want such a good person to "go to waste." Because to them that's what I was if I wasn't Christian: a waste. And no matter how good a person I was, no matter how morally upstanding, I would still end up at the gates of hell, wondering why I hadn't listened to my friends. And who was *I?* What gave *me* the right to think that my beliefs had as much clout as Christianity? Should I take the plunge to see what all of my friends have been trying to convince me of as the one right path for the past ten years? But my rational mind would not let me step blindly forward in tune with the beating drums around me.

At college, the dynamic between Christians and non-Christians remained the same, although since there are relatively few Asians in this school it's more difficult to truly separate the two groups. If you do interact with only one group, you're left with very few friends—given, of course, that you associate only with Asians. Friday nights with the practicing Christians meant a movie and buffalo wings while everyone else on campus was getting trashed playing pong in the frat basements. Friday nights with my non-practicing Asian friends usually meant going to the mostly Asian fraternity and taking care of my friends who were too drunk to walk home alone. I was living in two completely disconnected worlds. And I felt like a fraud in both of them.

Relationships with the opposite sex weren't much simpler. "When you first get to college, don't worry about studying for the first few weeks," my mother told me. "Find yourself a man. The good ones go fast." She was joking, of course, but as the saying goes, under every joke there's a little bit of truth. "And remember, there are men other than Asian guys out there. Don't limit yourself. Try dating a few white or black men." Whenever my friends and I complain that there aren't any good-looking men on campus, we are implicitly referring to just Asian men. It's as if other races aren't even an option. And it's not as if I find other men repulsive. Quite the opposite. Asian men are short and skinny. The nose is too flat, lips are too thin, and mustaches and beards are things that many Asian men can only dream about (not that I actually care for facial hair, but a woman wants options!). They don't have those rugged good looks that I find so appealing. The sharp jaw lines, square faces, and strong features that I associate with men blend into a soft unthreatening face when placed on an Asian male. And eyes. Eyes are the most beautiful. Large green eyes with hazel specks draw me in and trap me when I look at them. Do they really change color according to mood? I never find out the answer because I always date men with dull brown eyes. Opaque brown eyes that are more like padlocks on a gate than windows to the soul.

Maintain the pure Asian race. Do not taint yourself with the white man. Although many Asian families follow these philosophies, I'm thankful my parents do not, and I have no qualms about "tainting" my Asian heritage. This would probably shock and horrify my relatives in Japan. "Fuyuki, how can you ignore your background? Your roots? You are 100 percent Japanese. Do you want to ruin that with white blood?" Sure, why not? What's so sacred about my blood anyway? Perhaps I've been brainwashed by the individualism that America prides itself on, but in the larger scheme of life, there is nothing that truly separates my blood from the blood of the white male sitting in front of me in my psychology class.

I take relationships seriously. One-night stands and flings were things that I heard about but didn't actually believe happened. It's beyond my comprehension how people can so easily separate the physical from the emotional. "Yeah, I slept with her, but I don't really care about her. I don't even know her last name." College life opened my eyes to a whole different culture of sexual abandon. Saturday mornings are beautiful here in these rural mountains, when the trees blanket the sleeping sun that's barely peeking over the horizon. I'm usually staggering toward the equestrian team van for an early morning start to our show, while the ghosts of Friday night slip past me in wrinkled clothing and with alcohol on their breaths as they continue on their "walks of shame."

Before I came to college, I had never kissed anyone. I had dated several guys, but for some reason, something had always stopped me from letting their lips touch mine. I wanted the perfect kiss, from the perfect guy. I felt embarrassed talking about it with my friends. "What?!" they asked. "You haven't even kissed? Is there something wrong with the guys you date?" Inside, I was afraid they were wondering, Is something wrong with *you*? Maybe there *was* something wrong with me. I should loosen up. Have a few drinks, relax. But I shouldn't have to adjust myself to keep pace with everyone else. I'll find the right person when I get to college.

So, when my freshman roommate, Karen, spoke to me about having had sex with her past boyfriend in high school and that she was contemplating whether or not she should go "all the way" with her current boyfriend, I felt like crawling under my bed. Change the subject before she asks about you. She'll think you're a freak if you tell her the truth. I'll be a story that she'll tell her friends about—the roommate who's never even kissed a guy. They'll laugh and agree there's something seriously wrong with her. I started making up a story that I could tell her about almost going all the way, but feeling that he wasn't the right one. What should his name be? John? Ryan? I glanced around the room, hoping that there'd be some way of escaping. I stopped. Wait, I don't want to start off my college career lying to my roommate. Starting off as someone I wasn't. So I told her. I've never kissed a guy. She sat back in her chair and blinked at me. "You've . . . never?" Never. "Why not?" I just haven't found someone I wanted to kiss. Then, she shocked me by saying, "That's kinda cool. I respect that." My lungs breathed out a sigh of relief—I had been holding my breath the entire time.

It turned out my first kiss wasn't as exciting and romantic as I wanted it to be—unless you consider the Number 9 subway train in New York City a romantic spot. But my views on relationships have basically remained the same over the past four years at college. The standards I had set for my first kiss were raised even higher for the first time I would have sex. I'm not against premarital sex, but I wanted to wait until I found someone I loved and who loved me back. I've met someone at college whom I connect with on so many levels that it was easy for him to reach my expectations. We've been dating for more than a year now, and we plan to remain together after graduation.

Perhaps strangely, as I've always been friends mostly with Asians who are friends with other Asians, my boyfriend, who's sleeping soundly behind me as I type this, is a full-blown twinkie. He was born and raised in Atlanta, Georgia, and he was one of the few Asians who went to his high school. The majority of his friends were white, so when he came to college, he didn't feel the division that I had felt. He barely gives a second thought to his Asian identity, whereas I feel like it's a major part of my life. However, I've probably learned the most from him about looking beyond color. When I have dinner with him and his friends, I feel completely comfortable. I am myself. I forget that I'm talking to white people, and I'm able to see them for who they are, not for the color of their skin.

My parents have never explained to me how they feel about premarital sex, nor do I think I'll ever ask them. Just the thought of sitting down and talking about such a taboo topic with them makes me cringe. Affection is something that should be hidden behind closed doors, forcing people to imagine and wonder if there are any warm feelings at all. I've never seen my parents kiss or even hug one another.

Now I'm in the exact opposite position that I was in freshman year. I didn't tell anyone that I had lost my virginity until recently, and then only two of my closest friends. Perhaps it's better that way. Safer. Even though Asian women comprise about 5 percent of the population in this college, the percentage of Asian women who reported sexual attacks on campus one year was more than 40 percent. Forty percent?!

White males see Asian women as exotic sexual objects to be claimed and conquered. They want to see if that long, black Asian hair really feels like silk. We are meek, subservient, and want to be dominated by a strong white male. In essence, we are geishas trapped in the wrong century, waiting for the right man to free us from our independent minds. At least, that's what Asian women are like in movies and television, right? There's a term we use for white males who are only attracted to Asian women—*mongophiles*. We scorn and pity these men who have created this perfect image of Asian women, because we know they would be deeply disappointed by the reality.

College has led me to reflect on much more than just friendships, relationships, and gender issues. Coming to this school led me to question my own intelligence, for example. It wasn't because I did poorly in my classes or that people around me were brilliant. The main reason I doubted my intelligence was because everyone had specific expectations for me—to excel in math and science. I'm supposed to do well in those areas because I'm Asian. Any creativity I may have been born with has been suffocated because I'm too busy working on formulas and memorizing the periodic table. All Asians are nerds who lock themselves up in their rooms all day and study until the words become blurry. Then they take a shot of green tea and study some more.

The stereotypes continue. Athletics is a foreign concept, and I certainly am not supposed to join any sports teams. I am a sexual prude who giggles with my other Asian friends as we melt demurely into the background. Yet I am none of those things. And I am, simply stated, tired of those who label me as such before they even get to know me.

People always seem quick to adhere to stereotypes but slow to understand genuine cultural differences. There's a mentality among Asians to be tough and not let other people see that you actually have feelings—to cover up pain, anger, frustration, and depression. *Meaku kaketara dame.* The direct translation of this phrase into English is difficult because Americans do not follow this philosophy of life, whereas it permeates the inner soul of every Japanese man and woman. Loosely translated, it means, "Do not unnecessarily burden yourself onto others."

"Mom, can I sleep over at Christine's house?" "*Meaku kaketara dame.*"

Don't burden Christine's mother with your presence. If I started misbehaving at a restaurant, as little kids often do, I was stopped short with "*Meaku kaketara dame.*" Don't burden the other customers with your disobedience.

It's been a struggle to bring together the teachings of my parents with the American values of individualism. Americans pride themselves on speaking their minds and standing by their beliefs. Asians also stand by what they believe, but they are not as blatantly aggressive. We quietly express our concerns and suggestions, but we take into consideration *meaku kaketara dame*. So, how do I tell off a person who has just flashed me in the subway? I don't. I look away, the way an Asian would, and hope that someone else deals with the situation. But afterward I imagine all the curses, witty comebacks, and martial arts moves I should have used, the way an American would. They all seem to melt away, of course, the next time something like that happens.

So, I find myself attacking the one person whom I know won't fight back—another Asian woman. I play Ultimate Frisbee, a very athletic soccer-like game with seven players to a side. Across the field, an Asian woman lines up against me. Do I feel that warm bond of kinship that connects two minority women on a field dominated by white women? Definitely not. I am overwhelmed by an irrational sense of competitiveness, and all I can think about is how much I want to prove that I'm better than she is. The pain from my twisted ankle is pushed to the back of my mind as I try to outrun, outthrow, and outdo her. I must not take a sub before she does. I want to be the best; and if I can't achieve this on absolute standards, at least I can be the best Asian ultimate player out there. This fierce competitive streak within me only seems to manifest itself in sports. I try to deny the truth, but I'm forced to admit that I have a treacherous desire to beat my own kind. Perhaps secretly I want her to push back. To show me that she can take what I give, and then say, "No, I'm not going to just stand here and take this, I'm going to fight." On opposing teams, we can drive each other to be better.

I feel this need to represent the Asian race not only on the field but also in the workplace. As a minority, you stand out even when you're trying to blend in. Who knows if I'm the first Asian employee my boss has hired? If I don't hand in the report in time for the deadline, I may be jeopardizing the chances of all other Asians applying for this position in the future. It sounds ridiculous, but this subconscious message played in my mind every time I was asked to work on an assignment during my summer jobs.

So, where am I now as I'm writing this?

It's senior year, and after four years of college, I think I can look back with objectivity at the way race, religion, and my family and friends have affected my life. The majority of my friends are still Asian. However, now that I don't feel that need to connect with the white race, I find that it's much easier to make white friends. That aura of fakeness that pressed down on me when I was around my freshman roommate has disappeared. No longer do I feel the urge to impress anyone, and I feel comfortable being myself.

As far as my spirituality goes, I believe there is a God—just not the Christian God. And in looking back, I can see that I was always more comfortable in the non-Christian Asian group than in the Christian group. I felt that a number of my Christian friends frowned on some of my activities. Some of my closest friends are Christian, but I haven't told any of them that I'm no longer a virgin. Premarital sex is a sin. Drinking is a sin. Let's not even consider what they would say if they knew I've taken drugs. I've experimented and grown in college, and I need friends who will understand and accept all of me.

People often ask me if I have liked my college. How was going to school in the quiet countryside, where the mountaintops glistened with white powder and the woods echoed with songs of tradition and brotherhood? Honestly, in retrospect, although it hurts to admit it, I probably would have chosen another school—one where diversity is not quantified by the number of minorities accepted through admissions, but accepted as part of life and a part of the campus. I felt that it was my job to fit in, and if I didn't, it was my fault. The lessons I learned were difficult and important. But it makes me sad to think that perhaps my experiences here were indeed lessons in life, a glimpse of more to come.

I think about the façade of diversity I saw on campus, and I wonder what life will be like after college. It scares me. Out in the workforce, the world is white. If you can't make friends with white people, you may not have any friends at all. Once again I'll have to rediscover my place and how my Asian face fits into the picture—or if it even should at all. Over the past few years, I've learned how to balance on that all-too-narrow hyphen sometimes found in the middle of "Asian-American." I'm hopeful I've learned enough to keep me standing even when the bumpy road threatens to throw me off.

Slowly, I unstrap the load that I have been carrying for the past four years and allow myself a moment to rub my shoulders. Peering inside the secret folds of my burden, I strain to see what could possibly have caused me so much heartache, joy, and confusion. My eyes adjust to the darkness to find that—there's nothing in there. Was it my imagination? Was it all in my head? But no, the weight is real, and it's time to move on. As I brace myself to lift the familiar load again, something else catches my attention.

Sitting next to me on the floor is a new bag.

Fuyuki Hirashima is currently pursuing a career in medicine, something she had never imagined for herself, but she is thrilled to be on this path. She lives in Norwich, Vermont, and attends Dartmouth Medical School. The man she wrote about in this essay is now her husband, and they will soon be happily celebrating their one-year anniversary.

Leah Lee Korea Is My Heart and Soul, America Is My Mind and Spirit

I was eight years old when the 1988 Summer Olympic Games were held in Seoul, Korea. I was sitting with my mother on the couch in our family room in Connecticut, watching the soccer game between South Korea and the United States. I sat quietly, my heart beating fast and the blood rushing to my face whenever my mother would yell at the TV screen, imploring her nation to strike fast to victory. Then a penalty. A South Korean player committed a foul, and the United States would have a free kick outside the box. Instinctively I clenched my hand and pulled it inward, a "Yes!" emitting from my mouth. My mother's head snapped back at me and she shouted at me, her hands moving in great big circles, "What do you mean, 'yes!'? Who are you cheering for? You're cheering for America?" A pause. Then, "How could you?" I wasn't sure.

When the United States team scored a goal, my heart sank. All of a sudden, I wanted Korea to win. Then Korea scored a goal to tie the game at one apiece. My heart sank again. *Oh no*, I thought, *what if America loses? They can't lose. I want them to win.* My heart fluttered throughout the entire game, and I felt panicked watching the game alongside my mother who kept shouting, "Shoot! Shoot the ball!" In the end, I went upstairs to read a book and hoped that the game ended in a draw. I don't remember who won the game that day—I didn't care to find out and I prayed that those two countries would never be pitted against each other again, ever.

But, of course they were—over and over again. Even now a daily battle wages in my heart and mind between these two countries. I wish it would stop. I am set off balance by these two parts of my life that are so drastically different from each other. I don't know how I can take what has made me who I am and alter it to fit who I want to be made into. My friends tell me, "What's important is what *you* want." And yes, that's true, but only partly. What I want only matters if I do not throw away my duty as a daughter, a woman, a second-generation Korean American. I can't throw away where I come from. I can't throw away where my parents come from, and I can't throw away their values for the sake of what *I* want. The thing is, though, I can't move forward unless I let go somehow—but I don't know how to do that, either.

At this point in my life as a twenty-one-year-old Korean American woman, I feel as though I am stuck, trying to make sense of my femaleness and my Koreanness and to accept the two as essentially who I am. Being female is so closely tied to being Korean that at times rejecting (or accepting) one means doing the same with the other. I get stuck when I think about how much I like being American because I wonder if I can embrace both cultures—American *and* Korean—and form an identity that is composed of both. Or must I choose between one or the other? Can I hold on to the value of autonomy, of independence, of self-actualization that is so admired and sought after in American society while keeping the values of family, community, duty, and obligation that are the cornerstones of Korean society? Can I be happy with the same things that make my parents happy?

I get stuck, too, when I think about what it means to be a girl, a *woman*, and I realize that I think I ought to have been a boy. What I wish for myself is that I would be able to freely mix and match my Korean side with my American life, my traditional obligations with my spirited self, my blue-collar perspective with my upper-class upbringing. I want to be able to mesh all those things together and make for myself a hybrid life, but as it is, I can't. Instead, I feel like I am one or the other, but never both; one is what I have to be, the other what I'd like to be.

Even though I say I can choose to be one or the other, I also feel as though I don't really belong anywhere. When I am here in America, most Americans identify me as Korean. When I am in Korea, most Koreans identify me as American. I think I am more American Korean, but the correct term seems to be Korean American. I stopped thinking about it a few years ago because it gave me such a headache, and I decided that I was strictly Leah, the American with Korean parents. And then my friends found out my Korean name and began to call me *ChungHee* every once in awhile because it was a novelty to them to have this foreign-sounding name be associated with me. When I was last home for Thanksgiving I forgot to take my shoes off at the foyer and was so embarrassed when my mother looked at me like I was crazy and said, "What, have we turned into an American girl now?" But in truth no one in this country would ever look at me and *not* think that I was Asian first and American second. At least, this is what I perceive as the truth.

So, I would cringe whenever my mother would ask me to call the bank, or contest a speeding ticket, or argue at the customer service desk. Of course, I could never be fully American if, at age twelve, my English was better than my mother's. I cringed when my mother spoke to me loudly in public because now everyone would think I wasn't born in America. "CHUNGHEE!" That call in the supermarket, at Macy's, in the bookstore—it made me cringe, and then I would hurry to my mother, calling out loudly, "Yes, Mom?" so everyone would know that I spoke English perfectly without an accent and that I was really from America.

I was five years old when my neighbor Frank's dad invited me to play peewee soccer on his team. At five I was happy to tag along and follow Frank wherever he went on the field. I loved it when my mother was the orange mother for the game and took charge in passing out the orange wedges during halftime. By age eight I joined a girls league, and by age ten I made frantic gestures to my mother on the sideline, willing her to *please be quiet!* when she would yell at the top of her lungs, "CHUNGHEE! CHUNGHEE! GET THE BALL!" It wouldn't have been so embarrassing if she had used my American name.

At twelve years of age I asked my teammates for rides to the games and told my mother, "Don't worry, Debbie's giving me a ride, so you don't have to go." When I was fourteen my mother came for the first time to a tournament at which my select team was playing and on the way home apologized profusely to me for not being at my games all those years. "I didn't know *everyone's* parents went. Since you always said you got a ride, I thought parents didn't really go to the games. . . . I'm sorry." At age sixteen I told my mother the morning before every game that she didn't have to come, but then glanced wistfully over at the sidelines every ten minutes, hoping I'd see my mother's slight frame sitting at the end of the bleachers, wearing her big red straw hat and chatting with Debbie's mom, who once asked me, "Leah, is there a reason why your mother always calls me 'Debbie's mother' and not 'Susan'?" The question embarrassed me and I went home that day and demanded that my mother call Debbie's mom *Susan* because that was her name and she should know that by now. Forget about how uncomfortable it was for my mother to do that since in Korea you rarely call anyone by his or her first name unless you are great friends. Everyone is "so-and-so's mother" or "so-and-so's father."

This constant attempt to belong wasn't restricted to when I was home, though. I went to Korea every summer until I was seventeen years of age, and every summer I would either play games on the buses and subways, pretending I was a real, live Korean girl engrossed in reading a Korean book of poetry (even though it took me fifteen minutes to read one page) or I would talk to my sister in English so that I could confirm for everyone that yes, I'm from America if you couldn't already tell from the way I dressed and the way I slouched in my seat with my legs taking up half the aisle.

It is because of little things like this that I feel as though I have no country and no identity. I belong to neither America nor Korea. In both communities, I am an outsider. My mother tells me that I should be thankful that I have two countries to call my own, two cultures to pick only the good things out of to make me better. But I can't help but feel that I am neither truly Korean nor truly American, nor can I blend the two together. Korea will never be my country because I don't want it to be. And besides, when I go to Korea, I am always introduced as "Jae-Choong's older daughter from America," or if I make a mistake in manners, my aunts excuse me with, "It's because she's from America."

At the same time, America is not, and will never be, completely my country because I look different from what comes to mind when you picture an American. I am never called simply "American"—it's always "Asian American" or "Korean American." Third- and fourth-generation white Americans' perceptions of Asians will never allow me to fully call this country, in which I was born and raised, my own. It is as though I have internalized all these subtle messages from my environment, that white is power and therefore I am unable to claim for myself what is mine. Perhaps that is why I think about marrying someone white even though my parents are so adamantly against it, so that if not my children, my grandchildren at least will have the privilege of being called an American without any qualifiers. But then I think about how if everyone thought like me, what would happen to our race, our culture? It would die out, and isn't that just a subtle form of genocide?

It is in instances like these I see just how complex this issue of my identity really is. I think that it has hurt me more deeply than I can understand right now, causing me to always feel like an outsider and never quite right. I wander between the two cultures, my heart wavers then tears in two, and

I wish I could tear my body in two as well so that I can give the American part to my mind and spirit and the Korean part to my heart and soul. Then at least I could belong to both.

Much of my tug-of-war between America and Korea has to do with being raised in a rather unorthodox manner. My mother's views on how to raise children were extremely liberal. Both my sister and I were raised by being given a choice from the moment we could express ourselves. Every single time we asked our mother if we could do something, she answered with, *"Nee-ga ahl-a-suh hae."* "Do what you think is right." I was raised to make my own decisions, contingent on the fact that my mother trusted me to make the right choice. Her method of child-rearing was completely contrary to the typical style of Korean parents who would nag their children to practice piano, do their homework, study, study, study. I was given all the freedom in the world to do whatever I wanted, but I would always do the right thing, of course, since that is how I had been raised.

So, in one respect I was raised in a very nontraditional way, but in other ways my parents were extreme traditionalists in terms of maintaining Korean culture and custom, even in America, even with their American-born daughters. No matter what part of American culture we were exposed to every day, we were going to keep our Korean roots and remain *Korean* in America. My mother's favorite insult to reprimand us whenever we did something "wrong" was: *"Jae-jum-ba. Me-gook-ae ga dwes-sa."* "Look at you. You've become American." The way she said it, it was classless to be American—it meant having no manners, running wild on the streets barefoot, and raising my voice to my father.

To understand my mother and to see where she comes from in the way that she values her culture and homeland, I have to consider the family that she was raised in. My mother and father both were raised in exceptional households, and their values and sense of duty and obligation are quite profound. My mother's lineage can be traced back thirty-five generations to Korean royalty, and her subsequent upbringing was that of the complete privilege, tradition, pride, and honor of an elite class. Raised in an enormously wealthy family with intense ancestral pride, she was taught to believe that the more you have means the more responsible you must be, and so my mother's prized possessions to this day are her self-control and dignity.

Within this kind of upbringing, my mother's personal convictions were manifest in the way she quietly hid her lunch every day at school because she was embarrassed to have a meal consisting of a bowlful of hot rice, marinated meats, and tender sprouts when all the other children had no more than a handful of leftover rice and pickled cabbages in a war-torn era. Her dream was to be a nun like Mother Teresa, until her mother told her that she ought to be married. So, my mother obeyed—she met my father, went out with him three times, decided their values and backgrounds were compatible, that he had enough good qualities, and married him. Her duty as a daughter was to obey.

My father's family, too, shapes its values on the principles of self-control and dignity. My grandfather was the oldest son of a dirt-poor farmer in a northern province in Korea. The honor he perceived in his duty as the eldest son gave him the will and conviction to stow away on a freight boat to Seoul when he was fifteen years old and to find work in a steel mill. He slept on street benches until he saved enough money to buy a little shack and then brought his younger brothers to Seoul, leaving the second oldest brother in North Korea to take care of his parents and sisters. My grandfather worked in this steel mill to put his brothers through school and to put food on the table. He started a small business using the leftover scraps of metal that he picked up from the mill, and today, he owns an international steel corporation. My grandfather is eighty-nine years old. He has not seen his parents, his sisters, or the brother he left in North Korea for seventy-five years. He still goes to work every day, even on Sundays. As he sees it, it is his duty, as the eldest son of his parents, to take care of his family no matter what. My father grew up in a family tradition steeped in duty and familial obligation.

My parents have tried to pass these qualities of duty, self-control, dignity, and obligation on to me, but I simply don't share in their values of the ultimate importance of those things. I grew up in America, in a society that demands instant gratification and applauds independence. To be true to yourself is the best thing that you can do in America, and most of my values have been shaped by the American society in which I live. I believe that I should put myself first in everything and follow my heart. Do what I want. But I have been grounded and rooted by my parents' values and culture where to be true to yourself means to be true to your family. What I want should be what is best for my family, which, in turn, will be what is best for me. But as I grow older and shape my own values based on lived experience, some of my own values conflict with those of my parents and their culture.

Still, they are my parents. That is one Korean value that has remained steadfast in the center of my heart, despite the daily assaults on it by the

American culture in its many forms. They are my parents, regardless of what they do, what they say, what they think, what they want. Regardless of all that, as long as I know they love me, even if I think or *know* that they are wrong, they are my parents, and it is my duty and my obligation as their daughter to honor them, trust them, and obey them. My life is not only mine; it belongs to my mother, my father, my sister, my community. I want to believe that my life belongs to me alone; I want to believe the American mind-set of individualism and independence. But I cannot so believe because my parents were born and raised in Korea, and that ties me to Korea in a way that I cannot break without completely destroying my life and my family. That I was born and raised in America does not make that much of a difference in such a cultural mind-set. My parents are Korean, and I can't ignore that for the sake of what I want. The qualities of duty and obligation that my parents prize so much have been internalized by me as well.

When I think about duty and obligation, I think about my father and his relationship to his daughters and my mother. It seems as though my memory of him only begins when I was thirteen years old and he returned to Korea to fulfill his duty as a son. My father is the second son of his father, and when my uncle, his older brother, passed away of liver cancer when I was age twelve, my father became the eldest son. His duty then became taking care of the family business his brother used to take care of, including taking care of his parents. So, he left for Korea and at thirteen, I became the caretaker of my family because that was *my* duty.

When I speak of responsibilities, I don't mean things like chores or doing my homework; I mean the deeper responsibilities that you have because of your status, your class, your place in your family. The burden that I felt in my family as the older child who should have been a son—this is the responsibility that I felt on my shoulders as a thirteen-year-old when my father began his extended trips to Korea. No one told me explicitly that I had to take care of my family. But it was the cue that I picked up from hearing the stories my mother told about the role of the eldest child, the stories my grandfather told by being the oldest, the constant accolades and praise I received for being "such a good daughter."

My little sister, too, is my responsibility. Ever since I can remember, my mother would sit us down and say, "Nahee-ya. Your big sister is the same thing to you as a mother." And to me, "Chunghee-a. You are like a mother to your little sister." We were only 2 ½ years apart in age, but my sister has never once called me "Leah." She is not allowed to call me by my name, for it is a sign of equality in relationship. She has always called me "un-knee," which means, "elder sister." It is a sign of respect, just in the way that we call our parents Mom and Dad and not by their first names. We are not peers, nor friends; I am her elder sister, and as such, it is my duty to take care of her like a mother. This is not a huge burden on me, I don't lose sleep over it at night. But I do know that I can't tell my sister things that I would tell a friend. I do not show her any signs of weakness because what mother would show her daughter any kind of weakness? I am my sister's keeper.

Recently my sister and I have made great strides in closing the gap in our relationship. I have made the conscious effort to treat her more like a friend now that she, too, is in college. I know I still mother her, like a hen pecking at her chicks, but I also share with her parts of my private life that reveal I have my own problems, worries, confusions, and disasters. I even have joked with her that we ought to switch places; that I will give her my birthright as elder sister and she could have it all. We kid around, of course, because we both know that giving up your birthright in Korean customs is unheard of. But my mother, when she snatches bits of our conversation, turns a sharp eye toward us and says, "Oh, that's really funny. Joking about all sorts of things, I don't understand you."

My grandfather had always made funny comments to my dad because he didn't have any sons, just two daughters. My dad never said anything about wanting a son, and always said how lucky he was to have not one but two great daughters. Still, I couldn't help but think that if I had been a boy, my grandfather would treat my dad better and my dad wouldn't look so stressed all the time. If my dad was going to be away taking care of his parents, then I was going to be the boy in my family and take care of my mother and sister. From that point on, the face that I revealed to my parents was that of the utmost confidence, strength, and reliability. That's what sons are like, and regardless of the fact that I was only a thirteen-year-old girl, something inside me locked and for seven years I did not shed a tear in front of my mother.

When I think rationally, the root of the problem is me. I have this image of the American father that I can't get out of my head. The American dad plays baseball with his boys in the backyard before dinner, coaches his daughter's soccer team, and kisses his wife saying "I've missed you" every evening when he gets home from work. The American dad takes care of his family, makes his wife laugh a lot, and convinces her to leave the kids with grandma for a week while he takes her on a vacation. These are things

I did not see in my parents' marriage—not because they didn't love each other but because their idea of marriage as Korean parents is so different from mine as a product of American society. The American dad is who I want to raise my children and be my husband. He does not leave his family because he has an obligation to his own father.

My father had no sons, and though I wasn't a boy, I was going to be so strong and so able that no one would remember that I was a girl. I was going to show my grandfather, who when told by my mother that she was pregnant with a daughter and would he send them a name for me, sent her three pages full of boy names, and at the end included two girl names in the "accidental case" that she had a girl. I was going to show my grandfather that my dad wasn't losing out because I had to sit down to go to the bathroom. My parents never told me the politics of being a boy versus being a girl in Korea in my grandfather's time. They never once said they wished they had a son. My dad loved his girls more than anything else, and he never failed to tell us just that, even though Korean dads usually don't show their love through affection and don't say much except words of discipline. But it's hard for me to shake the feeling that maybe I could have been a better child to my parents if I had been a son, and I deeply resent this one aspect of Korean culture, which fosters feeling this way.

Perhaps as a result, since high school, I have always been more comfortable around white people. Many Asian students have claimed that they hang out with other Asians because they are more comfortable with them. Not me. When I am with other Asian people, especially a big group, I am constantly aware of who is looking at us. What are they thinking? What do we look like? Do they know that I don't only hang out with all Asian people? I suppose that I don't feel comfortable hanging out with all Asian people because it feels to me as though it draws so much attention to the fact that I am Asian, and to the fact that I blend in so well. Who can pick me out in a sea of flat, yellow faces? We all look alike according to white people anyway. I don't like being with Asian people because it reminds me too much of my own Asianness.

In the simplest terms, I am embarrassed to be with Korean people. I feel so self-conscious when I am in a group of Koreans; I feel as though other people are looking at us as a monolithic group but not at me as a person. I feel as though they are making judgments about us, so I do not feel comfortable interacting and socializing. I always feel slightly removed from the conversation, the activities, the jokes, and laughter. I don't know why I feel this way but it bothers me so much, and I am sure that it is partly the reason why none of my friends at college are Korean. I hate how I feel, but I can't ignore or stop those feelings. I wish I could.

Sometimes, I feel superior to my classmates who also are Korean American. Even with those Korean classmates to whom I have never spoken, I feel this uncomfortable sense of conceit creeping into my stomach whenever I see them. I began feeling this way in high school, and though I have forced myself to suppress these feelings in college, they still sneak up on me every once in awhile, leaving me a little sad, a little lonely, and wholly unhappy with myself.

I think that to a large degree, I have these feelings because I have internalized white America's culture of power. American standards of beauty—tall, thin, blonde, prominent facial features—as well as American standards of what are the correct ways to act and socialize are for me the better ways. I have a sickening sense of pleasure whenever someone tells me that my eyes are "a lot bigger than normal Asian people's eyes," or that I "look mixed." I am so glad that my hair turns a reddish-light brown color in the summer.

I am proud to be Korean, in terms of being able to speak Korean fluently, to read and write in Korean, and to know all the customary manners and traditions of Korean society. But, for as much as I *like* the way I look now and am glad that my eyes and hair are dark, my nose a little flatter, my frame a little slighter, I am still very aware that I am so different from what an American looks like, and I know without a doubt that I have internalized my appearance as not as good.

Perhaps I compensate for this internalization as a result, and my social life directly reflects this aversion to Koreanness. My friends at college are all white. My friends in high school were mostly white, except for at church, where they were all Korean, and I boasted to them about how my friends at school were white. On a very simple level, my friends are my friends because they are whom I feel the most comfortable with. We match. Around them, I don't notice that I am not white. No, that's not entirely true: I *do* notice but am not bothered by it at all. I have always felt more comfortable being the minority in my group of friends.

When I am in a group of white kids, I do not feel any tension associated with being the only minority. I don't feel as though people are looking at me and thinking I am the only Asian person in the group. I feel as though I fit in. I feel as though it is natural. When my ethnicity is called out, I enjoy telling people that I am Korean. Not Asian, but Korean. I like telling my friends about my culture at home and my family's customs. But I am never conscious of others looking at me as if I don't belong. I never wonder what other people must be thinking. My place in this white country is nothing new to me, and I have found a comfortable niche within white communities and, more particularly, my white group of friends.

I must have internalized this notion of white being better, though—why else would I think that I was better than another Korean just because I had white friends, was comfortable in a white community, or dated white boys? Perhaps I think that I have succeeded. I have "made it" in the white person's world, been wholly accepted and liked by them. I have learned to dress like them, talk like them, socialize like them, and to like it. But I haven't given up who I am; I haven't traded in my Koreanness for their whiteness. Because of my family, I have maintained and retained my Korean language, my Korean culture, my Korean manners. My family is my sole link to being Korean, and I am proud that I know all the customs, know how to do a proper full bow, and know how to speak, read, and write Korean with ease. I can slide from one world to another depending on whether I am at home or at school.

Of course, it is so unfair and immature of me to think that I have succeeded and other Korean Americans have not. I have no idea as to what their dreams are, what they want, how they feel about being Korean. I should not be so audacious and presumptuous as to think that I have a better life than they do—but the fact is, I *do* think that in the bottom of my heart, and I wish so fervently that I did not. I wish this because I cannot escape the knowledge that even though I think that I have succeeded in this white world, able to slide from one world to another with ease, I am still not able to mesh my two worlds together. The fact that I am uncomfortable when I am with a group of Asian people is a clear indicator that I am still not completely comfortable with myself. As long as I have the approval of my white friends and the approval of my family, I am fine. But do I have my own approval? I don't think so. In my mind, I cannot be both Korean and American. I can be either, but only one at a time. I have not yet learned to appreciate myself enough for that to happen. But I wonder, as long as I am living in America, and as long as America sees Asians to be different, not really American, can I ever reconcile the two?

The hardest part of this Korean American dichotomy for me to overcome has to do with relationships. I am scared that I will never marry because I will never find somebody to fit both my Korean and American sides. Fitting my American side is about appealing to *me*. Am I attracted to him physically? Do I have an emotional connection with him? Does he challenge me intellectually and personally? Does he believe in God? Do I feel safe when I am with him? Does he like to read? Can he make me laugh? Is he interested in my past? Is he interested in my culture? Am I proud of him? Is he humble? Does he try? Does he love me? Do I love him? Am I in love with him?

Fitting my Korean side is about appealing to my mother. Is he Korean? Does he come from a good family? Are his parents divorced? Does he have a bright future? Is he Korean? What are his parents like? What are his grandparents like? What are his roots? Does he have the right manners? Is he Korean? Does he have class? Is his home stable? Is he proper? Is he Korean?

More often than not my Korean and my American sides do not overlap. My dilemma is that because of my dual identity I cannot have one side without the other. The values that my mother and I have when it comes to relationships are so vastly different that I am scared to even consider the subject. Yes, almost all the things that are important to me are important to my mother as well. She wants me to be happy just as much, if not more, than I do. But what is most important to my mother has nothing to do with what I look for in romantic relationships. What is important to my mother is *so* important to her that she cannot let go of it. She trusts that I will come around and eventually see her way. I have been told explicitly that I am to trust her because she is my mother.

I once had a boyfriend whom my mother thought was not right for me at all because he was white, because he didn't go to one of the best colleges, because his parents were divorced, and because he had had a serious girl-friend in high school. But I wanted to be with him because he was the most genuine person that I knew, and we laughed all the time. I thought he would be an "American dad."

My parents never met him. They rejected him the moment I told them that I had a boyfriend. I never told my parents about other boys before because I knew they wouldn't like them. None of the others really treated me very well. But I told them about this one because I didn't like hiding that part of my life from them, and because I thought they would like him if they would let themselves get to know him. I knew that my parents wanted me to marry someone Korean, but I thought they weren't racist, that personal qualities and values would be the most important thing—along with my happiness. But they didn't like what they heard about him; I was told that if I spoke with him again I would be disowned, and I don't doubt that would have happened. I resisted, and my mother got deathly ill. They never even bothered to meet him.

So, in the last six to seven months, I have sacrificed much of my happiness to be a good daughter to my parents. It has been an exceptionally emo-tional struggle for me to give up someone close to my heart for the sake of my parents' wishes. I don't think this is the last time in my life that I will have this struggle tearing me in two. Conflicting values, the enormous yet unwanted faith I have in my mother, my duty as my parents' daughter, be-ing in love with someone who is forbidden for reasons I understand but cannot agree with—the separation that I feel inside between my Korean and American sides is manifest most seriously and strongly in these issues.

Being the daughter of my parents means that when they tell me to do something, I do it. I trust and obey them without complaint or anger be-cause they are my parents. They love me, want the best for me, and have more experience with life than I have. This is how a good Korean child is expected to behave. It doesn't matter that I am twenty-one years old. My parents are in their fifties and are wiser and know what is best for me. Trust and obey, I will not go wrong. "Why can't you trust me?" my mother im-plores, her heart racing from the panic attacks she has from thinking about me with someone she thinks is wrong for me, her eyes filled with tears be-cause all her life since I was born she has only lived to make my life better. "Please just trust me."

I don't know why I cannot trust her. My mother is the closest person to my heart, and I do not question her motives. But there is an American value about *self* that has been so ingrained in my belief system that I cannot trust the person I trust the most when it comes to decisions about *me*. I cannot help but think that this is *my* life. At the end of the day, I will return to my home and my husband and children and to the life that I have built for my-self. At twenty-one, I have the sense and intelligence to make decisions for myself. Why can't my mother trust *me*? If I make a mistake, I will learn from it. That is how I've lived my whole life. I have made many mistakes and feel that I am a stronger, better person for having made them. I have learned a great deal about people and life through the bad choices I've made in the past. I feel as though I should be given the right to choose for myself whom I want to date.

I wish that I could just agree with my parents and be able to go along with what they want without reservation. But in all honesty, Korean men scare me because I know that the kind of guy my parents think is right for me is bound to ascribe to traditional beliefs and ethics that elevate "role" and "obligation" as a way to freedom. But that is precisely the Korean part of my life that I want to reject: the emphasis on duty and responsibility. I am tired and cranky that I have to take care of this and that, not because I want to but because I have to. I think that for once I would like to be taken care of, given no responsibilities except the ones I make for myself.

I have not had a crush on someone Korean since one time in high school. But he ran with all the troubled kids, the cool, non-Asian boys who got all the girls and wore leather jackets and had five o'clock shadows by noon. He was racially Korean, but not really, not in the more important ways of conforming to Korean cultural expectations for being a dutiful son. At college almost all my guy friends have been big athletes, which says to me that I look for someone who I think can take care of me in the way I want them to. Physical size represents to me the ability to be a caretaker in a very non-Korean way.

A lot of times I just get confused about how I should think or act because I am trying to be this great Korean daughter but can't quite deliver. For example, my mother always taught me to serve my husband, because that was a woman's job. That is, it is a Korean woman's job. Things are changing very much today, yes, but I only know Korea in the context of my parents. When my mother was married, she quit her job and stayed at home because my dad didn't want her to work, even though he barely made enough money for them to have two meals a day. She obeyed her husband, and I was taught to do the same. I still hold those beliefs, about the man being the head of the household and the woman being the constant caregiver. These are very traditional views, and I have internalized them because I was raised in a Korean family in which my mother made sure I saw that she treated my father the way a proper, self-respecting, well-mannered Korean woman would.

What I learned from my mother was very different from my own image of the ideal, independent woman. I remember these thoughts swirling around in my head during my freshman and sophomore years in college: *American girls have a lot of sex, and that's okay for them. I'm not American. I'm Korean. My mother would kill me then die if she knew that I let a boy touch me that way. I don't want to be Korean, I want to be American, I want my mom to be okay with me having sex.* Never mind how unjust those thoughts are, never mind how they are nothing more than gross assumptions. In my head, I didn't know left from right, night from day when it came to boys and who I was around them. It didn't occur to me that when my mother spoke about serving my husband, it had nothing to do with sex and everything to do with respect. But the lines blurred somehow, and I equated the sex part to America, being American as bad, and I wanted to be part of it. It was a way, I thought, to be more American.

My mom came to visit me at college a few months ago and was talking to a friend of mine. She said to him, "I feel so bad for my children. They have one foot in Korea and one foot in America, and they are stuck there. I am so sorry for them sometimes. You know, my heart, it feels very sad sometimes." As does mine when I think about how much my family and my Korean heritage has given me. I am today what my parents gave me in the form of a Korean upbringing and values. But there are so many times these days when I feel that who I want to be is less Korean and more American. Korea is my heart and soul, and America is my mind and spirit. I don't know how I can balance the two, but I have to, if I am ever to find peace within myself.

The issue of balancing my two lives is a sensitive one. Recently, I have begun to think that I can understand the balancing of my two lives this way: I was born in the late twentieth century in California, but my life began over a thousand years ago along the shores of Hwang-He-Do, a small fishing province off the northwestern coast of Korea, and in Seoul, before it was a city that belonged to a divided country. As a twenty-one-year-old Korean American college senior the story of my life goes back that far, to my ancestors who planted their roots in the mountains and valleys of the Land of the Morning Calm. It begins with them, for I am merely a twig on the outermost branch of my family tree that has survived thousands of years. I live by feeding off the water that is taken in at the roots, but to see me from the tree's base, you'd have to crane your neck way back and squint to catch a glance of me whispering high up above the clouds. The distance between me and the base of the tree—between my life today and the lives of my oldest ancestors—is so great that I often can't remember how I came into existence. I enjoy the breeze and the clouds that the roots will never experience or appreciate. But snap me off the branch, disconnect me from my roots—my heritage—and I die. The question is, how can I snap myself off and still live?

After graduating from college, Leah Lee spent several years as a middle school teacher and outdoor trip leader before returning to graduate school. She now lives in New York City.

ORIGINS AND ETHNICITIES

Asha Gupta   In Search of a *Sangam*

As the plane descended into Indira Gandhi International Airport in Delhi, India, the chattering of Hindi from my fellow passengers grew louder. I had been anticipating this moment for seven months. It was the fall term of my junior year in college, and I was going to India to research educational systems through a grant I received from my college's center for international understanding. It had been eight years since I traveled to India, and I knew that the trip would be a challenge for my identity as an Indian American female. Would I be comfortable? Would I be able to relate to the people? Would I feel as lost in India as I did in America? I had decided not to force myself into a process of active soul-searching. Rather, I would open myself up to the culture and accept what naturally occurred.

The moment I walked out of the Delhi airport the hot midnight air enveloped me. I felt a distant and singular sense of familiarity. There was a mass of people waiting outside. Family members waving, pointing, and yelling excited greetings. This is the way it is in India. I had forgotten. When loved ones travel, especially internationally, it is a huge family event. I scanned the crowd and my eyes landed on my *maasi* (aunt), then *naanaaji* (maternal grandfather), my *mausa* (uncle), and finally my nine-year-old cousin. They all rushed forward to give me a hug and welcome me home.

I felt like a foreigner for the first few weeks I was there. While I had memories of previous visits and had a connection to the country through my parents, I was detached from the daily goings-on, as if I was only an observer. As this "foreigner," I did not think much about the implications of the culture on my life. After all, I was there to observe schools as an American and my relatives viewed me as an American; that's what made me interesting to them.

Since starting college I had been neglecting my "Indian side," and it eventually became normal to go about my life without connecting to it. I did not participate in the events of the college's South Asian group because I felt they marginalized the culture by perpetuating stereotypes. Their "culture nights" tended to focus on superficial things that would easily entertain, though not necessarily educate: midriff-bearing fashion shows, dances from Bollywood films, brainless skits that mocked what they were supposedly celebrating. These were not the things I associated with being Indian. As it seemed there were no outlets to express that side of me, a sort of deactivation occurred. But once I was back in the country of my ancestors it was not long before I began to feel India in me. For better or worse, the land and people and sights and smells and tastes and sounds could no longer be compartmentalized in the back of my mind. The objective mindset of an observer/anthropologist was slowly and surely being replaced by the personal subjectivity of a participant. I remember thinking on several occasions, "This country is *me*. This is where I come from." It was overwhelming to feel a sense of place, a kind of responsibility to the land because it had become a part of me.

This does not mean that I love everything about India. On the contrary, there are many things that infuriate me about the way things work there. For example, it is rare for a woman to walk down a street without getting ogled by men who feel entitled to let their eyes and mouths wander wherever they want, embodying the power of the patriarchy. I experienced this everywhere I went. In a small town, a group of young men once followed me, trying to take my picture, as though an Indian girl in a tank top and sneakers was the most incredible thing they had ever seen. Also, corruption is apparent in everyday life, as bribery is a common method of getting things done. And, as expected, the level of poverty and division of classes were extremely difficult to come to terms with. A society structured on such obvious and ancient hierarchy left me questioning my own biases; how could I judge something I didn't understand? But while I had to accept these things to a certain extent, I was accepting them in an entirely different context than before. I was personally offended by the negative things I saw and proud of the positive, as if I had something to do with it. Limbless beggar children and beautiful ancient temples struck a similar sense of ownership within me. My many emotions—fury, excitement, anger, confusion, and fondness—were heightened and transferred to a part of me that hadn't been tapped in years.

These sensibilities were intensified when my mother joined me about a month after I arrived in India. We traveled together quite a bit. She was hesitant at first, wanting to stay in Delhi with the family, but I insisted that we explore the country, as we both had seen little of it. We touched all sides of India, even venturing into Nepal, and these travels gave us a perspective on the culture and land that we had never before experienced. Every place we went was like a mini-country within India, each with its own language, food, dress, and lifestyle.

We traveled to two places known for their *sangams* (meetings of bodies, be they geographical, physical, spiritual, intellectual)—Allahabad and Kanya Kumari. Allahabad is the village that sits on the convergence of the rivers Ganga, Sarasvati, and Yamuna. It is considered sacred because of this *sangam*. Once every twelve years, millions of people travel to Allahabad for the *Kumbh Mela*, a Hindu bathing festival of rebirth. Kanya Kumari is the southernmost tip of India. The *sangam* here is again one of water: the Indian Ocean, Bay of Bengal, and Arabian Sea—three immense bodies coming together at a single point, creating a breadth and depth of endless blue waves. Breathing the air was intoxicating; all that water, all those different entities from different places that had seen different things coming together to create one being. I felt very connected to these *sangams*. The separate waters are akin to the mishmash of different origins I have felt within myself, never knowing where I fully belong, *if* I fully belong. Being in Allahabad and Kanya Kumari gave me some comfort with these issues, made me feel that my own distinct parts were as natural as the bodies of water themselves. My mother's presence personified these challenges of identity, and gave me a soothing sense of foundation.

Our travel experiences, combined with spending time with family members (some of whom I'd never met prior to this trip) and being in the country of my heritage, gave me a new take on myself—who I was, where I came from, where I was going. While I did not feel that I could completely identify as an Indian or as an American, I became more comfortable with both the distinctiveness and synthesis of these cultures within me. My mother expressed her personal struggle with immigrant identity when I asked about her own cultural identification on our journey back to America. She looked at me with confused eyes and said, "You know, Asha, after living in America for thirty years and going back to India this time, I realize that there are things about each place that I both identify with and don't. Truthfully, I feel kind of lost." That moment was one of the closest between us. Despite our disparate personalities and opinions, and the number of fights we'd had about our battling cultures, I will never forget how well we understood each other then.

That moment of understanding with my mother was particularly meaningful because my parents and I grew up very differently, so we rarely relate to each other's personal cultural experiences. Both of my parents are from India. My father was born in a section of India that is now in Pakistan. He is the eldest of five children from a religious Hindu family. His family was poor, and they experienced terrible hardship traveling to India from newly formed Pakistan during the 1947 Partition of India. They settled in Delhi, where my grandfather started a business that still operates today. My father had to play parent to his younger siblings for much of his youth, as his father was hard at work and his mother was preoccupied with health problems. Despite these hardships, he excelled academically, and in the early 1960s earned a scholarship to an American institute of technology, journeying across the world as the first of his family to come to America. My father later earned a PhD at an Ivy League university. Following his schooling, he returned to Delhi to meet the women his family had selected for him as possible wives. One of these women was my mother, whose story is quite different.

My mother's family quickly grew prosperous after their own struggles during Partition. The eldest of four children, my mother grew up mainly in India but also in other parts of the world, as her father worked for the Indian Embassy. Her family was very close; my mother's mother was extremely loving and fulfilled her maternal duties above and beyond the expectations of a good Hindu. My mother also excelled in school and was one of the few women at her college in India to study chemistry. She also studied the hard sciences in America, until she returned to Delhi in 1970 to consider marriage.

My mother and father were introduced with the intention of marriage. They went out a couple times and decided they were a suitable match. Six weeks after they met, they married and subsequently returned to America to start their lives together. Four years later, my sister was born. I came along six years after her. My mother did not pursue her love of the sciences after my sister was born, as she chose to devote her life to her family and home.

Upon setting foot inside our house there is no question that we are an Indian family. Many of our paintings are of traditional Indian scenes. Our living room is full of Indian furniture, painted wooden screens, and sculptures (one of Gandhi and one of Buddha). Small bronze figures of Indian gods and goddesses, a miniature replica of the Taj Mahal, and a large map of India add to the thematic décor, and the scent of *agarbathi* (incense) permeates the air. Most evenings, my mother can be found preparing dinner, usually spiced *daal* (lentils), *chawaal* (rice), *achaar* (Indian pickle), and some form of *sabzi* (vegetable).

My parents raised my sister and me very "Indian" and sought to integrate their host-culture into their native cultural lifestyle. As a result, I grew up being proud of and interested in my heritage, no matter how frustrating it was trying to balance two cultures. As a child, I liked telling people that I came from India and spewing out random facts, such as, "Did you know the Taj Mahal is in India?" or "My aunt lives in India and she talks British!" and the eternally proud pronouncement, "I've *been* to India. I'm *from* there."

By grade school I had traveled to India quite a few times. The experiences I had of the heat, countless people, poverty, sounds of street merchants, itchy mosquito bites, spicy foods, and loving relatives only intensified my attachment to the culture. It also helped that one of my father's brothers lives near us with his family. My sister and I are close to these cousins, who are the same age as we are. As we grew older, we talked through a lot of cross-cultural issues we had with our parents, laughed at the family idiosyncrasies, and shared a rare mutual understanding that was not possible with our "American" friends.

Many Indian families in our area, including mine, used to go to a devout Hindu man's house every Sunday where his living room was transformed into a religious space. The floor was covered in white sheets, and we'd all sit cross-legged, shoes off, listening to his words. He would read aloud sacred texts and preach, and we would all sing *bhajans* (religious songs) while he played the harmonium. At the end of the service we would all stand and sing the traditional ending song, the *arthi*. During this song, people would go to the front of the room one by one and hold up a plate with a lit *dhiya* (wick made of cotton dipped in butter) and edible and monetary offerings, moving their arms to make an *Om* shape with the flame. Afterward, we would all eat the *prasad*, the blessed food, which was usually *halwa*, a saccharine and oily sweet. I never questioned these religious customs, nor did I feel strange taking part in them. On the contrary, when remembering these times I feel a sense of safety and warmth. Everyone knew each other. I have grown up calling my parents' friends "Auntie" and "Uncle"; it is these sorts of traditions that have kept our Indian community close.

I was the quintessential "daddy's little girl." My father is wonderful with children; they love him as much as he loves playing with them. He spoiled me and we had very happy times together—he made me laugh harder than anyone I knew. I always wanted him to put me to bed because he invented the best stories, came up with fun games, and created the greatest songs. I was a smart kid, which made my parents proud; there are few things more important to Indian immigrants than their children's education. I have no complaints about my childhood; my home life was worry-free and secure, and as the cute and precociously bright baby of the family, I could get whatever I wanted. I was happy.

Things started changing when I was in middle school. I transferred the idolatry I had for my parents to my big sister, who was in high school. I became her confidante, her partner in crime. I lied to my parents when she had boys over and went to the "library" with her when she was actually going out with friends. I felt a bit guilty for lying, but by age twelve I related to my sister better than to my parents and our solidarity was in some ways necessary. I was beginning to like boys, listen to rock music, question religion, and realize that I did not always agree with my parents' values. All of this made them unhappy and apprehensive. My father and I were not getting along, and it seemed his temper was becoming our fifth family member. My mother's worry that I was straying from my academic focus became overbearing, and I suspected that things would get much harder when my sister left for college.

After I was the only child in the house, my parents and I started arguing more and more. I began to note the differences between the way my family and the families of my white, non-Indian American friends worked. With the new choices and decisions that came with my age, I found it harder to feel normal, given my parents' reaction to the changes I was experiencing. For instance, they expected me to remain obedient and unquestioning, ignoring the fact that I was getting older and forming my own value system, which often conflicted with theirs (seemingly unavoidable when raised in one culture under the guidelines of an entirely different one). When I disagreed with them it was taken as a sign of disrespect. A typical response to my questioning was, "We are your parents. You do not question us. We know what is best." This upset me because I felt that I should be most comfortable expressing my views and standing up for my beliefs with my parents, which is, admittedly, a Western ideal. I was different from my sister, who usually internalized her discontent in order to prevent a conflict. This led my parents to believe that she had been more obedient than she actually was, which made my "disrespect" even more unexpected to them. They thought the issues with my sister had prepared them to have better experiences raising me, but I usually ended up speaking my mind, knowing it would likely escalate into hours of screaming, crying, and slamming doors.

The fights with my parents continued through high school. During that time I never could keep my mouth shut—I *had* to speak my mind and do some things I knew they disapproved of. I knew this would lead to more fighting, but I had a real problem with not being allowed to say what I thought to my own family. It was so hard to deal with the pressure I felt from them and from myself to achieve the über-identity of the perfect mixture of a dutiful Indian and an independent American girl. I was to excel at school, obey my parents, maintain their traditional values, repress any sexual desire or questioning, be home by ten at night on weekends, get into a good college, respect my heritage, participate in extracurricular activities, star in the school play, and so forth. It was confusing for me to maintain this identity and also experiment with things I felt were natural for my age, but which my parents most certainly did not. I did not want to fight with my parents, but I felt it was my right to express myself regardless of whether or not they agreed.

Despite the negative situation at home, I managed to accomplish a great deal in high school. I maintained high grades, participated in community service activities, was involved in drama, had good friends, and won awards. My parents and I agreed that these activities were important and expected. While I fulfilled these expectations, however, I never received the praise I wanted from them. I still wanted more than anything to please them, yet the only recognition I received was from other people. I just wanted my parents to tell me they were proud of me, without my having to ask, but they only told me what I was doing wrong and did not really understand why I needed to hear *from them* that they were proud of my accomplishments. This hurt and left me confused about what they wanted from me, and what I wanted from myself. How much did I have to fit into their mold for them to be happy with me? I could not be the perfect Indian daughter, having been raised in America. I had low self-esteem, despite the positive qualities others thought I had, and was struggling hard to maintain some sort of control over my identity. This confusion and need for control manifested itself through a mild eating disorder and an omnipresent sense of unhappiness.

It appeared to others that we were a happy family. I never talked with my friends in detail about my situation at home; I did not want to air our dirty laundry, and I did not think anyone but my sister could understand. I felt that I had no control, and although I stuck to my beliefs, the two people who mattered most to me never accepted them.

As easy as it is to paint my sister and me as victims, we both know, despite our own resentment, that our parents cannot be demonized. They had reasons for being so angry and disappointed with us. I believe much of it has to do with their upbringing—just as my sister and I are confused about our identity as American-born children of immigrants, so too do our parents struggle with assimilation while trying to preserve their heritage. Their own parents' ideas about raising children in 1940s and 1950s India were the models my parents followed in America, where blind respect and obedience are far less easy to come by.

My sister is the only other person who understands the dynamics of our family, and we depend on each other for advice and sympathy. Our connection is unbreakable. I could not have handled many of the issues I've had to deal with without my sister's support. She is my blood, my kin; she is a part of me. Whatever happens in my future, I need to be close to my sister, my *didi*. I would not feel complete without her.

While my family has had a profound effect on my identity, I have also been influenced by the relationships I've had. I fell in love for the first time during my freshman year of college. We were an interesting match. He was a moderate conservative from a close family, loved heavy metal music and girls who looked like Southern belles, and was extremely logical. Then there was me, the die-hard liberal from a dysfunctional family. I hated heavy metal, dressed more like a hippie than a belle, and existed for emotion. But these differences were what made us interesting to each other. My boyfriend challenged me, and we made each other look at things from another perspective. Granted, we argued all the time, but we were learning so much and our love was new and exciting. We gave each other our virginity and our promises.

After some time, however, our differences got in the way of our happiness. I found myself becoming so dependent on him and feeling inadequate. He seemed to consider what I said unimportant, and when we disagreed he would be condescending and arrogant—a definite change from when we first got together. I didn't like who I became around him; I was silencing myself trying to be the girl that he wanted me to be, and this was infuriating. He had no real interest in my family or my roots, and I drifted away from those things. I felt most fully "American" with him, because those were the ideals he held high. During our junior year, we spent six months apart while studying abroad (I was in India, then London), and we realized that we were no longer meant to be together. I knew that I needed to be with someone who could respect all parts of me, especially after I reconnected with my heritage in India.

In London, I became involved with a female student. It was my first experience with a woman I was truly interested in (this was more than typical experimentation), but I was quite relaxed about the situation. I have always thought it natural to be attracted to people of the same sex, and I have many gay, bisexual, and queer friends, but I knew my parents and extended family would be horrified if they knew. I was in awe that this woman wanted to know things about me that my ex-boyfriend never seemed to care about, and I was inspired by her dynamic and radical personality. We continued to date for a short while after returning to school, and her influence on me made me more politically active and aware. We have since remained good friends. Our relationship made me more conscious of and comfortable with my attraction to women, though I am primarily attracted to men. I view my sexuality as a fluid and flexible thing, and I do not label myself as this would only serve to constrict my sexual identity.

I was happier with my last boyfriend than I had ever been with anyone. We were together for a year, ending the relationship when I graduated from college and he was still a student. We shared many interests and beliefs and were deeply in love. He loved me for who I am, not who he wanted me to be. We shared all of ourselves with each other. I felt whole with him and comfortable in my skin. He was so giving, loving, and accepting, which made me more conscious of how I could be a better person. He raised the bar as to what I expect from a partner, particularly that he or she will bring out all parts of me with reciprocal pride and comfort.

Though these represent my most recent relationships, my romantic life really began at age fifteen, when a high-school senior started paying attention to me. He was smart, funny, charming, and caused me much heartache and teenage trauma. Other romances include a hippie I met at the beach, a bisexual actor ten years my senior, a heroin addict, a born-again Christian, an egomaniac with an Asian fetish, and a fun-loving goofball who had had a short stint in prison. These romantic partners and others I have experienced, though all very different, have one thing in common: they are all white.

I have never been involved with a person of color. Although I think this is merely a matter of circumstance, I know it is no accident that I have never been involved with an Indian man. I think this has to do with fear; the fear that an Indian man will want to impose on me the subservient role that Indian women have had for generations. Many Indian American men I know see how their fathers are treated by their mothers and view that sort of relationship—being pampered, treated as masters, and feared—as the ideal. These men often have dated white girls throughout adolescence, but when it comes to marriage, they want an Indian girl, often one from India. Of course these are generalizations, and I know not all Indian men are the same, but my fear nevertheless prohibits me from objectively entertaining the idea of being with an Indian man.

Most of the men I know are white, and they tend to be more compatible with my personality than the Indian men I know. It has crossed my mind that I may be rejecting the idea of being with an Indian man to spite my parents or to transcend tradition, but I do not believe this is the case. I keep my romantic life hidden from my parents for the most part, so it is not something we discuss. Furthermore, I want to please them. Although I do many things that go against their beliefs, I have often wished that my values were in line with theirs. I would rather reach a level of understanding with them instead of doing things that make them angry.

I have thought about ending up with an Indian man, and I do see the benefits of such a situation. We would have a sense of understanding that I could not have with a partner from another culture. If we were to have children, it would be easier to have a common history. It is true that I have not actively sought out an Indian man, but I don't feel any need to at this point in my life. I admit that I should work on my bias against Indian men, but I believe that will happen by meeting more Indian men to whom I can relate—not typical "good Indian boys."

I am not the typical "good Indian girl." Feminism, activism, sex, and drugs have played a part in my life. If my parents knew they would be appalled. They could never imagine their Ivy League, highly motivated, work-driven daughter would even think about doing drugs. Neither of them has ever smoked or consumed alcohol—the result of an unbroken promise made to their parents and each other. They have reconciled the fact that I do drink occasionally, but it makes them uncomfortable.

The codes of my culture even travel with me to the bedroom. Sometimes while being sexually physical, my mind wanders to thoughts of my ancestors and certain family members. I think about how appalled they would be if they could see what I was doing and feel what I was feeling. My obsession with making my family proud and honoring my culture is at the crux of my struggles with identity. This worry extends to almost every aspect of my life, but I nevertheless cannot deny myself the things that bring me joy. I am not promiscuous; I am young, curious, and safe. I am not an addict; I experiment lightly. I am more an artist than a scientist. I am a good Indian girl . . . just not the one my parents have in mind.

I began to achieve a greater sense of security with this cultural duality in my last year of college. My trip to India gave me a renewed outlook on my identity and how to stay connected to my Indian side, so I decided to involve myself in South Asian cultural activities at school. I joined three groups in one term. When I expressed my objections to the Asian culture nights and the stereotypes I felt they perpetuated, people listened and many agreed. Changes were made and an activist mentality began to influence the way these Asian groups thought about their culture.

I also wrote about my experiences and talked about my trip to India. For a comparative literature course, I wrote a lengthy prose and poetry piece about immigrant mothers, their daughters, sexuality, exoticism, and the balance of cultures. The work came naturally, as these were all issues I had thought about a great deal. I was extremely proud of this piece, and part of it was published in a student literary magazine. I read some of the pieces at an Asian drama group's production (which I helped organize) centered on the deconstruction of stereotypes of Asian women. I spoke to a group of freshmen at the college president's house about my trip to India and also held a discussion about the trip and how it affected my life when I came back to campus.

All this action was driven by my new-found connection to my culture, my personal culture—what I had made of myself after serious thought and introspection, visiting the country of my ancestors, experiencing relationships with people who validated the whole of me, and really connecting to the different aspects of myself that make me who I am. I was able to relate who I was through the work I was doing and sharing with others. I feel strong now, and confident in my cultural ties to both America and India. My confidence has strengthened my relationship with my parents, and I think we are beginning to understand each other better. It is really all about sharing. As we learn more about each other's cultural contexts, the previously closed doors of communication begin to open. And while it is still at times an uphill battle, I am eager to take on the challenge, and not just with my parents. I love expressing these issues and my thoughts rather than keeping them buried and unexplored. It is as though a well within me was tapped and a rush of different rivers flowed out together, shaping me, shaping others, creating a *sangam*, a meeting of bodies, identities, and cultures.

After graduating college, Asha Gupta lived in Europe for two years, working in the field of education. She returned to America to pursue a master's degree in education and currently works with adolescent girls in public schools. Asha's relationship with her parents has continued to progress and is naturally replete with complexities. Her interest in cultural identity has remained strong through her academic, creative, professional, and personal life.

Aly Rahim A Muslim Citizen of the Democratic West

I drove up to the crossing in my month-old black Volkswagen Jetta. I had never been apprehensive or fearful about going back to the college and crossing the Canadian border into the United States. Usually it was a largely perfunctory procedure: I would show my student entry forms with my passport, which would then be stamped without much scrutiny, and I would quickly be on my way to our little rural corner of New Hampshire.

But on this crossing the border agent opened the back door of my car and unzipped a duffle bag nestled in the back seat. In the bag, a traditional South Asian garment caught his eye. He looked up and asked, "What religion do you practice?" This was a simple question that I had answered countless times, but this time was different. This time I was afraid to say who I was. I did meekly provide the truthful answer, but the experience left me with the poignant realization that everything had forever changed for me. Regardless of my confidence and pride in who I was, a new emotion was now unavoidably attached to my identity—fear. Until that moment I had never feared answering questions about my religious identity, but now I could not help feeling this question was loaded—especially coming from an official of the U.S. government. I did not understand what consequences my answer would bring, or what the agent's intent was.

In fact, the agent did not harass me when I told him I was a Muslim. He merely commented in a sympathetic manner that he had assumed this because he had seen my "prayer clothes" in the bag, perhaps apparently unaware that a Hindu or a Buddhist could have worn the same South Asian garments.

During a vigil a week later I spoke to 250 of my peers about the post-

9/11 backlash and about the fear experienced by a large segment of American citizens ranging from Buddhist Tamils to Arab Muslims. Looking out over the diverse crowd, I reflected on my small but telling incident and what it meant for my life as a Muslim in North America. "As I crossed the border a little over a week ago my heart was heavy with grief—for the innocent victims of a horrific attack, and for a world awaiting new and interminable cycles of violence." I paused, and then added, "There was another sort of emotion, however, that I harbored in my heart. An uneasy amalgam of fear, anxiety, and apprehension, for I knew my sense of identity was forever changed. I was and am no less confident of who I am, my confidence has not been shattered. But I cannot say the same for the society around me. For many in this society, my society, our society, confidence has been shattered. It is a sad truth that many members of our society will forever see my identity as an irreconcilable contradiction."

Growing up in Vancouver, British Columbia, I never entertained the thought that my identity as a Muslim and a Canadian could be perceived as any sort of contradiction. Religion was always an important part of our family life, and we were very involved in the Shia Ismaili Muslim community, a closely knit, mostly South Asian community with a significant immigrant population in both Canada and the United States. My father had come to Canada in 1972 as a political refugee from Uganda following Idi Amin's expulsion of South Asians. He had arrived as an educated professional eager and willing to integrate himself into his new society. My parents taught me that my faith was no more of an impediment to my full participation in Canadian society than that of our Christian or Jewish neighbors. Granted, instead of going to church on Sunday mornings, we went to the *Ismaili Jamatkhana* (the mosque and community center) on Friday evenings. But religion seemed to be an important part of many of my non-Muslim friends' families, so I did not think its role in mine was unusual.

I never really experienced the proverbial second-generation identity crisis. My family was intellectually progressive and deeply spiritual at the same time and a strong sense of Indo-Pakistani culture imbued our home. This dualistic ideal in our family life finds its origins in the unlikely marriage of my parents. My father grew up amid the Ismaili South Asian diaspora in East Africa. The norms surrounding marriage there differed significantly from the norms in Pakistan. Having been under British rule for so many years, many East African Ismaili families adopted the Brits' more liberal customs and attitudes about dating and marriage. In fact, almost all of my father's brothers and sisters married partners of their choice. Two of his sisters married Hindus and his younger brother married a Roman Catholic Italian—hardly traditional arrangements! For my mother's family in Pakistan, dating was an alien concept. Marriages among middle- and upper-middle-class families remained semi-arranged. Such was my parents' marriage.

My father left Uganda in 1972. Upon his arrival in Montreal, despite being penniless, he secured the single spot available to a foreign student in McGill's dermatology training program, beating out more than one hundred other candidates. By 1979 he was a licensed dermatologist with a private practice and a comfortable lifestyle. Consumed with providing for his family as they settled down in Canada, he had not given much thought to marriage. He was thirty-one years old, and most of his family had given up on his ever marrying. Unlike his siblings, my father was not particularly inclined to date or have girlfriends. He remained single and yearned for something more traditional. More than any of his siblings he felt a strong affinity for Pakistan, South Asian culture, and Islamic values. In the summer of 1979, he decided to move to Karachi. He closed up his practice and made arrangements to sell his Montreal apartment, but this plan would not ultimately prevail. My father eventually returned to Montreal, but as a married man.

My father arrived in Karachi in every way a foreigner. His Urdu was barely passable, as his mother tongue was the North Indian language of Kutchi. He spent his first month traveling—in the late 1970s it still was relatively safe to explore the beautiful northern expanses of the country, and he made his way to the verdant mountains of the Hunza and Gilgit. He delighted in the spectacular vistas and the simple but genuine hospitality of the mountain villagers. My father's dream was to purchase a jeep and administer medicine in these far-flung regions. He also wanted to find a well-educated, cultured Pakistani Ismaili wife. The ideal place to start was the *Jamatkhana*, the Ismaili place of worship and community center.

One evening my father went to the largest *Jamatkhana* in Karachi. Though not many African Ismailis came in search of Pakistani brides, there was a very structured network of matchmakers in the community. The head of the so-called marriage committee in this area of Karachi happened to be Noorjahan bhai, my *nanima* (maternal grandmother). My father was given her address and told to pay her a visit. After a long meeting with my father, my mother's parents arranged for my mother to return to Pakistan from Los Angeles where she was in a postgraduate training program at an accounting firm. After only a few meetings, chaperoned by her nineteen-year-old brother, my mother, who had rejected several previous suitors, made her decision to marry my father.

My father had a very different background from my mother, having grown up in Uganda and having spent seven years living in Canada. Yet my father continued to feel a strong affinity for the subcontinent, particularly for the emergent aspirations of the new state of Pakistan and the South Asian Muslim culture it celebrated. Although his siblings had adopted more liberal marriage practices, I think that my father felt that by marrying a wife who was brought up directly in the traditional culture and had the common foundation of Ismailism, he could create a family more in line with the values of the "homeland."

In many ways, therefore, the beginning of my family was not so much a continuation of tradition as it was a conscious return to tradition, if also a traditionalism infused with modernist intellectualism. Towers of books have always filled an entire floor of our home. The library shelves long ago reached their capacity, and new books find a place in some haphazard pile. Scanning the spines you might see Chomsky's *Manufacturing Consent*, a book on Sufi mystical traditions, and a volume of Wordsworth's poetry stacked together. Education is a common theme in immigrant families of any ethnic stripe—computer science, engineering, business, and premed are considered legitimate academic pursuits by many South Asian parents—and I observed this phenomenon with cousins and friends of my generation.

However, in my family the function and value of education differed from the norm. My brothers and I never felt any pressure from our parents to change our academic orientation, although such pressure is not unusual in immigrant communities. My eldest paternal cousin is a striking example. My father's success as a dermatologist has become a sort of model for our extended family, and my cousin's parents pressed him to pursue premed studies through his undergraduate career, constantly reminding him of the standard of living enjoyed by my father and our family. When time came for my cousin to apply to medical school, my dad's counsel and my cousin's efforts paid off. My cousin gained admission to the medical school at the University of British Columbia. It took him four years of undergraduate toil to get in, and another two and a half years in medical school to realize that he was living his parents' dream, not his. He dropped out. I never confronted such pressure.

I sometimes reflect on why my parents' educational ideals were so different from those of many of my South Asian peers. Our economic comfort was not necessarily distinct; many of my friends' parents were successful in business or medicine, yet they still pressured their children to pursue an education in those fields. The Ismaili community has an especially strong bent toward success in business.

It was a crisp but sunny Vancouver afternoon. The spring rain for which the city is famous had abated for at least a day, and my parents and I were enjoying a walk along the seawall. On our left the Pacific inlet lapped up against the concrete walkway, and on our right loomed the backdrop of the majestic coastal mountains of British Columbia. The last quarter of junior year would begin in just a few days, and being home for spring break was a much-needed sojourn. My parents loved these walks and insisted I join them when I was in town. We'd inevitably cross paths with a few West Vancouver Ismailis. That day we were chatting about my recent experience volunteering in Karachi, when we ran into Zubeen Suleiman, who had attended school with my father in Kampala, and his son Rafiq, with whom I had graduated from high school. "How are you, Uncle?" I asked, using the term of respect used by most Ismailis when addressing male elders.

Mr. Suleiman, a wealthy Vancouver hotelier and the quintessential Canadian Ismaili businessman, asked me, "So, Aly, have you decided what you will be doing after next year?"

I hesitated, knowing that Mr. Suleiman would be puzzled at my reply. "Well, I'm going to continue with my studies in international affairs. I'm hoping to get my master's degree before I start working."

"OK," he said uncertainly, "what will you do after that?"

I tried to explain as succinctly and confidently as possible. "I'm interested in international security and want to work in foreign affairs for the Canadian government or for an international organization like the UN."

"There's very little money in that you know," he retorted. "Malik Mansoor's son is graduating from Dartmouth," he said, referring to an Ismaili student who was graduating that year. "He'll be working in venture capital in New York. Why aren't you doing something like that?"

I tried to explain why I wanted a career that reflected my intellectual passions and moral convictions, but Mr. Suleiman could simply not comprehend this: "Someone as smart as you could be earning so much. You must have some great ideas; why waste all the effort and expense of being educated at such an expensive school in America?"

Mr. Suleiman was not at all uncharacteristic of other immigrant Ismailis of his generation. As immigrants from one diaspora in East Africa to another in North America, the Ismailis distinguished themselves primarily as savvy, dynamic businesspeople—a perception that is a central part of the Ismaili identity in Canada's multicultural fabric. During the last recession, Prime Minister Jean Chretien joked that what his hometown of Shawinigan, Quebec, lacked was "a dozen Ismaili entrepreneurs." An enterprising and affluent entrepreneur epitomizes the Ismaili immigrant success story. Many members of the community are therefore baffled if a young Ismaili attempts to pursue something outside the realm of business or medicine. Education is undoubtedly considered vital, but most older Ismailis regarded it as a means to an end, not as a time for intellectual and personal development but as preparation for professional success.

My parents always stressed educational attainment, but I never was expected to conform to the conventional image of Canadian Ismaili success. They considered professional success important, but education was an end in and of itself. I was raised to see college as a time to engage the ideas that have animated civilizations; to grapple with the social, cultural, scientific, and political issues confronting societies in wide-ranging disciplines; to read great literature; and to unravel the lessons contained in the history of the world. Though politics were my passion from a young age, I was dedicated to the notion of a liberal arts education—a concept that has little currency in Canada, let alone in the Canadian Ismaili Muslim community.

Increasing numbers of Ismaili Canadians are turning to what they see as the next level of educational attainment by applying to Ivy League and other top-tier U.S. schools; most are applying to graduate schools but more and more are also looking to U.S. colleges. Again from my anecdotal experience, an overwhelming number still focus on a narrow range of disciplines. As an Ismaili undergrad pursuing a liberal arts degree with a major in government and having no inclination to pursue a corporate career, I am not entirely unique, but my choices are contrary to the conventions of success in my community. My parents sometimes explain to their Ismaili friends that other Dartmouth students with the same major continue into investment banking or consulting careers, earning between $50K and $100K their first year out of college. While their friends are often puzzled as to why I would not immediately grab such an opportunity, my parents state this fact with pride and believe that I have made choices based on my convictions rather than on the conventions of success in our community.

My social experiences have also diverged significantly from those of most of my peers. During my senior year, a professor invited me to join a discussion group of about ten seniors. Each week the professor assigned us literature that was to touch off a discussion. The objective was to examine life, following somewhat from the Socratic principle that the unexamined life is not worth living. The group met every Monday night for an hour or two to examine a topic that brought meaning to all our lives. The ten of us, who were varied in academic interests, gender, and ideologies, showed up simply to experience an unusual and sustained form of shared introspection.

One evening, when we were discussing choices we make in life, the professor posed a question: "If you could remove any incident from your life, what would it be?" This was a compelling question, and I racked my brain for an answer, trying to recall some childhood blunder, life-changing decision, or traumatic event.

Bill raised his hand and began, "Well, there was this time sophomore year . . . " His story began comfortably in the everyday trappings of Dartmouth life both figuratively and literally—his story started at a computer at the Collis Center. Bill explained that he and his girlfriend had set a date at Ben & Jerry's, and that his friend "blitzed" him and said to come by his room before he met Jennifer. When he got to his friend's room, a marijuana pipe was being passed around. Bill couldn't resist and got "really high." He forgot his date, she found out why, and the romance came to an end.

Where Bill left off, Danielle started eagerly into her story. "Well, I first started dating Michael during senior year in high school and then I left for Dartmouth. . . . " She earnestly explained the story of her "hometown honey," recounting how she "was torn between my loyalty to Michael and all the new and interesting men I was meeting at Dartmouth." I clenched my teeth. If this theme persisted, I would have to say something.

Josh piped in next about an ex-girlfriend at Dartmouth who found out he had gotten back together with his high school girlfriend. After each sorrowful admission about how some relationship was lost because of thoughtlessness or stupidity, the rest of the group would murmur in collective understanding. But I just sat there, nervously, trying to make my silence inconspicuous.

Nevertheless, my turn did finally arrive, and I mumbled rather inconsequentially, "I don't have much to offer on this theme, but . . . "

"Wait a minute," the professor interjected, interrupting me in mid-sentence. He had remained silent up until then, but it seemed that he had picked up on something in my voice, something that betrayed the fact that there was a deeper issue at heart. Furrowing his brow, he looked at me intently and asked, "Is there something more here? What do you mean when you say you don't have much to offer on this theme?"

One requirement of the group was a high degree of openness, but I hesitated, not knowing whether my fellow students would understand. I tried to shrug off the probing, saying, "Well, it's quite complicated; I'm not sure I should get into it."

The professor did not relent; "There's enough time to explain. We'll hear it if you'll say it."

And so I began, "I have never had a romantic relationship in my twenty-one years. . . ."

As a Muslim, I will not have sex before marriage. Issues of dating or physical intimacy have always been wrapped up in questions of my faith and culture. I never so much as kissed a girl during my four years at Dartmouth, a fact I'm reluctant to admit to any but friends. I'm not embarrassed, but I also don't want to have to explain. Unlike many Muslims, I anticipate having some degree of physical and emotional intimacy with women before marriage. But I see dating as something I will engage in only a few times and when there is sufficient reason, such as when I meet someone with whom I connect ethnically and religiously. This person must be emotionally and intellectually attractive to me, and there must be serious potential for her to be a life partner. Thus, for me, dating is really an activity for finding a life partner.

Sex underlies so much of the social interaction on American college campuses. My decisions to remain a virgin and to date only if I see a potential life partner already placed me on the margins of the social scene. Because of my faith I do not drink. Since sexuality and alcohol are cornerstones of the collegiate social experience, mine was a pretty atypical college experience. The Dartmouth I experienced over four years is probably a very different place than what many of my peers will remember. I have no stories about sexual encounters with girls I met in frat basements, no nostalgic tales about that brilliant and beautiful girl dated during junior year, or whimsical anecdotes about drunken escapades. Even my most mild-mannered friends can share at least something about one of these experiences.

Despite my lack of some typical social experiences, during my first three years at Dartmouth I never felt particularly marginalized because I was a

Muslim student. I had always been vocal on a range of political issues and prided myself for being a political liberal. While at Dartmouth I headed a number of nonpartisan political affairs groups and never felt that my involvement or leadership was questioned because of my Muslim heritage. After 9/11, however, the comfort zone started to contract. Having an openly Muslim identity in an increasingly hostile public arena is a daunting experience. I have read virulent columns by tenured professors at elite universities attacking Islam as intrinsically violent and hateful. I have sat through lectures at Dartmouth at which my religion was derided as a dangerous ideology. These hateful currents are increasingly strong, and a growing interest in the Islamic world has created fertile ground for provocative and incendiary opinions. I find myself being more and more on the defensive, having to explain why I can be both a part of North American society and a Muslim. It is draining to constantly feel that you have to be on the defensive, to justify who you are, which I am beginning to increasingly resent. These challenges seem relentless and are not always separated or impersonal.

A little more than four months after the terrorist attacks, I found myself at a luncheon with a visiting fellow at Dartmouth. This former U.S. intelligence officer was invited to share the insights he gained during his extended activity in the Middle East. Fifteen of my peers were comfortably seated in a large, homey living room, while the visitor sat stiffly in an oversize armchair. The questions and discussion wandered through the quirks of Middle East history and U.S. foreign policy. I raised my hand and asked, "What can be done to support democratization in the Islamic world?"

By this time the speaker was well aware that I was a Muslim. He looked at me sharply and answered pointedly, "Islam and democracy cannot coexist. You cannot at the same time accept the principles of democracy and Islam. Islamic democracy is an oxymoron." He went on to substantiate his answer with what he felt was relevant evidence drawn from his reading of Islamic doctrine.

I sat in shock at his answer, which affirmed the fear I had referred to in my speech a few months earlier. I was confronting head-on "the sad truth that many members of our society will forever see my identity as an irreconcilable contradiction." Uneducated anti-Muslim rants I could handle, but sitting face to face with a former member of the U.S. foreign policy establishment and hearing such a specious opinion expressed as scholarly "evidence" was terrifying. I looked around at my peers. How did such words affect them? I sank into my seat, my stomach knotted with anger and confusion. I was immobilized by his stinging implication—that I cannot be a true member of this democracy if I am a Muslim.

I worried that his explanations would convince my peers that I was confronting some sort of epic decision where I would decide between Islam and living in a democracy. Although no such decision has confronted me or millions of other North American Muslims, the myth of divided loyalty has been perpetuated by hate-mongers and buttressed by self-proclaimed Islamic experts. My loyalty is undoubtedly being called into question, and I cannot help but have a new and uncertain sense of vulnerability. I know that I do not feel a contradiction in my identity, that I do not consider myself a false Muslim or a false Canadian, and I am unsure how to respond to such ideas.

During the spring of my senior year the former Prime Minister of Israel, Ehud Barak, visited Dartmouth. His visit coincided with heightened tensions in the Middle East, as troops were being mobilized in and around cities throughout the West Bank. After a speech that characterized the United States and Israel as kindred sprits in a war against terror, which most of the audience seemed to embrace, I got up to ask Barak a question. I asked him why the number of settlers in the West Bank had increased by 100 percent after the 1993 Oslo peace accords if the Israeli government acknowledged a Palestinian right to sovereignty over the area. I have never been hesitant to stand up and state my political views, to challenge arguments I do not accept.

After the lecture, a friend of mine overheard a comment outside the auditorium. A student said to his friend, "That Aly Rahim, if he was not Canadian and a bleeding-heart liberal, he would have a bomb strapped to his chest." When my friend told me this, for the first time I felt an intellectual insecurity. I had to wonder, if I tried to voice a dissenting opinion about foreign policy that involves Muslims, would I be branded by some as a potential terrorist?

There is another dimension of my post-9/11 experience that I had never expected. Visible and violent hatred is deplorable, but at least it can be easily identified. But the insidious workings of educated minds cause me great concern. Two months after 9/11 I was talking with two of my close friends, intending to highlight what I thought was unjustifiable ignorance. I innocently related an experience my brother had had a few days earlier as he flew from Toronto to New York. "My brother was flying back to Princeton," I started. "He was sitting a few seats back from two twenty-something Indian guys. The two guys happened to have beards and were sitting next to each other. Some passenger told the flight attendant that these two seemed suspicious. In a few minutes the police showed up and escorted the two men off the plane, based simply on that tip. The plane was grounded for an hour as it was searched." I was indignant about what I felt to be a ridiculous incident, but my friends' response led me to realize I had not grasped the reality of my post-9/11 world. I discovered a type of visceral reaction that was shared by many more people than I had anticipated. I looked at the odd expressions my two friends wore and said, "Well, that could have been me. If you didn't know me, and you saw me on a plane, would you be scared? Would you report me as suspicious?"

My friend Adam looked cautiously at me. "I wouldn't report you, but . . ." and he stopped. It seemed he was too sympathetic to follow through with his answer.

Nevertheless, his "but" had already given me an obvious answer. If Adam did not know me and he saw me on a plane, he would be afraid. I was not willing to leave it there. "You know me, you have other South Asian friends—Indians and Pakistanis, Muslims and Hindus—but you'd still feel scared if you saw someone who looked just like your friends?" By now I was agitated. Brown skin does not redden easily, but I was probably approaching some shade of crimson. I prodded, "Does this seem rational to you?"

Adam's reply gave me remarkable insight into not only what my friend was thinking but also what others and I would confront in the post-9/11 world. It was not malice, or ignorance, or hatred. It was something entirely different. "I know it's not rational," Adam explained. "In my mind I know it's nonsense and doesn't make sense. It's a fear I can't reason away. I feel miserable that I feel it, but I am being honest."

"But you would not act on your fear?" I asked.

"No," Adam replied. "That I can reason away. I know the fear is irrational."

Our friend Terence said he would react in the same way. Despite having close friends of South Asian descent, these two bright Dartmouth students said they would feel a visceral fear if they saw someone with my skin tone on a plane. At least they were aware that this had nothing to do with any rational processes, that it was an instinctual response, and they had the capacity not to act on what they knew was irrational. But what would happen with other people who could not recognize that their fear was irrational? How many people around me felt that the fear of being on a plane with someone of my ethnicity was rational? I had assumed that such fears belonged to ignorant people I would not have to meet, but my friends' comments left me shocked at how pervasive such fear was. If, as my friends said, this fear could not be reasoned away, then could nothing be done to alleviate it? It was utterly bewildering to think that people like my friends could find my ethnicity a source of fear.

Since 9/11 I have not been beaten or been the target of racial epithets. My challenge has been a more subtle and insidious assault on my identity. I am far more fearful of educated intolerance than of sheer ignorance. The university professor who uses authoritative scholarship to explain why Islam and Muslims are anathema to the West terrifies me far more than the evangelical pastor preaching from the pulpit. I still cannot comprehend the fact that some of the brightest young people in America viscerally fear someone who looks like me. I have always been proud of my distinct identity and have never had a desire to be assimilated. Being considered a dangerous presence in my own society was not part of the picture, but it is since 9/11. I am not going to feign assimilation to gain security, although I have found myself considering this option.

But I have chosen not to be silent or to merely blend in. I know that educating the people around me is the most effective thing I can do to help them understand who I am, to learn that I am not a threat. With that in mind, I chat openly with friends or acquaintances about how I live Islam every day as an American college student. I have spoken to middle school children so they can see that Muslims are not necessarily menacing bearded men in some distant part of the world. I have given speeches, spoken to administrators, sat on panels, and given interviews to my college newspaper about my experience after 9/11 in the hope that my fears and the fears of my fellow Muslims are understood. During one panel discussion, presented with three other Muslims, I sat before more than two hundred of my Dartmouth peers. At the end of my talk, I summed up in five words the message that I am so eager to convey—"I am not the enemy."

The Islam that has informed much of my twenty-one years has always been spiritually liberating and intellectually stimulating. It has taught me to be accepting of diversity and to have a strong cosmopolitan outlook. Growing up in Canada and attending college in the United States has never been impeded by my faith. I have attended some of the best schools and pursued an eclectic mix of intellectual interests, and I have enjoyed an active social life (albeit sans sex and alcohol) with friends of many religions and ethnicities. I have always been open about my faith, and although people close to me have been very accepting, I was always aware that in many circles, educated and uneducated alike, Islam has been and continues to be derided as some sort of vast institution of backwardness. I never paid any attention to this viewpoint, which I dismissed as mere ignorance. But since 9/11 I have become hesitant to be open about my identity with all people, especially when I sense this sort of ignorance. But even though I have experienced a derisive comment here or a slur there, I still am boldly optimistic that the democratic world's pluralistic ethic will prevail. I am and will remain a full-fledged Muslim citizen of the democratic West.

After graduating from Dartmouth, Aly Rahim went on to earn a master's degree in international security studies from Georgetown. Subsequently, he spent two years as a conflict and development specialist for Africa with the World Bank. Aly presently works on conflict prevention and peacebuilding for Canada's department of foreign affairs. He is married and lives with his wife in Ottawa.

Dean Krishna   American Pie

When I was four, my preschool class walked a few blocks down the street to release our classroom ducks into the pond in the nearby park. My mom was one of the parents who were chaperoning us. As we were walking, one of my classmates asked me: "Is that your mom?"

"Yes," I said.

"She's *ugly.*"

I looked up at my mom, the wind blowing her black hair all about. She was wearing black sunglasses. Everyone else in my class and all their parents did not look like her: they were all white-skinned, with light-colored hair. On this trip to the pond, my mom really was an ugly duckling. I agreed with my classmate.

The next spring, once we all began wearing shorts to school, I noticed that I too was different: my knees were darker than were everybody else's. I played outside a lot, and my mom was always rubbing dirt off me from the crease of my elbow, so I thought I had somehow gotten a lot of dirt on my knees. I vigorously rubbed my knees the first day I realized this, hoping to get clean. I kept rubbing them the following days, and they would turn red for a bit, but they would always go back to blackish brown. I asked my older brother about his knees and noticed they were the same as mine. I consigned myself to the fact that we were different, and we were ugly. I wished I could be like the rest of them.

These two early experiences are the first memories I have of thinking of myself as the *other* because of the color of my skin. I grew up in West Des Moines, Iowa, so my family was one of the few non-white families in the area. In an effort to fit in with our peers, my brothers and I, as I see it now, distanced ourselves from our Indian heritage. My parents themselves encouraged such distancing—one immediate example would be the names they gave us: Alvin, Dean, and Golden. These are not Indian names; they are Western, non-Christian names that my parents hoped Americans would have an easier time pronouncing than their traditional polysyllabic Indian names. My parents believed that the more American we were, the easier our lives would be in this country. Unfortunately, the reality is that what I think of as myself on the inside is not what people see me as on the outside. After spending a childhood trying as hard as I could to be like my white peers, it was right after high school when I became more in touch with my Indian heritage and started feeling comfortable blending the more traditionally Indian aspects of myself into my American identity.

Growing up, my beliefs and personality traits were strongly shaped by my Indian heritage. My parents are both Indian immigrants, and their backgrounds—particularly my father's—continue to strongly influence how I view myself.

My father grew up in a poor family in Hyderabad, India, the second child out of six. In a country with so many people and so few higher education positions available, the academic competition was tough, but my father managed to succeed. For college, he won a small scholarship, and he had enough leftover money to buy his family their first-ever fan. Early on, he exhibited a pattern of excelling and then giving. When my father finished college, he decided to come to America because it was the route for advancement in society—options in India at that time were limited.

What follows is a story I have heard told about three hundred times, and I am sure he will tell it to his grandkids at least that many times. In the fall of 1968, he received acceptance to the engineering program at the University of Kansas, and he borrowed $1000 from friends and came to the United States the following January. At age twenty-one, my father stepped off the plane at snowy Kansas City, Missouri, with a suitcase, the sandals on his feet, and barely enough money for tuition. He did not know one person in the entire country. He once again beat everyone in the classroom, and he supported himself by doing various janitorial jobs around campus. One summer, he and a few of his friends stopped in West Des Moines on the way to look for jobs in Chicago. It turned out he got a job there; he has lived in West Des Moines ever since.

My dad went back to India to visit in 1974. It was on this return visit that he married my mom. Their marriage was normal for the times—his mother picked out various women from their caste, and my father had to choose from the lot. He initially did not like any of his mom's choices, but then at his brother's wedding she introduced him to the woman who would become my mom. After talking for just an hour, my parents decided to get married. They were married three weeks after they first met.

The most defining characteristic about my Indian father is that he is a very practical citizen. He always gushes with approval of the recommendation made in airplanes: "Give the oxygen mask to yourself first, and then to those dependent on you." He wants us to get our act together first before trying to help others. My father has centered his life on this philosophy. Since he financially established himself in America, he has given much money to his family in India, and he generously donates to causes in which he believes.

My father tried to pass this philosophy of practicality on to his children, and that has often led to conflict. My freshman year in college, I became a vegetarian for environmental reasons. My dad was very upset; he talked about how hard it is to fit in already, and how my move was a step backward from the measures my parents went through to have their kids fit in. When we were younger, my father used to take my older brother, my younger brother, and me to McDonald's once a month so we would get used to eating American food before we had to start eating school lunches. When arguing with me about vegetarianism, my dad maintained that I should at least eat meat occasionally for socially practical reasons.

In his unwavering belief in practicality, the issue of preserving our Indian heritage has been left behind. To put it simply, preserving Indian traditions is not practical where we are. This lack of emphasis on our Indian heritage is something that sets my family apart from the rest of the Indian community.

My father literally embodies the American dream. He immigrated to this country with nothing, and he became rich by starting his own business. I am so proud of *my* country for making this dream possible, and so proud of my father for accomplishing it. I understand the struggles my father faced, and how his very practical mind-set helped him achieve the things he has.

But from very early on, it was clear that my father was not like my brothers and me: he was a foreigner, and we were not. For example, my dad's social advice in elementary school to walk up to people at school and say: "Hi, my name is Dean. Will you be my friend?" Who does that? Even at a young age, we knew our peers would laugh at that. In Little League, it seemed that everyone's dad either coached or came to the games. But my dad was always working, and he did not seem to care about baseball or any of the other things we were into. It was pretty embarrassing to have a dad who had no clue.

My mother also perpetuated our notion of our parents being different from us. Unlike the parents of my American friends, my mother did not go to work each morning; she was a homemaker, who did all the cooking, cleaning, and child-raising. More important, the idea of power sharing with my parents was traditionally Indian: my dad made all the big decisions. My father was the authority figure whom we feared, while my mother gently nurtured us. Growing up, we knew that our parents' division of responsibilities was not going to be like ours. My mom herself kept telling us: "You're never going to find a wife like me in this country." So, from a really young age, my brothers and I thought of ourselves as American, and we thought of our parents as Indian. No one ever explained to us the idea of hyphenation or compound racial identities (being able to embrace and identify ourselves with both cultures), and we certainly never thought of things that way.

While I thought I was American, my early childhood experiences left me with the feeling that my skin color made me inferior in some way. The media in particular compounded these feelings. Growing up, one of my favorite cartoons was GI Joe. The theme song said, "GI Joe, a real American hero. . . ." Sure enough, to me, GI Joe was America: there were white people in charge and white people everywhere. There might have even been some black soldiers. Never was there an Indian American soldier. I liked America, and I kept wishing I could be white like Americans were.

From GI Joe onward, the media shaped my idea of what is "American." Television characters were seldom of Indian descent. One time, there was an Indian actor in a movie called "Short Circuit." The actor had a thick accent, with all the ups and downs in intonations that so sharply contrasted with the more monotonic American speakers. This Indian and his accent was a form of comic relief. He was certainly not American. Later in my childhood, I saw a second Indian character on TV—Apu on *The Simpsons*. Apu also had a thick accent. Indians in the media were always foreigners; they were never Americans in the way I viewed myself. As I look back, I realize that the media is such a powerful tool in determining the American identity. This is especially true for children of immigrants, who turn to the media to seek their definition of what is American, because they oftentimes do not view their own parents as being American. I feel the media failed me during my childhood, as it provided me with only two images of skin colors that could be American—white or black.

At home, our language ingrained our thoughts. Sometimes I would have friends over from the Indian community, or sometimes I would have my "American" (meaning white) friends over. Whenever talking about another person, one of the first questions asked in my family would be: "Is (s)he an American?" My parents also spoke to each other in their native language, Tamil. They spoke to us in English and did not encourage us to speak Tamil. From an early age, the distinctions were clear: one could be Indian or one could be an American. The thought of a middle ground never crossed my mind, and it certainly was never suggested to me.

Growing up, my brothers and I distanced ourselves from the Indian community in our town. We thought we were more American, and therefore better, because it was our country. The older people had accents, and we thought their kids were losers. Why did so few of them follow sports? How come the Indian kids never came out to play YMCA basketball or Little League baseball? Most of our friends were Americans, and we belonged more with them than with Indians.

Perhaps most emblematic of our rejection of Indian culture was our rejection of Indian food. At home, my mother cooked Indian food every night for my father and herself, but my brothers and I refused to eat it. We were not Indians; we wanted American food.

So, over the years, I grew up ashamed of my Indianness, wishing I could be white, because I really felt like I was an American. I was happy that I at least had lighter-colored skin than the other Indians; this way, I could blend in better—I thought the darker-colored ones were too "Indian" and could never be as American as I was. I was also happy that my parents were so much more Americanized than other Indian parents. They had many white friends, and more important, they did not have accents. We were mixing in well.

One day early in high school, I was telling one of my Indian friends how I thought his mom had a thick accent. He said, "*My* mom? No way! If anything, *your* mom has a bad accent." I responded with an exasperated groan; there was no way he could be right! To settle our argument, we asked a white friend of ours. He said, "*Both* of your moms have accents." I responded with disbelief. I wanted to know how thick it was, and if it was very noticeable: Did she pronounce her w's as v's? Did she roll her r's? I realized then that I had probably not noticed an accent simply because I grew up with her and heard her every day; to me, her voice wasn't Indian, it was "Mom's." At any rate, I was ashamed of my mom's accent, and for the rest of high school, I took pains to notice and correct any mispronunciations she made.

I have noticed that this embarrassment to be Indian by second generations is not unique to my family. One weekend during college, six of my Indian American male friends and I decided to make a road trip down to Boston. We were supposed to go to an Indian American conference there, but we left late enough so that we would arrive for only the last event—we were more interested in just spending a night in Boston to party.

Our packed minivan stopped at a small-town McDonalds for lunch. Have you ever seen a large group of Asians together in a small town? We definitely stuck out. As we were walking in, we ourselves were commenting on how we were going to turn heads. As we formed a long line at the checkout counter, we spoke our perfect American English to each other. I made sure to speak perfectly enunciated English to the cashier. I had to prove to the people in the restaurant that we were Americans, because I felt if I had lived there, I would think that we were a van full of foreign tourists. It is certainly what I would have thought when I was growing up in Iowa. One or two or even three at a time is okay, but there is something indecent about a large group of foreign-looking people. It is amazing how I have been acculturated to stereotypes about myself that do not even fit me.

The group of people I was with were not the Indian American activist type. Our ties with the original culture were minimal, as a majority of us had never been involved with our campus's South Asian organization, and we did not go back to India regularly. More traditional Indians also watch Indian movies and listen to Indian music; we wanted none of that. We viewed ourselves as much more on the American side of the Indian American assimilation spectrum.

During lunch, we were laughing about how we managed to get so many uninvolved Indian people together just for a night out in Boston. Somebody mentioned that we might miss the last conference event if we didn't hurry, and one of my friends said angrily: "Fuck that. Fuck Indian people!"

The entire restaurant was silent. A woman a few tables down turned toward us with a look of disdain on her face. There we were, the only minorities in a small-town restaurant, and we were cursing out our own kind. And on the way to an Indian American conference of all things. I could only put my head down in embarrassment and laugh at the irony. What an absurd community we have made for ourselves!

I sensed the bitterness in Ganesh's yell; it was an expression of a lifetime of a second generation's angst. We are not Indians in so many ways. In particular, the continued presence of Indian immigrants gives us clear reminders that they, the true Indians, are not like us. I am not close friends with the Indian international students on campus; they grew up in a completely different culture and have completely different interests. I think they came to college just to perform academically, whereas many Indian Americans came to college for a more wide-ranging experience. When I see an Indian immigrant walking around campus, I think of my father. You have to respect him for his academic diligence, but you know that he is not you.

Another important difference is how we view other races: Indians have less progressive views on race than we do, and blacks in particular earn their scorn. An Indian aunt told me about a black man walking toward her down the street one afternoon. Since she is afraid of blacks, she exclaimed: "I turned around and ran!" My relatives are so comfortable in their racism. My father talks about how we are the Brahmin caste, so we are meant to be the leaders of society. He talks about how lazy everyone else is, and how he came to this country and beat all the Americans academically. This Indian notion of innate superiority is contrary to our second-generation American notion of equality, and we are distanced from Indian culture. The idea of superiority also sets up high expectations, and we feel anger and frustration at our community when we are unable to meet them.

My other brother, Alvin, failed to meet those expectations and that led to his even greater distancing from the Indian community. The fall term of my freshman year of high school, I was in the same English class as Alvin, who was then a sophomore. I earned an A in the class; he got an F. In fact, I got all A's that term, and he got all F's. I was as shocked as my parents were. I knew he wasn't doing so well in English, but I never realized he was *failing*.

I was thirteen years old, and I did not think about it too much. I was that good kid that all my teachers liked, who always did his homework and did well in class. I loved school—always had—and I was immersed in my own little world. I had joined the debate team that term and had done well for a first-year student, and I was looking forward to tennis beginning in the spring.

That term was not a temporary glitch in my brother's academic career. Instead, it was the beginning of its end. He failed all his classes again for spring semester, and for his junior year he transferred to a school in a neighboring, more rural district. After five years of high school, Alvin never finished enough classes to graduate. He just did not seem to care.

I was sixteen years old when Alvin was in his second senior year, and it was only around then that I began analyzing his situation more. By the middle of senior year, my grades would no longer be reflected in my transcripts for college, and I began to relax a little. I began to come out of the machine mode that had made the last three years of my life a blur. I began to become more self-reflective and caring.

I realized then that a lot of my brother's struggles had to deal with the fact that our parents are from India. Growing up with Indian parents and relatives, the only adult examples we had, we were overwhelmed by their near perfection. My father had to distinguish himself among millions academically in order to earn a right to be educated in the country, and he now has a successful business. All of the other Indian parents that we knew seemed to be doctors. My father was on the early end of the first wave of immigration from India, and my brother and I are the older part of the second generation. No one comes across the world to be a social worker or teacher—the only adult models we had were those of extreme brilliance and financial success.

And then there is me. I was in so many ways the stereotypical Indian American child. I always got A's. I would come home from all my after-school activities around 7 to 8 o'clock each night, and I would go straight to my room to do my schoolwork. I was the standout student since I was young—I even skipped a year in elementary school. I was the Energizer Bunny—I would just keep going and going, and no one could catch me. And like the Energizer Bunny, I was not quite human either. I was driven and goal-oriented, but there was not much beyond that.

My cousin commented to me once in high school how our house is like a hotel: five of us lived there, but no one but my mom ever knew where everyone else was. I remember even making it a point not to know where my brothers were—I thought this was the American way. It was only during my senior year that I let that comment affect me. To be honest, I do not think I learned how to feel until then.

I think what happened with my brother is quite simple. He could not compete with me, and his inability to attain our Indian standards of perfection made him feel like a failure. He was older than me, but I was getting all the glory—it just did not seem right.

Alvin's frustrations heightened his disdain for Indians. Their academic standards were very high; they were not like him, and he was not like them. There was a feedback cycle where Alvin became more and more alienated from the Indian community. I, however, never felt such a degree of alienation because I met those high academic standards. During a conversation about our culture that we had while I was in college, Alvin asked me: "How can you *stand* Indian people?"

Of course, at the time, I never talked about these things with Alvin. In our house, we usually did not talk about feelings. My parents are task-oriented Indians: asking each other questions like "How are you doing today?" simply was not a part of their culture. Growing up, my American brothers and I did not challenge that lack of personal communication; we too failed to see the value of it.

But perhaps more important, I did not talk to Alvin because I felt powerless. He was my older brother, and I was somewhat jealous of his life. Academic success was not important to him, and he seemed to be getting along fine without it. I could tell that he had dismissed me long ago as his geeky little brother. I was part of the problem; I was the enemy, why would he listen to me? Besides, I was not at home that often anyway. On the odd chance that we both happened to be home at the same time, we would talk about Iowa State football or the Chicago Cubs. Always sports.

At the end of his high school attendance, Alvin drove out to California with his friends, and he decided to stay there. I think being away from home made him aware of how hard living away from home is. His friends enrolled in a community college up there, and he wanted to do the same. He received his GED from California that December, and in January he enrolled in a community college. He stopped going to classes after a few weeks, though. I remember talking to him one day that February. He said that he really respected our dad, and that he realized how hard our dad had had to work to get to where he was. Alvin had never said such a nice thing about our father before. I felt that things were changing. Maybe it was better that he was away from home; he seemed to be maturing.

Alvin moved home that April. He started working at a hotel in town, and he has been working in hotels ever since. He has had a girlfriend for over a year now, and she has helped with my brother's emotional struggles. I think he is going places, and I am glad he now seems motivated. Being at the front of the second generation has been an emotional ride for him and my family, but things are getting better.

Looking back, what happened to my brother has helped our family become more American: we get involved in each other's lives now. We make it a point to have a family dinner at least once whenever I come home. Our house is no longer the hotel filled with five independent lives that it used to be. Alvin and I still are not very close, but we have grown closer as I have broken out of my machine mode and revealed myself to the brother I hardly spoke to in high school. My parents also regret the rush that was our childhood. I know my dad in particular feels bad that he was not around much when we were growing up, and he is trying to make it up by spending more time with my brothers and me when we are home.

These overt efforts at being more caring—more American—has affected my younger brother, who is more than three years younger than me. He also had the benefit of growing up with American brothers to guide him, instead of only the Indian parents that Alvin and I had. The difference is noticeable—he talks about feelings much more easily than Alvin and I did at his age. While he also grew up not liking Indian people, he has performed decently academically, so he does not hate Indians to the degree that Alvin does. Because he cares about his grades, Golden respects Indians' work ethic in a way that Alvin did not.

By not graduating from high school and not going to college, Alvin outwardly defied our parents and their values. This defiance goes beyond just our parents to all of the Indian community—the basis for my parent's values. As I have seen with my other friends, Alvin's dislike of his own kind is not unusual among second-generation Indian Americans. In our generation, there is a spectrum of Indian Americanness. Some remain very traditionally Indian, while others, like Ganesh, my brothers, and myself, rejected Indian culture because it was not American like we were, and we did not like the expectations and the stereotypes. But we are all still Indians, and are redefining what it means when someone says, "Fuck Indian people!" Certainly, our children will have different perceptions of what it means to be Indian, as they will be basing it on the spectrum of definitions they will see from their second-generation parents. It is going to be interesting to see what the future holds.

Because I grew up embarrassed to be Indian, I oftentimes assumed that my kids would also lack an affinity for Indian culture. However, my own thoughts about Indians changed when I went to India the summer after I graduated from high school. I had been there six times before, but I had not been there since the summer after seventh grade.

On this particular visit, I discovered what an amazing nation India is. I had never before learned about the rich cultural and artistic history of India. It had that many people? It had a culture as old as the oldest European ones? I had no idea. We had never learned about Asian things from kindergarten all the way through the twelfth grade.

But more significant, when I went to India, I was surprised to feel like I was at home. Everyone there looked like me. My family was Indian and practiced the Indian customs that I had shied away from growing up. This is my history, I thought. This is a part of my identity; this links me to my father's father's father, all the way back to the beginning of civilization.

I saw a beggar in Madras, with nothing but rags on, but who was my age, and had the same hair as me, the same color skin, the same *eyes*. . . . why him, there? And why me, in the United States? If I had come out of his mother's womb—and I very well could have—my life would have been so different. That summer, for the first time, awareness of my Indian identity was truly aroused.

I knew I would never be able to stop thinking about my brothers and sisters in India. I left the United States that summer as an Indian boy wishing he could be an American white, and I returned as someone determined to represent his race to the fullest degree possible. I was proud to be Indian. No, no, I was Indian American. Hyphenation, or compound nationalities, truly meant something, and it took me until then to realize that it meant *me*.

Over the course of that next year, I became more conscious of my skin color. My family and I made our annual trip from West Des Moines to St. Louis, Missouri, and because there are no major interstates connecting the two cities, we used two-lane highways. I remember stopping at a small-town gas station and being very aware of my race for the first time in all our trips. I journaled then, writing, "I felt intimidated walking into that gas station. . . . I wanted to ask those people, 'Do you think I'm an American? Did you think I was a foreigner when I walked through that door?'" Independent of what people thought, that self-consciousness of being a different color became an integral part of my identity.

I think that most of the time people do notice my skin color, and accordingly make associations with it—oftentimes that means they think I am a foreigner. On my flight back home after my first year in college, I asked the nine-year-old girl sitting next to me if she wanted a piece of gum as we were taking off. She looked startled and said, "Oh, I didn't think you spoke English." She was young enough to be honest, but I think a lot of people assume I'm fresh off the boat until I prove otherwise. As I look back, I can recount dozens of times when I've had this conversation:

"Where are you from?"

"West Des Moines."

"No, where are you really from?"

"Oh, my *parents* are from India."

I certainly do not blame people for making assumptions about me based on my skin color. In high school or before, I would have made the exact same assumptions had I seen an East Asian, or even another Indian. It has taken a tremendous amount of conscious un-learning in college for me not to jump to such conclusions. If the media and culture deeply ingrained such impressions on me, a young person of color, then I understand how much more ingrained such ideas may be to older white people—they grew up in a time when society was less racially integrated, and when the media had purely white images of true Americanism.

In the year following my India trip, I engaged in discussions about race and identity for the first time. I particularly remember one day when our student government went on a "diversity retreat." That day, we shared each other's conceptions of different races. An African American student spoke about when she was growing up her parents always told her to close the shades, unlike the "dirty white people, who had no shame." I identified with that. My parents were always telling us to close the shades, and they did not understand those Americans who showed the whole world what was going on in their home.

For the first time, that January day, I was having an open, honest conversation about race. I raised my hand and spoke about that boy I saw in India who had the same eyes as me. I talked about how I used to rub my knees because I did not quite understand that I was different from white people. But the substance of what I said was not important—it was the fact that I was talking about it for the first time ever that was significant. It felt great to share. It felt great to hear other people's stories and anxieties, and to hear how similar they were to mine. Over the course of the year, I started identifying with the larger minority community. I became more acutely aware of the stereotypes we all suffered from, and I became active in fighting those perceptions that I myself had bought into: Asians are not as American, Asian men are not as masculine, and so forth.

Despite the ideals I embraced that year, I am still in the process of shedding the parts of my Indianness of which I have felt ashamed. In college, I have always felt embarrassed when my mom talked to my roommates. I felt her accent made her seem stupid and ignorant. It was in my senior year, however, that I thought about my mom having a British accent instead. Why was it that I might be proud of that—because she would sound educated? I realized there was no reason to have this double standard between British and Indian accents, and that I was imposing racist norms if I were to think that my mother's accent somehow necessitated that she were stupid in some way. I was finally no longer ashamed of my mom's accent. In fact, the more I thought about it, I then became proud, because the accent symbolized my mother's ability to negotiate two cultures.

This negotiation of cultures has defined my life as well, and it will continue to do so for as long as I live. When I was six, my three-year-old brother brushed past a woman in a Hallmark store in the mall, and she said to him, "I guess they don't have manners where you come from." Part of me wants to go back to that lady and smack her. But honestly, if I were there again, I would let her know that yes, my parents come from India, and ancient Indian traditions are a part of me. I would also let her know that I was born and raised in Iowa, and that I played Little League baseball and watched Saturday morning cartoons. I have experienced the immigrant experience, and multiple cultures have fused into me. I am as American as apple pie.

While I struggle to be perceived as American, there is already one place in America where I feel my skin color truly does not affect perceptions of my Americanness: New York City. The first time I experienced the liberation of the city was after I had spent seven straight terms at Dartmouth and was ready for a change. My friend Tanveer and I hopped on the early train, and we arrived at Penn Station, New York, during the afternoon rush hour. I was looking forward to being in the city, but I was not expecting to feel what I felt.

There was no dominant skin color there; there were racial minorities everywhere—in fact, we were *all* now minorities. Suddenly, the color of my skin did not matter; I was no different than anybody else. I had not previously realized what an integral role my skin color had played in my life, and how I was always viewing myself with regard to the color of my skin. But as soon as I stepped into Penn Station, I felt this tremendous load come off my spirit. I realized that is how white people must feel—and what a wonderful feeling it was! Tanveer, who was from Bangladesh, was thinking the same thing: "Oh, wow," he said. "I had forgotten how New York makes you feel like you're home." And I did really feel *home*; it was the same feeling I had when I was in the streets of India, among thousands of my own people. But I was in America this time. I did not know such a feeling was possible in this country.

During the cab ride to Brooklyn, as I was absorbing the sights and smells of the city, I was thinking about race and the tremendous freedom I felt. I looked over at Tanveer, and I started thinking about how I even became friends with him in the first place. We had some interests in common, but I was not sure if we would have been friends if we were not both minorities.

When I meet people of color, I automatically feel some bond with them. I understand that people tend to see me for my skin color first, and I understand that the feelings I had felt and actions I had taken as a child were related to my minority status. My best friend in college, Jeff, is Jewish. I like to think that we are good friends because we have the same interests and personalities, but perhaps part of our closeness lies in the fact that we are both minorities in some way. I feel minorities understand me better. I do not need to educate them on how it feels to be different; they have felt it themselves.

It is not that I am constantly thinking of Indian history, and that I am upset at the European colonialists. I do not carry with me a soul full of anger toward whites for the oppression committed by their predecessors. I just feel a bond with all minorities, because they have felt the feelings of un-belonging that I have felt and experienced the separation and difference that I have experienced as well.

But that day in New York, I really, truly, felt I belonged. We were all minorities, with our own cultural idiosyncrasies. It was spiritually liberating; I had no idea of the tremendous weight of the racial load I was carrying until I was free of it. I was no longer *different*, since there was no standard to be different from. Maybe in the future, all of America will give racial minorities the same feeling that I felt when I arrived in New York.

In the meantime, however, as much as people like to say it does not matter, my skin color will continue to dominate people's perceptions of me. As a result, skin color will continue to dominate my perception of myself. At the end of junior year in college, my roommates and I were talking one night about girls. I mentioned that I had not dated anyone from school all year, and one of my roommates said, "Yeah, I guess there aren't many Indian girls here."

Why did it have to be Indian girls? I was upset at my roommate for saying that. At the same time, he had a point—although I had never told him this, I did in fact like Indian girls more. But why did my roommate assume I could not date non-Indian girls? Could he not see beyond my skin color to realize that I was as American as he? Did he think that because I was Asian that no other types of girls would be attracted to me?

From early on, I was reminded in so many ways that romance would be different for me because of my skin color. People who looked like me were never on TV, and I and one other Indian boy in my elementary school grade were the only minority kids in a class of ninety people. In fifth grade, two of my classmates came up to me and sneeringly asked, "Hey Dean, is your dick black, or is it pink like the rest of ours?" I gave them a look like I thought it was somewhat funny and I went on my way, but the message was clear: I was not the same. When we were on the cusp of the age of dating, something about my sexuality was not "like the rest of ours."

The first girl I ever dated was an Indian American. Even though we were both mainstream American, it felt weird—like I couldn't make it with other Americans, so I had to go back to my own kind and date from that pool. Our *parents* did that; we were in America, why couldn't I find someone more American (i.e., white)? I myself was buying into the notion that Indian Americans aren't quite as American as whites.

I did not tell my parents about Sejal. My parents never dated, and I was not sure what they expected out of their kids. Talking about such personal matters was definitely awkward, and it was easier not to talk about it. Also, I did not want them to know I was dating an Indian girl. When we were younger, my brothers and I had been so thoroughly anti-Indian that we had convinced our parents (and ourselves) that we would eventually marry white girls, and I did not want to deal with telling them about potentially changing my mind. Based on their reactions to our youthful promises, my parents—unlike other Indian parents—had made it clear to us that we could marry whomever we wished, no matter what the skin color.

When I was a senior in high school, I became close with Katie, a white girl who told me she liked Indian guys. Wow, I thought. Lucky me. There was something about being with white girls that symbolized being mainstream. It was not the cop-out of going back to my own kind; it meant I was more American and less like my parents. Once I became more aware of racial issues in college, however, I became angry with Katie for exotifying me. I felt that the fact she liked Indian guys cheapened what was more real between us. At the same time, I was torn, because I wondered if I would have liked her so much if she had not been white.

The idea of affinities for particular races manifests itself best for me through my friend Jeff, who makes no secret of the fact that he is more attracted to Asian women. He has been dating an Asian American for nearly two years, and they seem to have a healthy relationship. There is a danger in liking someone based on their skin color, which is what led to my anger at Katie. Liking someone for their skin color can lead to objectification of the other, and what is between the two might be more artificial. But now I see no reason why skin color can't play an initial role and then selection can occur from there. I, generally, am more attracted to Indian women and minority women in general, and that might be because of all this cultural baggage that I know they share with me. But if I were to date an Indian American woman again, I don't think it would be because I view her as an object, but because I like her as a person.

But again, there are tensions. Ideally, skin color should not matter, and people should be equal-opportunity daters. And even now, after a solid three years of being proud to be a minority, I still do a double take when I see a picture of myself with my white friends. I stick out so much. I cannot help but think to myself: "Gee, you're pretty dark. Remember to wear sunblock the next time you go out."

So, I buy into the idea that whiter is beautiful. I wonder why I do so. Is it simply because I have an innate desire to look like those around me? Or is it that society has told me what is beautiful, and that being a dark Asian male does not qualify? Honestly, how many Asian American males have you seen playing a lead romantic role beside a white woman?

In my fraternity, there are a few guys who have "Asian fetishes," and it's accepted. But the problem is that the guys who people joke about not ever getting girls tend to be the guys of Asian descent. There is an odd double standard in our culture about which gender of Asians can be more beautiful, and over the years, I unknowingly have let it apply to my view of myself as well.

This sense that I am the romantic *other* because of the color of my skin is another part of the long process of identifying as the *other* that began with my class trip to the pond. When I was young, this difference made me feel un-American, and therefore inferior. I let my alleged inferior skin color affect my affinity for my ethnicity, and I became embarrassed to be Indian.

But since my trip to India, I have been more comfortable with being Indian American. I think I am very aware of my standing as a person of color in this country: I speak my mind on race-related issues and pay close attention to larger minority political movements. I try to notice when people look at me or treat me differently because of my skin color, and I generally let them know how I feel about that. I feel like I have been helping racial progress in this country. But there is so much beyond race, and I discovered it as my junior year of college came to a close.

That spring, I was pondering much. Where was I supposed to go with my life? Up until then, I had been involved in activities that had consumed my life. I debated the national circuit in high school, and I concentrated intensely on getting good grades. I was heavily involved in student government in college, and spring semester of my junior year marked the end of my term as student body president. My 24-7-365 duty to my school was ending, and I did not know what to do next. The question of my *purpose* kept nagging at me. My job that summer was only forty hours a week and not having anything to take over my life helped me understand what was important to me. Since I was in New York, I did not have to think about race, and I saw how economic and educational privilege gave me much power there, and how I could use that power to help others—it did not have to be about race.

Senior year, I'm thinking about race less. I know my place in America and I accept it. Jeff used to always say to me, "You always talk about race." He has not said that as much this year. I am not friends with him because of a shared Indian bond. I am friends with him because we enjoy the same sports, have a similar sense of humor, support each other, and have similar midwestern backgrounds. My roommate George and I became close friends last summer; we have much in common. Our racial differences hardly come up. I know he sees my skin color each time he sees me (I would, too. How can he not?), but we are friends beyond that. Whenever race does come up, we talk honestly with each other; I might explain to him why my culture requires me to think a certain way or eat a certain food. Sometimes, we get in deep discussions about race-related issues like affirmative action, but they are by no means our most frequent topic of conversation.

I have my Indian American activist friends with whom I discuss race issues in more detail. One of my friends, Reena, is very involved in the Indian American community, both culturally and politically, and she is my friend who understands best when I want to talk about the Indian American community or my Indian parents specifically.

It is hard to divide my friends into ethnic and non-ethnic categories, because my ethnicity is clearly such an integral part of who I am. But I suppose I have had a unique experience, where I denied my ethnicity for so long that I came to have many interests that do not directly deal with race at all. I know I separate my friends to some degree based on being similar in all respects except that our races are different, or based on our racial bond being stronger. While there is much overlap between these groups, I have my Indian friends and I have my non-Indian friends. Each of these friends does not play the same function in my life, and that is fine. It is not all about race.

While I have managed not to let race dominate my life, I am still frustrated about how I view race. Last year, there was an earthquake in Taiwan. Although I felt sorrow, the feeling of remorse paled in comparison with the sadness I felt for the earthquake in India this year. I still have an affinity for Indian people, and that seems unfair. I feel badly for not caring equally for the victims of other earthquakes.

I do still think of my father's airplane metaphor about taking care of yourself before others. That philosophy may apply to me as an individual, but does it apply to my ethnicity, too? Should I take care of my own people before caring about others? Does not affinity toward one's own kind help justify and perpetuate the very white cultural domination that I resented? I continue to be torn.

I feel I should be impartial because I am American; I am not Indian, like my parents' generation. Naturally, they are more tied to their homeland. When I was telling my uncle about an Indian American whose leg was blown off while providing medical relief in Rwanda, my uncle's reaction was typical for an Indian parent: "Why did he go to Africa? Doesn't he realize that Indians need his help, too?"

But I do not belong in India, and neither does that Indian American doctor. In the movie *Congo*, they take the chimp Amy back to the African jungle because she does not belong in human society. The other chimps look at her and know that she is foreign. It is the same look I get when I go back to India. Almost everything outside my skin color—my dress, my demeanor, the language I speak—indicates that I am not one of them. The chimp does not know the ways of her ancestral clan. "Oh, no," said Amy's caretaker, "she doesn't belong here either, does she?"

That is me; I am the chimpanzee. I do not belong in India, yet I know that people continue to see me as a foreigner in this country. But I am firmly patriotic. I know that someday, as Indian Americans establish themselves, and as society and media images become more racially diverse, my kind will be perceived as American.

I am teaching in an inner city next year through Teach for America, so I can help my fellow Americans. For all the talk about hurt and identity and inclusion, all of it in perspective does not mean as much as other issues: economic despair, or lack of educational opportunity, is worse. The people I will be teaching are society's *other* in a more significant way than I was the *other* while growing up. I had access to a good education—and therefore nearly infinite lifestyle choices—because of historical happenstance. What if I had been born a poor child in India? In East St. Louis? I am not an Indian; I know the ways of America best, so I choose to help my people here.

I ask myself: Who would I want teaching my kids? Naturally, I would want the best educated and the most enthusiastic teacher possible. I know I can be that teacher. It is in my blood, it is my caste, it is my ancestral duty. It all ties together. I'll be giving people hope and access to the American dream that my father was fortunate enough to live. I want every American—no matter the skin color—to have the same opportunity my father had. So, while I choose to further break my ties from India by affirming my American identity through teaching in a non-Indian area, the reason I am teaching is firmly rooted in my awareness of my Indian father and my ancestral heritage. In the end, it all comes full circle: for all the psychological progressions I make about my future place in this world, I am constantly mediating my historical identity.

After teaching for two years, Dean Krishna is now in law school. He is married to Reena, the Indian friend he mentioned in his narrative. He has also found out that the Indian character in *Short Circuit* was actually a white man in brownface.

Sabeen Hassanali   My Permanent Home

Four days ago, I called home to Houston to see how my family was doing. It was relatively late, but everyone there seemed wide awake. My mom's best friend Rosie was visiting from San Antonio for the first time in several years, so they were having a sleepover. She had brought along her oldest son, Kamran. As children, my younger sister and I played house with Kamran and his younger brother. My outlook on life then was very simple: Kamran and I would grow up together and, when we were older, get married. It made perfect sense.

Fifteen years have gone by and we have seen very little of Auntie Rosie's family, so it was nice to hear that they were visiting. My mom sounded unusually happy as she said, "We were just talking about you." There were giggles in the background. I heard the word *marriage*.

When Auntie Rosie got on the phone, she pleaded, "Sabeen, dear, you have to promise me that you'll do as I say when you see me." Something began to gnaw at the back of my mind. I readily gave her my word, as she is not just a close family friend but also my godmother, and I have always held a special place for her in my heart. Yet, I was hesitant. When I talked to my sister, things began to make sense. She mentioned Kamran as well. "Sabeen, he's really cute. And he's nice, too. You should definitely check him out. He's perfect for you. He and Auntie will visit in December, so you can meet him then." I felt a slow and uneasy churning in my stomach as I tried to ignore what I thought might be happening. These comments from my mother, Rosie, and my sister had a subtle undertone that came in loud and clear on my end of the phone. In December, they're planning to come down so I can get to know him better. And were they discussing a marriage proposal? *My* marriage proposal? No! And yet, I had seen it happen often enough to other girls to recognize that that's what it was.

After I hung up the phone, I thought to myself, "This is incomprehensible. How could this be happening to me? I'm a college student, an undergraduate. I've never even been in a relationship. How do they think I'm ready for marriage?" Yet, I *knew* this had been coming. These subtle "jokes" about marriage had begun even before I finished high school, even though my family knew how much I despised even the casual mention of it. I was eventually able to ignore or dismiss whatever came my way, and I had assumed I would always be able to. But this time, with family friends and heightened expectations involved—I had certainly not expected my godmother to be arranging things—it was not so easy to dismiss the idea as a harmless joke. I also had not expected I would have to face this reality so soon. Maybe I shouldn't be too surprised, however. After all, my mom was my age when she got married. All of her seven sisters (she has no brothers) also grew up modestly in Karachi, Pakistan, and married fairly young, all arranged marriages.

The custom of arranged marriages is one of a number of values that my parents and I disagree on. For me, growing up as a Pakistani American with traditional parents has meant constantly dealing with fundamentally divergent attitudes, including those toward education, love, and "home." Reconciling these differences has meant that I have had to assert my independence and make choices that my parents do not agree with—in a way, I suppose, I have had to be an "American." Still, in this struggle, I have made a conscious effort to remain a "Pakistani," grounding myself in my faith and culture while asserting my autonomy. I understand that my parents may not agree with the choices I have made—I would not expect them to—but over the years they have also come to see that I have not abandoned them, and that I will continue to remain both Pakistani and American.

My father's family grew up in poverty in a community of mud houses in urban Karachi. His family of nine shared a 160-square-foot living space that had no electricity. The only bathrooms within walking distance were communal government bathrooms, which were rarely cleaned. Growing up, food was scarce and there were many mouths to feed. After completing tenth grade, my dad began working at a local bank, and his family moved to a one-bedroom apartment. The eldest male of seven children, he had decided to take on a job to help support his younger siblings and ensure that his brothers could continue their high school and university studies. His brothers, like all respectable Pakistani men, were expected to provide for their future families, and hence had to take advantage of educational opportunities. His four sisters, on the other hand—like most other poor women in their community—completed only elementary school and were expected to be ripe for marriage soon after. They did not need further schooling.

In a few years my dad had been promoted and began working at a bank in Qatar. Prompted by his mother—my paternal grandmother, or *Dadima* in Urdu—he decided to take a month off work to return to Karachi and find his future wife. "Shopping around" for wives consisted of going to families' homes, seeing the girls briefly, and conversing with their parents. An informal network of older ladies in the community kept tabs on the single males and females who were of marriageable age and how respectable their families were. They were the personals—personified.

While my dad and *Dadima* were looking in a neighboring town at the end of September, they came across a lady named Jena Bhai. At the time, my mom was a twenty-one-year-old teacher, having recently graduated with a BA from a local university, but she often tailored clothes for Jena Bhai, who was quite fond of her. Jena Bhai suggested that my dad and *Dadima* check her out, since she lived nearby. They heeded Jena Bhai's advice and visited my mom's home, asking to see her. As it happened, when my dad and *Dadima* visited, my mom was just getting ready to go to *Jamatkhana*, the place of worship; my mom's parents told her to serve the guests drinks on her way out.

In the tight, humid room, small talk between the elders wafted through the thick air. My petite, five-foot-tall mother hurried into the room, her *dupata*, a long scarf, flying behind her. She did not think to ask who the guests were. She quietly served the glasses of Coke to the now-silent bodies around her, careful to touch only the base of the glass as she passed each one. (I would be trained on this exact glass passing technique ten years later.) She left the room without ever having looked up to see any of their faces. She had no idea what serving those Cokes had implied.

The next day, Jena Bhai informed my maternal grandparents that my dad had liked my mom and wanted to marry her. My grandmother informed my mom of the proposal. And that was that.

I can't help but wonder what my mother's feelings must have been. Wasn't she surprised? Wasn't she scared? Was this what she wanted? How could she know he might be right for her? *She never even saw his face!* The engagement date was set for the following day, October 1, and because of my dad's work schedule, the wedding itself had to occur within ten days. That week, my mom and dad went out a couple of times for dinner, their only "dates" as an engaged couple. On October 11, with full faith in first impressions, their parents' decisions, and an unquestioned destiny, my parents were joined in marriage. A week later my dad left for work, and two months later, when her visa arrived, my mom left alone for Qatar, boarding her first flight wearing a new light-pink sari.

My mom and dad got along well in Qatar and were soon blessed with me and my sister, Nadya, who is two years my younger. My memories of living in Qatar are happy ones. It now seems like a dream—a quiet, happy life where my dad worked a nine-to-five bank job and my mom stayed at home. I cheerfully attended the local private school—all schools in Qatar were private—waking my parents up even on Fridays, the day schools and offices were closed, because I loved school so much and wanted to go even on holidays. I remember evenings at home when Nadya played with my dolls while I learned the multiplication tables with my mom at the dinner table. Sometimes my dad would be watching an American movie and would say something like, "Sabeen, come here. Look, that's snow. They have snow in America. It gets very cold there." Snow looked stunning and beautiful. My dad would often talk of how wonderful America was. I believed him completely—these were dreams and pictures of a land far away from what our simple world held.

When I was six, my mom became pregnant with our younger brother, Faisal. Around this time, my dad's bank began laying off many employees, and eventually my dad's number was up. Fortunately, they offered him a visa to either Pakistan or the United States in exchange for the layoff. After quickly discussing the matter, my parents decided to take advantage of the rare opportunity. My dad's younger brother was already in the United States, working as a successful businessman in New York, and having some family there meant we wouldn't be completely alone in an alien land. Soon after my brother was born, when I was seven, our family of five left the only home we knew and headed for a new life in America.

In New York, my dad took a day job at a donut shop and an evening job as a taxi driver, which worked out well because he loved seeing the sights of New York and he loved to drive. My mother, meanwhile, babysat some neighbors' children while taking care of my baby brother. We lived on the fourth floor of a five-story building in New York, not quite downtown, but en route to the outlying suburbs. The main room of the apartment was the living room, brightly lit with two economical, white tube lights. With its borrowed sofas, wooden wall unit, and doily-covered glass coffee table, our apartment personified the "fresh off the boat" image. Family pictures in dollar-store frames and plastic flowers in large vases colored the room, which permanently reeked of Indian curry, though we rarely noticed. The five of us shared a bedroom: my sister and I had bunk beds, my mom and baby brother slept on another bed, and my dad slept on the floor. Driving around in a cab all evening, he found sleeping on the carpeted floor to be better for his back.

As was my nature, I was excited to be in school after our recent move to the United States. My third-grade class was full of people with different colors of hair, skin, and eyes, something I had never encountered before. My teacher, Mrs. Jackson, had light yellow hair and blue-green eyes that fascinated me. Her eyes would change color every day. I yearned for a doll with yellow hair and desperately wished I had "colored" eyes. My black hair and dark brown eyes, I concluded, did not count as legitimate hair and eye colors. I was sad that I could never really be "American" because I looked so unlike one. Compared with these doll-like faces around me, I figured that I was and would always be too plain. Instead of worrying excessively about my appearance, however, I decided to focus on things that were in my control, such as the work we did in class. In my three years at Woodson Elementary School, I truly loved the experience of learning, especially when it meant a teacher, an actual "American" teacher, cared. Mrs. Jackson gave me the confidence and motivation to work hard in everything I did thereafter. Even now, after fourteen years, I am in touch with Mrs. Jackson, who is still a teacher in a New York public school.

I was in fourth grade when my family suddenly decided to move to Houston, where one of my mom's sisters lived. Leaving New York was painful because I was once again leaving behind everything I knew—and because I had only vague images of Houston as a town full of cowboys and horses. I wasn't even sure if they had cars over there. We drove down to Houston in my dad's cab, which he had bought at a discounted price and painted light gray. As we approached the Houston skyline (insignificant compared with New York's), I felt nothing but angry uncertainty. I had been told that I needed glasses, but my family could not afford them yet, so everything from our car windows looked hazy to me—especially Houston and my future in it.

Eventually, my family adjusted to Houston and worked to make it our permanent home. Since my parents would leave for work at 6 a.m. and not return until 6 p.m., I looked after my siblings and the house after coming home from school. The increased responsibility made me mature early, particularly as I began my adolescence. At the same time, my academic motivation continued to increase and became a way for me to develop an identity and make friends in the different schools I attended.

Because our family switched apartments often, however, my friendships tended to develop less from school and more from my relatively stable religious community. The sense of permanency this community provided also helped build a strong sense of identity within me. Our community of Shi'a Ismai'li Muslims consists of ten million people spread out across the world, most of Central or South Asian descent. One key distinction of our faith is that we have a living spiritual leader, an Imam, to guide us. The Aga Khan, who resides in France and was appointed Imam while completing his senior year at Harvard, is a direct descendant of the Prophet Mohammed, forty-ninth in a line of Imams who descended from the Prophet's time. Going to *Jamatkhana* to pray regularly and being involved with its social organizations, such as Girl Scouts, kept me very active within our *jamat*—our community. Service and intellectual excellence also fit in perfectly with the teachings of our Imam, who emphasizes living an ethical and balanced life. Islam has always been a part of my worldview, and I cannot perceive myself as separate from it. As such, I have always been a spiritual person, consciously meditating since I was ten (following in my parents' footsteps). I feel the comforting presence of God with me, through good times and bad. As the turbulent waves of adolescence entered and took over my life, my faith became the anchor that grounded everything else—family, school, traditions, and friends—and helped me realize my potential.

As a sophomore in high school, I found myself confronting several new stumbling blocks: I discovered that elections were popularity contests I could not win. Classes were becoming significantly more difficult, and I struggled to keep up. It seemed impossible to get into a competitive college in the Northeast. My friends all had boyfriends while I remained unattached. I found myself not fitting into a particular clique, failing to identify with one strong circle of friends. Reflecting on these troubles plunged me into a spiral of depression in which I no longer felt a connection with my school, my friends, my family, and even life in general. I longed for this connection but did not expect it and did not experience it. Instead, I shut myself off from everyone, hiding behind a casually pleasant smile and dedicating myself to academics, looking for the hint of appreciation in an "A" at a time when I needed nurture and love.

Interesting opportunities of service in our *jamat* and school would present themselves and I would always decline. In May I heard about a week-long youth camp, and although I declined initially, I was persuaded by organizers and grudgingly applied to be a counselor. The first day of training, I noticed someone I did not recognize: a bouncy, twenty-five-year-old South Asian American in a ponytail named Azim, who looked like a carefree surfer. He began the training session by having us all sing and dance in a circle, and the session continued along the same unpredictable, unorthodox vein. The counselors all had quizzical looks on their faces—this was not what we were expecting "training" to be. Yet, as confusing as it initially was, this concept of surprising people and keeping them on edge in order to teach them strangely thrilled me, and the intensity of my emotions baffled me. Being so accustomed to not feeling anything, I breathed in this rush of excitement with all my might. Throughout the training session I avidly participated in discussions, raised issues concerning youth, made analogies, and probed the minds of my fellow adolescents who, before this, I believed were doomed to hopelessness. Growing up, we craft such amazing dreams and fantasies for ourselves. Why do we let others over time allow us to give these up as childish or idealistic? At one point I thought of my secret image of Aladdin. After seventh grade I stopped telling people that *Aladdin*, with its aspirational message, was my favorite movie because it seemed too childish. Reality, I had learned, was not full of hope. I wondered, if only kids would hear affirmations that their hopes were real and legitimate, how much better a world would it be? How many more young Muslims, or youth in general, would grow up feeling comfortable in their own skin?

"Can anyone guess what my favorite movie is?" Azim asks, suddenly jolting me out of the maze of a hundred different ideas and hopes that were whirling through my mind. "*Aladdin*. This is our chance to show these participants a whole new world." I stopped breathing. Suddenly, everything else around me faded as I looked into Azim and saw the vision I had been thirsting for. In this "surfer boy" with a ponytail, I felt my potential, my *full human* potential, for the very first time. Throughout the camp, an invincible spark ignited me. I rarely slept that week because of an urge to instill hope in my campers, an urge so strong that it inevitably became a reality.

More so than the camp itself, my relationship with Azim gave me a reason to live and care once again. Azim saw the same potential in me that I saw actualized in him. He and I stayed in touch and worked together on a number of different youth leadership programs within our community. This renewed spirit also showed up in my classes and relationships with friends. During the spring of my junior year, when my family moved to South Houston, I quickly befriended some of the top students in my new school and gained leadership positions by working extremely hard. What could have been a horrible experience of once again starting anew actually pushed me to succeed even further, mostly because of a renewed faith in myself.

There is within me a spiritual presence so incredibly powerful that at times it is difficult to understand myself without it—a timeless and invisible friendship has seen me through the years, through the oppressive heat of Texas, and through the cauldron I call home. All year long there is a stifling heat in Texas that consumes you and makes you boil inside out. During the summer people stay indoors in nicely air-conditioned homes and malls, shunning the outdoors, where one is fried alive. Although the heat simmers outside, people become accustomed to being closed off from it so that it almost disappears. Almost.

Growing up, however, my version of this heat existed not outside, but indoors, at home: the scalding melting pot in which the traditional and the modern, the old and the young, the Pakistani and the American simmered and collided. It was a crucible my sister and I yearned to escape. In our first-generation immigrant family, the home became a battleground between the idealistic, assimilated American teenagers (Nadya and me) and our self-sacrificing, old-school parents. On the front lines—our dinner table—Nadya and I fired off staple English phrases, such as "You never understand," from our side, while ceaseless lectures in Urdu hit or missed our ears from the other side. The battles we fought (and still fight) revolved around going to parties, wearing shorts, highlighting our hair, or talking loudly. To my parents, who came home tired from twelve-hour workdays, these childish desires to be more American seemed like imposing threats from a culture they felt distant from. It was understandable that they could not relate well to the Americans they served at work. Facing the same foreign culture and language in their own home, however, must have been a much more alienating experience. Meanwhile, my sister and I detested our parents' dogmatic rules. For example, I never understood the American concept of grounding children while growing up, partly because the only permissible way to leave our home—regardless of our recent behavior— was to go to school, to a mandated extracurricular activity, or to our place of worship. To my sister and me, my parents' concerns seemed irrational, devoid of any faith in us and replete with fear of a corrupt, alien society.

Eventually, Nadya and I found two ways to avoid the bitter arguments: to live with the oppression or to defy it with lies. I chose the former and dedicated myself to community activities, while my sister chose the latter and lived a "full" teenage experience. The arguments with our parents eventually became less frequent, but the sense of feeling closed in grew. For my sister, acknowledging her identity as the difficult child of the family meant that she could get away with going to parties and piercing her belly button, whereas I was thought to be above these childish whims. I would usually relent short-term, because I knew that if I worked hard in school my time to escape would arrive upon graduation. In the meantime, with a renewed faith and the experience of making a positive difference in other youths' lives, I threw myself into community service and leadership positions, both in school and in my religious community. Part of my rationale for being so involved in extracurricular activities—rather than, for example, challenging my parents' restrictions—was that colleges valued them in addition to grades. Because my faith emphasizes meritocracy in school and hard work, my parents could not argue. I became the model child that all the parents wanted their children to emulate.

At home, however, my accolades and ego melted under the crucible of culture. My mother's endless tirades to shift my focus to cooking and cleaning stabbed at my morale. During my sophomore year in high school, I received a national honor recognizing my scholarship. My mom's way to congratulate me was to say, in Urdu, "Now that you've proven that you're smart, you should concentrate on learning to cook." Then, adding in English, "Ee-school ees not ev-ary-theeng." During high school, I became so involved with community programs that I dedicated whole weekends, and eventually entire summers, to work away from home. My mother said, "You serve all the world, but not your own parents." And it was true. I put the whole world before my own parents. I never cooked dinner for them. I didn't make it a daily habit to work for a few hours at our grocery store after school. I made them drive me to and from meetings and activities at odd hours. And I never massaged their feet after they had come home tired from working all day. I would sometimes see my friends doing this—massaging their parents' tired feet—and I would think, "Wow, how can they do that? They must really love them." I could never massage my parents' feet. It was too close for comfort. After years of listening to lectures about being too social and too involved in outside activities, the physical closeness of soothing another's feet was a sign of intimacy that I could not handle.

An emotional divide formed within me as I found solace in helping and connecting with others outside my home. I cannot remember the last time I kissed my parents. It would not occur to me to do this. Even now, three years after entering college, I still have trouble saying "I love you" to them. They must miss that, and certainly like to hear it, but I can only slip it in casually or playfully, rarely with emotion. Maybe due to a lack of strong bonds with significant others, maybe due to the fear of being seen as weak, and maybe due to my naturally introspective personality, I held my emotions inside. Although I loved my parents, by the end of my high school career my bottled-up emotions and my dwindling patience in dealing with their traditional impositions and endless criticisms made home a pressure pit where I was afraid of feeling, for fear of exploding. My only escape, and my culminating goal, became to leave home to attend a school far away.

My leaving for college was much more difficult for my mother than for me. I counted the days until I could escape the heat and breathe easily, on my own. I longed to have friendships and schedules on my own terms, without my family judging me for it. My mom and dad wanted me to stay at home through college. Although they knew that I was going to a prestigious school in the Northeast, and although they knew I had always wanted to leave home for college, they refused to accept it. Every time we drove past our local community college, they would say, "Sabeen, wouldn't it be great if you went to school at Sweetwater? You could just live at home. It would be so much less expensive, and we hear it's a good school." Even a few weeks ago, as a college senior, I heard their disappointment at my refusal to attend Sweetwater. I grew up hearing, "Family is everything. Friends and acquaintances are nothing, because when you're in trouble, you can only count on your family to be there." My act of attending college far away meant that I defied this expectation. I left my family, even when they needed me.

My dad and I pulled my bags from our rental car and searched each door in the hallway for my room. A girl wearing nothing but a towel passed us and smiled. I came to the end of the hallway, reached the room she had just stepped out of, and realized that this would be my first-year roommate. She realized the same and turned around. It was an awkward moment for us both—she in her towel, me with my bags, and my dad standing next to me, looking down at his feet. "Ashleigh?" I said, while she asked, "Sabeen?" At the moment, all I knew was that this redheaded, tanned Caucasian girl was a field hockey and squash player from Greenwich, Connecticut. I did not know what squash was, or that field hockey was actually played at some high schools, or that being from Greenwich put one in a very select and privileged group of people in society. It would take over a year for me to really understand the subtle differences between Greenwich and South Houston. She could take her dirty laundry home and I could not. Her younger siblings were bound for the Ivies and mine were not. Her parents often visited her and mine still have not. On the phone, she could jokingly curse out her mother and laughingly describe what a "blow job shot" (an alcoholic drink) was while I spoke quietly to my mother in Urdu about the upcoming college bill, wondering if we could pay it even with all the subsidies.

Still, Ashleigh and I found more common ground than the 180 square feet of our room. We were both the oldest of three children. Our younger siblings were the same ages. We both talked in our sleep. We both cleaned house in order to think straight. We both listened to Sarah McLaughlin to calm ourselves down during finals. We both ended up with the same major. And when our parents would call us, they often could not distinguish our voices. As we got to know each other better, our polar backgrounds remained in the background, while our similar personalities brought us closer. I have often said to people that I could not have wished for a better first-year roommate. During the day we had very different friends and schedules. At night, we would fall asleep talking to each other, sharing the quiet thoughts of two sisters and their new experiences away from home.

Every three months, while spending breaks at home with my family, I became accustomed to a conversation that occurred more and more frequently. My parents and I would sit at the dinner table discussing my future after college. One evening, for example, I mentioned that I wanted to get some experience before heading back to graduate school in a few years. I got an interesting response. "Sabeen, why you don't finish all of the school now? You must think about your future." I *was* thinking about my future—just not the future they wanted me to think about.

"I told you," began my standard response. "I'm not going to get married for another ten years. You'll just have to wait and accept it."

"*Aisa nahi bol.* Don't talk that way. You have to think about future. Two years maximum. Then you have to settle down. What will people say?" My mother's words poked at my patience, causing me to shake my head, cringe, and roll my eyes all at once. What followed was a list of girls' names, girls with whom I had grown up, who were now either engaged, married, or married with children. After that, they would mention some guy or another, a computer scientist or a businessman, very wealthy, from a good family. . . . By that time I had not only tuned out but had left the room.

Only recently I came to perhaps the most important realization of my upbringing and its impact on me. It was an underlying foundation, present in our home for as long as I can remember, something so subtle that I only became aware of it upon visiting Azim's home and seeing how differently his family functioned. In my family, "home" was a temporary dwelling that you had to leave sooner or later. *Home was an interim situation before I was married and settled into my "permanent" home.* This sudden truth shocked me simply because it made so much sense. Being with Azim's family demonstrated the contrast in our situations: His home seemed permanent; even I felt a sense of belonging there. My home, however, seemed to have a looming expiration date stamped on it. Maybe this is why leaving Houston for school or activities was never difficult for me. Maybe my parents have prepared me well for leaving for my "permanent" home. Regardless, a silent sadness remains in my heart, knowing that my parents brought my sister and me up with the intention of having us leave.

As I prepare to go home for winter break, I'm not quite sure how to react to this potential marriage proposal with Kamran. This idea of an arranged marriage was a thing of the past, a thing of the uneducated masses, a thing that living in America dispelled, or so I had assumed. At our weddings, the bride has to sit quietly, look pretty, and rarely raise her eyes to the crowd. I feel uncomfortable as I imagine myself in that bride's shoes. Every parent and aunt and cousin I know has been through an arranged marriage. Even though it is a sign of respect for elders and a tradition in my family, for me it means the official stamp that I was unworthy and unable to find love on my own.

Azim is keeping my faith in love alive. He and I have built a strong relationship that, at first, was difficult for me to put in perspective. Azim, eight years my senior, would ask me to travel with him and work on various projects. I felt subordinate to him at first and doubted my abilities. As the years have progressed, however, I have learned that we make a dynamic and empowering team. I have also opened myself up to his friendship, realizing that he needs me just as much as I need him. The closest parallel I can give is that he is my older brother. There are times when I can feel our souls talking with each other. I can sense when something is going wrong in his life even without having contact with him. He knew what college I had chosen even before I had a chance to tell him.

Sometimes, I feel my relationship with Azim is strong enough to carry me through without the need for a significant other in my life. At other times I feel our relationship has deterred me from having boyfriends, because the care and love he has shown me sets a high expectation for others. In either case, the fact remains that through junior high, high school, and college, I have never been in a romantic relationship. About two years ago, I began feeling that my spiritual, intellectual, and emotional growth was being stunted by this empty space in my life; dealing with this space meant acknowledging a need for acceptance. Some nights, my walls and pillows soak up soul-filled cries and tears as I slowly surrender to faith and sleep. I want to care about someone who also cares for me. However, I cannot get past the wall of finding a second person for this relationship.

Throughout adolescence I was always more concerned with the emotional benefits of relationships, partly because I knew that physical experiences for me would be limited. I knew I would not have premarital sex, and thus I was not really concerned with that aspect of intimacy. Recently, though, I have come to understand the power of relationships to threaten people's deep-seated morals while promising to satisfy intense physical needs. In a way, this experience humanized me.

During my junior year, I met someone in Chicago and was shocked at how attracted I was to him—and how attracted he was to me. Sam was a Pakistani American who shared my religious faith and was one year older than me. He was handsome and well built, and he seemed sure of what he wanted in life. My attraction to him was shocking and new for me—I had never felt such an innate *physical* drive to be with someone. Yet, parts of him morally repelled me—Sam was a mysterious, immoral, flirtatious rebel who lived life by taking risks. And yet again, this opposition of character seemed to fuel the attraction even more. After our initial meeting we talked on the phone often, though "just as friends." Sam had a longtime girlfriend at the time. Whether we were together or not, however, my body lost all control when thinking about him. I felt like a raging, hormonal teenage boy on his first date, eager to sexually devour his unsuspecting companion. Maybe these urges were normal experiences that all adolescents felt, but they were new to me, and as a twenty-one-year-old without any prior experience, I felt lost at my lack of self-control. The three months during which we interacted were like one continuous, intense state of arousal. But, as we began to know more about each other (as people and not solely as sexual beings), I came to learn that he did not care for me enough to tell his girlfriend about us. I became scared at the prospect of meeting again. Long-distance conversations were fine because they were just talk; however, if we were to meet up again (as we expected to), I knew it would be a test for my morals. Before this experience, I had never really understood the power of sexual attraction in a relationship. Sam seemed too great a threat to me at the time, both physically and emotionally, and although I knew I was forsaking a potential relationship, I concluded that it was not founded on a strong basis of mutual love and concern. At my request, we stopped talking after three months and never met again.

Azim and I often discussed my relationship with Sam, and he was always quick to remind me that I deserved someone better, someone who genuinely cared about me. Azim has shown me how much another person can care for me, and although our relationship has never been romantic, I would value that type of intimacy in my future relationships. In considering future boyfriends, I do not necessarily limit myself to dating only other Ismai'li Muslims or South Asians, or any specific minority. When I get married, however, it will be to an Ismai'li Muslim. It is a given that my family expects me to marry another Ismai'li, and there is no other alternative (unless the non-Ismai'li decides to convert). Still, the decision to marry an Ismai'li is solely mine, not one that my parents or Pakistani culture enforces upon me. I see the bond of marriage as transcending the two individuals, to including the union of two families and a shared sense of faith that ties this new, larger family together. As a Pakistani American and an Ismai'li Muslim, I hope to instill this sense of faith in my children and in my children's children. For me, this faith lies in my religion and community.

The faith I speak of is an intimate connection with God that guides me in my daily interactions. One of the reasons I chose to come to Dartmouth was to share this complex faith and culture with others. Coming to Dartmouth also challenged my faith because I would not have a religious community around me. The closest *Jamatkhana* is two hours away. Meetings and work often interfere with prayer times. Yet, my faith has persevered and has become even stronger. I pray every night and morning. I try to live an ethical life. Most important, I have made an active effort to remain in touch with the Ismai'li community through service, which has been a defining factor in my life.

Another defining factor invaded and shaped my life when, on September 11, 2001, the two World Trade Center buildings and a side of the Pentagon collapsed after being hit by hijacked planes. During the first days after the attack, my body and mind throbbed at night from the pain I felt for those who had lost loved ones. As the days wore on, however, talk about terrorists and Muslims sparked another emotion within me: fear. Flags sprouted everywhere, including in my parents' corner store. My mother conscientiously wore her red, white, and blue ribbons, encouraging us to do the same. I went to the grocery store to pick up some bread, and was even more aware than usual that I was wearing a traditional Pakistani garment, a *shalwar kameez*. "Please let me get back into my car safely," I remember thinking.

All the South Asians I knew became experts on the latest incidents of backlash. We saw a glimpse of what to expect on September 12, when instead of the World Trade Center coverage, the local news reported that three mosques in neighboring suburbs had been shot at that morning. Islamic schools were shut down in fear of being attacked. My worst fears were heightened when a Sikh owner of a gas station in Arizona was shot and killed a few days later. Sikhs are South Asians who wear turbans to cover their hair, which they do not cut out of respect for God's creation. Sikhs are not a terrorist group, but by virtue of being brown or wearing turbans, they became a ready target for ignorant and scared individuals in America. These incidents of stabbings, shootings, and murders of South Asians pierced my heart. Every morning at 6:45, my dad (a Pakistani immigrant and a U.S. citizen) opens our corner store in a small suburb in Houston. The town's burgeoning population is mostly Caucasian, many of whom have come to know and respect my parents as decent people. Yet, in the wake of the traumatic September 11 events, everyone feels the loss of a sense of security. My parents work in our grocery store all day long; I hate the fact that they are so vulnerable to the ignorant lunatic driving by with a gun, and that there is little more they can do than to put up our flag and wear our ribbons, both in support and for protection. Everyone feels sorrow for those who lost their lives and their loved ones. Everyone feels anger and helplessness at those who could conceive of such atrocities. However, those of us with darker skin and hair must now also fear being the next victim. I shudder knowing that my mom and dad in their store or my brother or sister in school could so easily become the next target. This fall was one of the few times I felt uncomfortable leaving my family as I headed back to school in late September; I felt even more helpless about ensuring their safety while at college. In light of the attacks on September 11th, my family has become a high priority in my life. I call home often, just to make sure they are safe. The tragedy has brought me closer to my family and given me an outlet for beginning to express the emotions that I have had such a difficult time sharing with my family.

As a senior in college, at a time when I should be excited with possibilities of jobs, graduation, living on my own, and becoming an adult, I find myself apprehensive of what the future may bring. I know that I must face certain pressures from my parents while living up to the expectations I have set for myself. I know that my parents have sacrificed their youth and adulthood to ensure that their children will realize the American dream, and I feel a sense of duty and honor in returning the favor. I know they want me to return home to Houston after graduation. Yet, having physical distance from my parents during college has actually helped bring me closer to them. I would like to continue to strengthen this tie, something I feel I cannot do in Houston. I know they want me to get married soon so that they can be happy, seeing me settled in my "permanent home." Yet, I refuse to give in to the pressures of arranged marriages, fighting for the chance to feel mutual love on my own terms. At the same time, I am no longer that restless eighteen-year-old desperate to escape home. I find myself caring more about the well-being of my parents and wanting to look out for their future. In a sense, these four years away from them have made me able to be my whole self, my Pakistani American Ismai'li Muslim self. Regardless of the challenge or opportunity, I always end up relying on my faith to carry me through. In the end, this *faith* is my permanent home. It continues to define my values, my practices, my culture, and my identity. It guides me and follows me wherever I go.

Sabeen Hassanali graduated from Dartmouth College with a BA in government-comparative politics. Upon graduation, she moved to Washington, DC, to work on issues of international development. She recently completed her MEd in international education policy at the Harvard Graduate School of Education in Cambridge, Massachusetts, and currently resides in Washington, DC.

WHAT ARE YOU?

Ki Mae Ponniah Heussner   A Little Plot of No-Man's-Land

The first few minutes of the bus ride were uneventful, even pleasant. I had taken a seat on the bus across the aisle from a particularly talkative classmate of mine and found her unending stream of conversation comfortably distracting. So while Whitney and I exchanged our first-grade pleasantries, the bus made its way to school, quietly bumping up and down the length of Bedford Road. It was not until the bus rounded the corner and stopped in front of Sterling Drive to pick up two older boys that our chattering came to a standstill. Like every younger child on that bus, I too inquisitively noted the arrival of those older boys. My curiosity was replaced by apprehension, however, when I realized they had taken the seat directly in front of mine and were peering down at me over the back of their green vinyl seat.

I was just a little girl with long black hair who had confidently boarded the school bus that morning, proud of the care she had taken in dressing herself for the first day at her new school. But all too quickly I became embarrassed, conscious that my black-and-green plaid dress looked foolishly formal next to the grubby jeans and T-shirts of the boys in front of me. And the black patent leather shoes that had been my favorites up until that moment found no friend among the rest of the sneakers on the bus. But I had not noticed any of these things until those two boys noticed me.

Under their scrutiny I felt alone. Under their wide and watchful eyes I felt dwarfed by everyone else who seemed suddenly so much bigger and tougher and better. The aisle that separated Whitney from me seemed impassable, and the back of my seat felt twice as high as it had before. I had never felt more trapped, and I had never felt more on display. And then, as though attempting to classify a bird or snake in a pet shop, one of the boys sort of cocked his head to one side and asked, "What are you?"

What am I? I thought. I do not remember ever having been asked that question before, and if I had, it certainly had not been offered in the same way, with the same stare, and with the same suspicion. I did not know what he wanted to know. I did not understand what he hoped to find out. *What was I?* I was a girl. I was a first grader. *WHAT am I?* Not who, but *what*, as though I had more in common with Cookie Monster than I did the human race! He must have noticed my confusion, because he continued, "You know, are you Japanese? Or Chinese? What are you?"

"Oh," I said with pride, finally recognizing what it was that he wanted to know. "I'm part Malaysian."

I was on familiar ground again and could offer information that had elicited appreciation before. But he had never heard of Malaysia, and he started to reel off other races, as though I was wrong and had to pick one with which he was familiar. So I timidly clarified my answer for the confused boy, providing him with a response that characterized how I saw myself from that day onward.

"Well, I'm a quarter Chinese, a quarter Indian, and half, you know, American."

And it was the first time in my life that I realized that I was any different from anyone else. Before that moment I had not known that people could consider me unlike them; I was not aware that there were whole worlds to which I did not really belong. At the international school I had attended until that day, the uniforms of black, gray, white, and navy were the only colors that all the schoolchildren had in common. It was only upon leaving that school and moving to my new, predominantly white Connecticut suburb that I became conscious of race.

I have been asked that question—What are you?—countless times since that day, and by now, at twenty-one years of age, I am used to it. I do not mind the question, and I have memorized my response. To be honest, there are times when I even enjoy the frequently interesting conversation that follows. But often, when I recall the height of those green vinyl seats and the width of that impassable aisle, anger and frustration replace my usual composure. I'm no longer angry at a little boy who didn't even know that he had the power to make me feel so diminutive; he was barely older than I was, and as little as I understood about the meaning and implications of his question, I'm sure he understood far less. Any anger or frustration I feel now is directed instead toward a society that still has not learned its racial alphabet and still must search for a lexicon of acceptance. And because I quickly and quietly tucked away my personal racial questions, it is only recently that my own racial vocabulary has moved past that of the first grade.

That little boy couldn't have had any idea that his innocent question would leave such a lasting impression. I am sure he would be surprised to discover that I still remember him and the first words he ever spoke to me. But, although he may never know, the awareness and the consciousness produced by our little elementary interchange quickly stole the limelight from my stage. Before I met that boy, I was a Little Orphan Annie, always harassing my parents until they allowed me to sing my favorite song for their dinner guests. I did not sing at all that first day of school, and I did not sing for a long time afterward either. I became a very quiet girl who caused very little trouble.

Recognizing that my differences had the potential to create discomfort for the people around me—often the people closest to me—I invariably tried to blend in as best I could in other ways. I grew far more introverted than the Lion the stars predicted I would become and often felt more comfortable with the fictional characters in the books I read than with the real live children in my classrooms. While children on the playground might note my dark hair and different features with cries of "mutt," and the adolescents in my classes might find amusement in teasing me with whispers of "beast," the characters in my story tales and novels never said a word. As a child, I recognized that my visual differences were the source of these names and my troubles, yet I did not know how to reflect upon the origin of these differences. I never thought to blame race; instead, I just blamed myself.

Ashamed, embarrassed, and convinced that these encounters revealed truths about my flaws and imperfections, for far too long I silently kept these stories inside. It is only recently that I have begun to disentangle these tales of the bus, the playground, and the classroom for my parents. And when I do, I sometimes hesitate, wondering if they can possibly understand the experience of a daughter who has led a life so different from their own.

My mother was born in Klang, Malaysia, to my Chinese grandmother and my Indian grandfather, and although she too grew up as a racially mixed child in a race-sensitive society, I often forget that this is an experience we share. My mother recalls that the few other children of racially mixed marriages were teased and excluded by the "purely" Chinese and Indian children, yet her memory of her own childhood is not colored by the recollection of these experiences. My grandfather was the principal of the school that my mother and her siblings attended, and their status as his children elevated their standing among their classmates. Moreover, after marrying in spite of severe opposition from their church and communities, my grandparents were fiercely protective of their mixed family and tried very hard to instill pride in my mother, my aunt, and my uncles. As the youngest of four children, my mother recognized the support and pride of her family and easily faced the crowd of her racially "pure" classmates.

In the end, her racial and cultural impurity played a significant role in setting her apart from and ahead of the crowd. Having no other common linguistic ground between my grandmother's Cantonese and my grandfather's Tamil, and recognizing the political value of English at a time when Malaysia was still occupied by the British, my grandparents insisted that their children speak only English at home. At that time, many Malaysians could speak English but few could claim it as their first language. My mother's unusual proficiency in English played an integral role in distinguishing her from her university classmates in Malaysia.

While my mother was singing hymns at a college that was left as a gift to a developing country by British missionaries, my father was still tossing footballs across a high school stadium in Bay Village, Ohio. While my mother was awaiting her marriage to the first man she had really known beyond a few conversations, my father was preparing to escort his date to the senior prom. And while my mother was preparing for a life that would not take her very far from home, my father was hoping to take his intellect and athletics from his small midwestern town to the Ivy League.

About five years later, in Boston, only a couple of years after my father graduated from college and my mother had left her first marriage, their different worlds overlapped at a joint lecture between their two graduate schools. As the story goes, they met one afternoon, went for a cup of coffee, and married soon after at the university chapel. Seven years later they had me, and one-and-a-half years after I was born they divorced.

There have been times, perhaps out of anger, I have wondered what my parents could possibly have been thinking to believe that two people from such different backgrounds, histories, cultures, and countries could actually remain happily married forever. There have been other times, perhaps out of puzzlement, I have wondered if my parents were merely intrigued by the exoticness of the other. And, finally, there have been times, perhaps out of loneliness, I have wondered if they ever thought about what it might mean for their child to grow up in a no-man's-land between their two cultures.

At my worst, I have questioned their motivation in deciding to have me at a time when their marriage must have already begun to unravel. How dare they bring a child into the world when they were still struggling to find within it a place for themselves together? And what kind of parents could they possibly be if they failed to imagine what it would be like for their own child to grow up—inherently like them both and yet nothing like either of them?

Perhaps it is not my place to determine if my parents' marriage broke down primarily along the fault lines of culture or love. But in seeing that the worlds my parents have entered and cultivated since their divorce exaggerate the differences that existed before they married, I think I will always blame culture, at least in part. I know that whatever tale I tell will not be able to capture completely my relationships with them and their respective worlds. And I know that even the boundaries of these worlds I imagine are not as strict and defined as I often think they are. But still, regardless of the overlap that exists, these worlds are much more antagonistic than they are compatible, as the word *divorce* suggests.

My parents' split took them swiftly to their new separate lives. And in the process, it ruptured the integrity of my multicultural world and set in motion a lifelong seesaw ride between their two cultures. I am learning to put my parents' past behind me, yet I cannot pretend that the past does not frequently take hold of the present. When I feel inextricably caught between their two worlds—rejected by both, or too quickly accepted by one—I wish to be solely of one heritage. I do not think people often realize how much of a luxury it can be to have one group to fall back on, one to blame, or one to identify with and one to reject. Perhaps it's easier to wear your racial consciousness on your sleeve when you know that you can always hide behind the garb of an entire race if things get too bad, or if the opposition comes on a little bit too strong for you alone. Most will never know how much more difficult it is to speak out when you feel as though you have to pick a side, even though *neither* side is really your own.

For as long as I can remember, I have searched my parents' faces and their collections of old photographs, hoping to find some connection between who they have been, who they are now, who I am, and who I will be. Most children cringe when neighbors and relatives tug them closer and exclaim at the resemblance between parent and child; I stood a bit taller on the few occasions people saw my parents in me. Even when I was in the prime of my adolescence, the peak of my rebellion, I remained the well-behaved daughter who desperately wanted to please *all* her parents—biological and stepparents alike. When I should have been attempting to create an identity and an ideology of my own, I still held back.

If my bus ride to the first day of school marks the first time I recognized my differences in relation to the people around me, an evening with my father a year or two later marks the first time I really recognized the significance of my differences in relation to my own family. And although the initial recognition came over a decade ago, it is primarily over the past few years that I have learned how much more painful and difficult it is to negotiate differences within a family than with the people outside of it.

After a busy day spent touring another one of New York's many cultural gems, my father, Bonnie (then his fiancée), and I found respite on the living room floor of my father's West side apartment. It was almost time for me to go to bed, but after flipping through the television channels, we decided to watch the end of the Miss America pageant. During one of the commercial breaks, in a good-natured attempt to compliment Bonnie, my father commented, "What do I need to watch this for? I have the most beautiful woman in the world right here."

Instead of merely accepting his flattery with appreciation, being sensitive and female herself, Bonnie looked over at me and quickly interjected, "Dale, don't you mean the *two* most beautiful women in the world?"

At first my father looked completely confused and did not understand the reason for her prompt. It was only when he followed her glance over to my face that he recognized my disappointment and revised his previous remark.

I will admit now, with a tinge of embarrassment, how much it mattered to me that my father revised his original comment, but at the time I was too embarrassed to say a word. Perhaps it is not important for a parent to think his child beautiful, but when I was seven years old and just recognizing that I looked different from most people around me, my father's casual comment struck a chord I did not know existed until that moment. I was not a vain child in need of praise, but I did not want to be excluded from my father's definition of beauty. I did not want to feel any more self-conscious or be reminded yet again that I did not look like my father's daughter.

Now, I accept our lack of resemblance and no longer agonize over the reaction our differences inevitably provoke. When I was a teenager too tall for her age, however, I used to fear that, without Bonnie along, people would mistake me for my father's girlfriend. And when my father, Bonnie, my brother Jesse, and I would wander about Westport, Connecticut, I would worry that people might assume that I was Jesse's nanny and not his sister. In a town where most Asian women are nannies, who would expect that the one Asian female walking with a little blond-haired, blue-eyed boy and his equally Caucasian-looking parents could be related to them by blood?

Over time I have grown comfortable with the place I occupy within and between my two families, and I have come to value the unusual pictures we paint together and apart. But it is only recently that I have been able to appreciate and navigate this space that often feels very lonely. In the twenty-one years of my life, my father and I have spoken only a few times about our cultural differences. And although we frequently laugh about the unexpected family portrait we must present to onlookers in restaurants and shops, I sometimes think he underestimates the extent of those differences. Both he and Bonnie have always encouraged me to speak my mind, but I really do not know how I would begin to enumerate to them the differences between life at his house and life at my mother's house.

When they ask for my "honest" thoughts on how they raise Jesse, how do I tell them that, because I was raised in my mother's house where tough love reigned and gifts were never used to temporarily appease, I have often wished that they were not so generous with both me and Jesse? And when I open up the trash can and see piles of still edible food and still usable plastic utensils, how do I honestly reveal that, because my stereotypically penny-wise Chinese grandmother would cringe at the amount of things wasted in their home, I tend to inwardly cringe as well? Moreover, how do I honestly express that it is guilt and dismay I often feel when I recognize that many of the characteristics I criticize in my father's world have managed to find a place in me? I have no blueprint to follow, I have no paradigm to respect, and I cannot always tell if honesty is healthy or hurtful.

At my mother's house, I am not alone in negotiating multiple worlds—my mother and my stepfather's marriage also crosses racial and cultural lines. But because my stepfather has spent almost as much time in Asia as my mother has in America, they have been able to help my sister Maylien and me to navigate the blurred cultural cross sections that characterize our lives. Yet, even so, there are times when I have to stop myself from too easily following my mother's and stepfather's bad habit of prematurely dismissing those who have not tread the same ideological path they have.

Both professionally and personally, their lives have taken them to more countries than most people in our town are probably able to identify, and as a result they recognize the degree of global inequity far more deeply than even our most well-traveled neighbors. Their model of justice is based on a global understanding of the injustices they have perceived in the world, and they have passed this understanding on to my sister and me. The most difficult lesson for all of us to learn is to appreciate our own experiences without detaching ourselves from those whose lives do not cross so many cultural boundaries.

Here in America, the various cultures that have found a home under one roof have, over time, integrated harmoniously to form a new whole. The cultural differences, however, between my mother's family and the new family we have created emerge profoundly when we make our biennial trips to Malaysia and find ourselves held to the standards of a society we're only a small part of, and that is only a small part of us.

Although my friends are fond of reminding me that I inflect the tone of my voice far more than I should, the inflection and cadence of my own voice is *nothing* compared with the ruckus of my Malaysian family's conversation. When the whole "jinbang" is assembled, conversation is dotted with "ah!" and "Ai yo!" and phrases are punctuated with the local "lah." What might be lacking in vocabulary is compensated for with animation— lively hand gestures substitute for unnecessary words and volume often trumps text. If we are lucky, Uncle Vinci will surrender and buy the delicious, grease-saturated *roti chenai* and chicken curry. If we are patient, we will catch the nightly stroll of the *chee-chak* (lizards) who emerge from their daytime hiding spots. Yet, if my sister and I are loud, we, being female, will provoke the criticism of our older uncles, who will quickly remind us that we have become "too American."

When Maylien and I linger around the dining room too long after eating dinner, our uncles artfully push us along to the kitchen sink; when we are caught reaching for another biscuit at teatime, we are asked, with a pat on the belly, if we *really* want another. "Ai yo you girls," Uncle will say, clucking his tongue loudly, "you spend too much time in that country." Although he teases with a good-natured smile and mocks us with a disarming grin, there is firm conviction behind his words. He jokingly refers to his American nieces as lost causes, but I think he does believe there are standards set for Asian woman, and he certainly believes we should respect them. If Uncle Vinci had his way, all of the women in his life—sisters, daughters, and nieces alike—would match the image of his slim, young wife. Auntie Swee Gin has the smooth, long hair, the slim build, the pale skin, and the coy demeanor of the ideal Asian woman. And although the rest of us poke fun at the adoring glances and reverent words she bestows upon my uncle, there have been times, especially when I was younger, when I wished I could escape the tyranny of my uncle's criticisms by more closely resembling her.

In America, on the other hand, the coyness and reserve of the demure Asian female are met with mixed reviews. Although I may have been too loud for my Asian uncles in Malaysia, I think I have often been too quiet for my American family and friends at home. And if I attribute the silence of my childhood to the simple recognition of race, I believe that my adolescent reticence is due to the echoes of my uncles' warnings. I certainly did not back down from conflict and confrontation to please those uncles, but I think that I found in their model—or at least in the one they projected—the best balance to the imposing height and academic success that I sometimes wanted to hide.

I thought that if I could not change the appearance of "beast" perhaps I could distract people with the demeanor of "beauty." To a thirteen-year-old girl whose big, red glasses covered the upper half of her face, whose height seemed to give away her presence in a crowd of two hundred, and whose dark hair and slightly off-kilter features refused to cooperate to create something pleasing or familiar to look at, any distraction that might minimize the awkwardness was eagerly accepted.

Those painfully awkward years did not last as long as I dreaded they would. I amended the mistake of the large red glasses by trading them in for a pair of contact lenses. And soon after, I somehow sufficiently grew into the features and height that had plagued my early adolescence. I was no longer the quietest girl in my class, and as I grew older, so did my confidence and the strength of my voice. Yet I was far from outspoken. Even after I did not need the ideal demeanor to offset a less-than-ideal appearance, I still held on to the quietness and reserve that had characterized my earlier behavior.

Throughout high school I was considered a leader of my class, and I appreciated the distinction and respected the responsibility. But even though I could muster up the courage to address administrators and speak professionally with teachers, I found it difficult to interact with many of my peers with the same amount of confidence. A child of a practically TV-less home, it took me a while to recognize pop culture. And as a child of a multicultural, international home, it was more likely that I would identify the name of a UN agency than a Fortune 500 company. As a result, I would often find myself mid-conversation with little to say, searching frantically for common ground. Wanting neither to accentuate my differences by pleading cultural ignorance nor to check out of the conversation completely, I would linger at the edges, smiling and nodding appropriately, wondering when the trial would end. I was a good student and the president of my class, but when I interacted with many of my classmates I found myself constantly questioning the cadence of my speech and the formality of my language. I created multiple voices to fit the multiple worlds I encountered in my life, and when I could not tailor the appropriate voice for a given situation, I chose silence.

For a long time I think I believed that the integration of these worlds would come once I met someone who would let me be myself all the time. But when I was younger, I would become so enamored with someone that in his presence I would lose the capacity to speak. Although I might write pages and pages about how wonderful, unique, and perfect "he" might be, in the face of opportunity with him I would become so nervous that I would find myself unable to form thoughts and compose questions. And when our conversation eventually reached a standstill, I would be left wondering if the person I had created with my pen really did exist beyond the pages of my journal. As I grew older, confidence lent me the ability to carry on a conversation, but I still would never learn the true nature of my pen's inspiration. As the rules dictated in this odd game I would play, the second I sensed reciprocated interest, I would completely lose interest, until, of course, I felt that interest had been lost in me.

In middle school and high school I easily excused this pattern by declaring the high standards I held for myself. It was not that *I* was the one who lacked the capability to get to know someone beyond a first date or a first kiss, it was more that I honestly believed that my exceptional powers of perception enabled me to sense incompatibility from a mile away. I know now that I was deceiving myself. It was not always high standards or perception that prevented me from getting too close to anyone romantically or even platonically, for that matter. I was just too insecure, and I lacked the confidence to believe that anyone could really like me; if they did, then surely something about them must be wrong.

A few months after coming to college, however, I did meet someone who seemed absolutely flawless to my freshman eyes. And although now I sometimes wonder how Jon and I managed to maintain any type of relationship at all over the years, I think, at least to a degree, that what kept us together was equally responsible for ultimately pulling us apart. While my family life has been unique, his has been quite conventional. My views are liberal, his are conservative. And my background is mixed, his is not. Now that our three-year on-again, off-again relationship has finally reached its conclusion, I look back amazed at how long we attempted to make our relationship work. Sometimes I think that had we just been disciplined enough to stop ourselves from falling back to each other, we might have developed other more complementary relationships. But I also know that for a very long time, I refused to let go of the security and comfort my first serious romantic relationship offered, despite the many clues and conversations that indicated that our relationship would inevitably end.

The first time Jon forced us to confront our increasingly apparent differences, I thought it was the last time we would ever speak. We had certainly been aware of these differences from the beginning, but we enjoyed the sometimes amusing, sometimes exasperating conversations they created. Only four months after we started dating, however, those same qualities that had initially amused and intrigued us began to divide us. During the summer after my freshman year in college, when I was at home and Jon was at school, and our relationship existed over telephone lines and extended weekends, our incompatible qualities became irreconcilable differences. Toward the end of the summer, when I anxiously noted the infrequency of his calls and sensed the detachment in his voice, I asked him what was wrong. And he simply replied, "We're just so different."

Refusing to continue over the telephone, I drove up to school the following weekend to finish our conversation in person. Between a Saturday afternoon and a Sunday evening, we uncovered every foreseeable difference that could possibly limit our capacity to sustain a relationship. Toward the end of the weekend, when our religious, philosophical, personal, and political debate was already threatening to turn my boyfriend back into a stranger, he asked the question that I may silently remember each time I begin a new relationship. "Well," he offered timidly, "what if I don't know how I'd feel if my children didn't look like me?"

At the time, his question did not unsettle me any more than the rest of the conversation had. Instead of listening to what his question revealed, I simply dismissed it with a frown and stumbled my way through a response: "I just don't think you need to know that right now. . . . Shouldn't we just be thinking about *now*? I guess I just don't understand why we need to talk so much about the future. . . ."

I should have appreciated his honesty, and I should have followed his inquisitive lead, but I was not prepared to consider the possibilities of such a far-off future, and I was too scared to acknowledge the questions that could threaten that and future relationships. I thought I already knew the familiar, discouraging answer, and I forced myself to ignore it.

Aside from my family, no one else in my life challenged me to confront race in such a personal way, and at times, I was disappointed in the short-comings, within each of us, that were revealed in the process. Yet, three years of disagreement and reconciliation allowed us both to mindfully ex-amine, and sometimes adjust, what we had always believed to be true.

During my adolescent years, when my journal reflected the innocent musings of a naïve teenage girl, I thought that upon falling in love I would be transformed into someone more confident, self-assured, and independent. I had hoped that one person would be able to help me integrate the different worlds I had tried so hard to keep apart. It was not until after di-viding my worlds even further that I finally learned how to bring them together.

Whereas in high school I was a school leader and swore that I would someday "change the world," my first years in college were spent more concerned with social image than social awareness. Instead of setting off on my planned path of righteousness, I sharply delineated the social as-pects of my life from my ideological ones. I took advantage of the few aca-demic opportunities I had to incorporate my beliefs into my academic studies by writing about the gender relations and social issues that I did not tackle in my daily life. I would write papers for my English classes com-paring the roles of women in various plays, or taking a feminist stance against metaphors in Early American Literature. I was even a member of an a cappella group devoted to spreading messages of social awareness through song. Yet I did little more from day to day than sing about issues or write about them or speak about them when the occasion arose; I did not do nearly as much as I could have to actually *solve* the problems I claimed to feel so strongly about. I would write about social injustice, and I would sing about female empowerment, yet at the same time I became part of an organization—a sorority—that actively excluded women and a system that passively divided them.

Although I decided to attend the college I did almost in spite of its well-known Greek system, when the time came I still signed my name to the list of sophomores looking for a bid to one of the campus's many sorori-ties. I was the last woman in my class to sign up for rush and perhaps one of the least enthusiastic because I believed that I already had the most supportive "sorority" in my a cappella group. But even though it was mostly curiosity that led me to the system, it was vanity that enticed me to join. I was flattered by the offers of acceptance, and I was tempted by the trappings of belonging. I cannot go back in time and erase my name from the long list of sophomore rushees, but had I known then what I do now, I would never have threatened bonds of true friendship with the often superficial ones of "sisterhood." Now, while I am grateful for some of the friendships formed within my sorority, I think I will always see my participation in the Greek system as more of an educational detour than a step forward in life.

It was not until fall term of my junior year that the multiple worlds in my life began to grow together and the words I sang with my a cappella group began to resonate in my classes and in the friendships that I formed. I finally felt engaged and productive in classes that provided me with the tools I could use to someday do something more than simply sing freedom songs to distracted college students. In the education department I met professors and students who powerfully influenced my life—socially, academically, and ideologically.

In a class discussion that term, our teaching assistant asked us to write down how our life would be different if we were each a member of a different race. As my classmates furiously wrote their answers down, I just sat quietly and refused to write a word. People read their answers out loud and every answer began with, "If I were [insert racial difference here] I would [insert racial stereotype here]" as though with a flip of a switch you would call yourself by another name, changing only the attributes associated with that name. If I were a different race—if I were only *one* race—my entire life would be different, and to think that I could be expected to enumerate, isolate, and analyze how almost offended me. To me, the question implied that you are your race, you are only your race, and your racial identification is the one that is the most important. Of course I think that people should participate in interracial discussions but constantly defining people and groups along racial lines seems to me to be the kind of racial division that interracial discussions should attempt to move beyond.

In interracial discussions like the one my class had that day, I had always felt obliged to pick a side, as though if I did not, I would be a coward straddling a racial fence. In our racially polarized world, it often feels as though someone long ago decided that in order to have your voice count and mean something you need to identify with one party *or* the other. If you attempt to actually identify with both and take the time to look for the middle ground, you are selling someone short, or you are not realizing all there is in yourself, or you are taking the easy way out.

It was not until I went to China on a foreign study program the summer before my senior year in college that I fully recognized that there is no easy way out—the world's racial spectrum is far more complex than the black and white one many Americans think exists. I cringe at the implication that my trip to China was a quest for "roots," but in truth, I did go to China in search of a connection to the stories and traditions that peppered my childhood. My Chinese heritage is only a part of my cultural whole, but my grandmother's superstitions are still a fixed part of my daily internal dialogue. When my right eye shakes, I wonder what kind of good fortune will come my way, and when the palm of my left hand itches, I wonder how much money will soon be slipping out of it. When I forget to clean my plate I remember my grandmother's warnings that I will then marry a pockmarked husband, and when I wear red I immediately feel protected by the power of its lucky hue.

Before I arrived in China and during my first days there, I hastily assumed that these superstitions, and the other relics of Chinese culture inherited from my grandmother, were enough to secure for me a comfortable connection to the Chinese people I would meet. I thought that because many of the traditions I would find in China were the ones I was accustomed to at home, I would not experience the culture shock anticipated by many of my white classmates. My motivation for traveling to China was certainly more personal than it was academic, and I expected that it would be something akin to a homecoming—if not for me, then at least for my grandmother, vicariously, through me. But I soon and sadly learned that although my family's version of "Chinese" and the "Chinese" that I encountered in China share many qualities, my family and I are quite alone in our cultural habits and beliefs. Although many of the words we speak, the expressions we borrow, and the foods we eat are gifts from my grandmother's Chinese heritage, too many other cultures have added their own flair for us to recognize the truly "Chinese" in our lives.

As I walked and biked the streets of Beijing that summer, as I sat on buses and trains up and down the coast and back and forth across the country, and as I talked to and laughed with people and suffered their laughs at me, I found myself struggling to determine how I belonged to China and how it belonged to me. Visually, I blended into crowds of Chinese people better than I could ever hope to blend into crowds of Caucasian Americans. If you casually glanced my way and didn't experience the amusement of listening to my broken, incorrectly inflected Chinese, you might think that I had lived in China all my life. But because of my linguistic shortcomings and a mismatch between what I expected to feel and what I actually found, instead of experiencing the homecoming I had expected, I felt locked out of the culture I had hoped to be welcomed into.

One night, on a train bound for a coastal town sixteen hours northeast of Beijing, when my classmates had managed to achieve uncomfortable sleep and I was left to my thoughts, I realized that the best I could ever hope for was partial cultural understanding from any person I would ever meet outside my family. And I realized that even within my family—because of interracial marriage, divorce, and remarriage among my parents, my stepparents, my aunts and uncles, and even my grandparents—individuals are sometimes left quite alone to their cultural understandings and beliefs. On my mother's side of the family, it would be quite difficult to find two people other than my mother and her siblings who have an exact racial match. And although we have benefited greatly from the synthesis of all these races, I wonder what we have sacrificed and surrendered to become a family that has had to dilute each culture in an attempt to integrate them all. And although I often relish my lack of cultural commitment, there are many moments when I would like to be able to claim one culture, commit to one culture, and be comforted by one culture only.

The more of a mix any person becomes—of experiences, of ethnicities, of cultures that are racial or not—the more she becomes connected to other people, the more she is able to understand, and the more she is offered to share. But somewhere down the line in the sharing of cultures you realize that when each culture is done sharing for a little while and goes back to its own world, you are still left in the middle of them, dependent on them all—but alone, without any.

Most people receive their inheritance the day their parents die. I received mine the day I was born. And although I have spent much of my life running away from the little plot of no-man's-land my parents left for me to till, I am learning to enjoy the responsibility of cultivating this familiar, untapped place. The boundaries are not as rigid as I once thought they were, and the ground is much more fruitful than I originally assumed it to be. Sometimes its solitude halts my progress for a while, and sometimes I stop for a rest someplace else, but I return to my quiet lot with pride, for my entire family, for myself, and for the vision of what it might someday be.

Ki Mae Ponniah Heussner currently lives in New York City and is the Manager of Public Affairs and Advocacy for Lifetime Entertainment Services. Still enamored with the capacity of language to validate experience and provoke action, she designs and manages many of the network's award-winning public education and advocacy campaigns. She also suffers from insatiable wanderlust and exits the country as often as she can.

Anthony R. Luckett Multihued

On Being Asian
They asked me to write about why choosing
or choosing not to choose sides is relevant
in my life.
I told them that before my thoughts could travel from mind to mouth
I heard the universe whisper life into my mother's womb.
Lucky me.
I might have survived the sound of fate mumbling destiny
while reading a novel on a love unfilled.
He book marked where love had been emptied and
now I'm pessimistic.
I'd give up but which way is up to me?
Where is down to earth when I can't stop thinking about having left heaven.
I've danced with angels and solved multiracial differential equations
in three dimensions. I stand in the fourth now speaking
about the three axial frames of reference and not one of them
described what it was to be Asian.
Sometimes, when I'm not being Korean,
I speak Konglish with my mother and eat Kimchee
alone in my dorm so my roommates can't smell it . . .
I hum Ah-Ri-Rhang to my dreams so they and sleep can be lovers.
Under the covers in the dark I imagine myself with straight hair
and a grandmother that cooks for me every night despite her own desires.
But when I close my double eyes in private I remember my birthright
birthplace and inner fires.

If I had a log for every time I've been asked
whose side I would have taken in the Riots,
the earth would be a ball of flame and we'd wander lost in our lust to label
    everything
we see because for every sort of people you think I might be,
they all know they're not in me
and all I hear are voices in my head still asking questions that don't move me
    any more.
I'm black and Korean, devoid of sympathy for culture vultures that
circle over my head, a fateful halo reminds me that it's time to be free
of the 38 parallels I've seen folks draw on me . . .
They asked me to write about why choosing
or choosing not to choose sides is relevant in my life.
I told them that before my mouth was informed by mind that
I piggy backed the universe's spine and tapped into my Chi . . .
Lucky Me.
I might not have survived nearly four years of fate's interpretation of destiny.
But.
Here I am.

On Being Black
I feel as if I am an interloper in a land where the packed snow smells of
    watermelon.
And I traverse the hills picking snowflakes and spitting seeds that plant
    themselves in my journey.
Walking in circles.
My racial profile eludes my facial style.
I don't look the part.
and I am Black by association.
Misappropriate usage of my visage has been the ground on which I walk
    alone treading the Mason-Dixon poverty line.
Perforated like my spinal cordless phonetic Nile tones.
I'm light skinneded.
Where do I fit in next to "I've seen you before's" and "my cousin look just
    like you's"? And, because I've got Seoul in the windows of my soul, I've
    also heard "He ain't just Black I told you so's." So.
Sometimes when I'm not being Black, I speak in Ebonics and quote Ca$h
    Money's Greatest Hits.
I purposely fail tests just to see . . . just to see if I'm keepin' it real. I walk

slowly and strut, nod to say "what's up dogg, peace, ah-ight, that's tight,
    smoke? Nah, shit shorty and hey. My. Nigga."
I've got my finger on figuring it out but when I'm out of my mind what is in
    sane?
My father gave me the greatest lesson on what a black man should be by not
    being around for me to follow his bad example.
Now Jazz is my mother and Hip Hop my sample of what daddies be like.
I feel as if I've intruded into a land where the snow smells of watermelons and
    I'm no longer picking cotton snowflakes but bad decisions.
Ones that spit the seeds of a freer future plantation.
Walking in circles encircled by miracle manacles I be dazzled and unfocused.
Black by association.
And, I don't look the part that's played me.
only.
time isn't planted with watermelon seeds.

I felt the beat of my mother's chest against the side of my face. Drowsily
I looked up and out of the taxicab window. I fell back to sleep against my
mother's chest. I was snug and clinging to Mom as best I could. Finally, we
stopped. Mom nudged me awake and brought me out of the car. There was
a large wood house in front of me. There were two shadows in the door-
way of this house. I walked into the house and sat down at a table and put
my head down. My eyes were cracked open, and I caught sight of Mom
talking with one of the shadows. They spoke and spoke. Then without
warning, Mom started walking out the door and I ran after her. As I descended the steps in front of the house I saw Mom get back into the cab.
The tailpipe exhaust made the red lights eerie at night as the cab drove off
and I screamed, "Mommy! Where are you going? Mommy!" I couldn't say
anything else. I was so shocked that she would just leave me. All I saw were
the red taillights getting smaller and smaller and more and more blurry as
my tears fell.

The lady escorted me back into the house. As I sat down at the table,
the man and woman looked at me. She began to peel a tangerine and asked
me if I wanted any. No, I didn't want any! I wanted my Mom. I wanted my
Mom. The impact of my mother leaving left me speechless for a long, long
time. I remember sitting at that table for what felt like hours—long
enough for there to be veins of salt down my cheeks where the tears had
tumbled. There were things running through my body and soul that I
didn't have the words to fit to. All through my childhood, that image of the

dwindling taillights haunted me because I still hadn't come to terms with being left in the care of strangers. The household that I was born into had fallen apart by the time I was four years old. This is how my story begins.

I was born in Suwon, Korea, to a Korean mother and African American father. In less than a year, my mother, father, and I moved to London, England, where my mother had a job as a model and teacher, and my father was still in the service of the United States Air Force. We somehow ended up in San Francisco, California, where we lived near an air force base. I don't remember moving, just being in different places and different feelings that come with it. I don't remember having friends, and I wasn't allowed to be in the same room as my father when he and his friends watched adult movies and smoked. He flickered in my mind until his presence disappeared.

When I was left with the tangerine family, each day was like awaking from one bad dream into another. They were a white family. Looking back, I cannot remember a time when I felt like I was a part of that family, perhaps because my recollection of the negative outweighs the occasional happy moments that I can only vaguely remember. My memory serves me tidbits of history salvaged after a tumultuous beginning to life. One of the most enduring memories I have of my time there was the way I spent a number of my weekend mornings on nice days. The funnies were handed to me by one of my foster parents, Jim and Marcy. A hand on my shoulder turned me toward the side door, and I was asked to go outside and read. Jim gave me a hasty nod and told me it was OK to go outside in my underwear. I was uncomfortable but didn't know what to say. I walked slowly out of the door and sat down on the picnic bench with the funnies. Before I started reading I carefully screened the surroundings for onlookers. I opened the pages slowly, hesitantly, and read at an even slower pace. Systematically, I scanned the premises for onlookers as I read the funnies. When I was done with the funnies, I thought it would be all right to go back inside the house; I felt as if my reading the comics was a punishment. I stood up and walked up to the screen door, and it was locked. When I finally got back inside it wasn't long before I was outside again; at least I was clothed on my return excursions. The words were usually, "It's nice out, so why don't you go outside?" Those innocuous words never really sparked any real thought until I heard them repeated over and over again. Nobody ever wanted me *in* the house. It wasn't as if I truly wanted to be inside so much as I wanted to belong. I just wanted to feel accepted, but nobody wanted to know what I wanted. I missed my Mom, and I didn't like living with this tangerine family.

My unstable disposition was kept aflame by my anger and aggression. In school I was your typical problem child—the kid who doesn't keep quiet, who is always running around and won't listen. My rage would cause me to get into fistfights, and I can even recall throwing a chair across the classroom at another student and hitting the teacher by mistake. My tangerine family foster father, Jim, was called and that night he spanked contempt and embarrassment into my backside at the dinner table. It didn't hurt anything but my pride.

In retrospect, I suppose I should be grateful that a family would take me in and care for me for as long as they did. I suppose that I should thank them for providing a roof over my head and food for me to eat. I suppose that I would indeed be grateful if it were not for memories riddled with nightmares and a feeling of emptiness that fills my gut. Each day I was made to feel as if I wasn't wanted. The house was a large beautifully crafted wood house with a basement, two floors, and an attic. They kept bees on the side of their house to collect honey to sell. The garage was a bottomless pit of baubles, toys, auto parts, and other things that families accumulate over years. The pond behind the house was connected to a creek that was filled with tadpoles. The woods were deep and magnificent. Unfortunately, there was no home for me in that picturesque niche down a quarter of a mile driveway off of Whitney Road. When I think back, the darkness overshadows the light. There were things that happened in that niche that my mother does not know about to this day. The worst part about that tale is that Jim and Marcy knew—and did nothing to protect me.

Jim's father must have been in his sixties when I met him. He was a large heavyset man with gray stubble, a dirty T-shirt, and a dirty odor. I didn't care much for him so I never understood why they ever left me alone with him. They knew what he did on those walks out in the woods at night. He would lead me around behind the pond, and we'd sit on the bench. In a gruff voice he'd ask me if I liked him. I was frozen because even the first time it happened didn't seem like the first time it happened. His coarse hands would find their way on to my back and the friction would rattle my tiny six-year-old frame. His large body overwhelmed me as his large hands found their way off of my back and into my pants. I felt his stubble on my face and in my mouth. I wanted to scream but couldn't. Who would come? Jim and Marcy knew already, I was certain, and Mommy was not there. He touched me where I hadn't even discovered myself and asked again if I liked him. No, I did not like him! I wanted him to go away but I couldn't tell him that. I sat quiet and wished that it would end sooner and sooner each time. I hated walking with Jim's father.

Jim and Marcy were aware because one night after I had "taken a walk," they asked me what happened on the walk with Grandpa. "He touched me here," I said pointing to my groin. "And kissed me. Then he touched me here . . ." There was a pause as the two stood there. The sad truth is I don't remember that being the last night that he sapped, rubbed away, and swore to secrecy my childhood with his sixty-plus-year-old mouth, disturbing hands, and five o'clock shadow.

Of all the bad things I remember, the most difficult to deal with was the fact that something bad was happening to me, and my foster *parents* knew. They knew, and they knew that I knew they knew, and still nothing. No protection, no nothing—except for more walks with Grandpa. I didn't feel as if it was my *fault*, but for some perverted reason I thought that I might have *deserved* treatment like that. If everybody knew, maybe it was normal, but part of me knew it couldn't have been. I don't remember too much else about the tangerine family; their faces are murky images of exaggerated features. Fortunately, life is very different for me now. But family secrets have to start somewhere.

I had come to terms with what had happened during the summer after my senior year of high school, but I was twenty years old when I finally came around to writing about this incident.

The	night that cried for those
Hands	to stop
That!	Stop That! . . . Stops that
Rock	my brain,
My	pains to sleep in that
Cradle	made for one . . . I would still
Kill	the night that cried for
Me.	

There is a part of me that would commit murder to regain the innocence, security, and trust I had taken from me on those walks. Motherfuckers! I will never forget what I lost there. I often wonder what life would have been like had I not lived with that tangerine family: Jim, Marcy, and their children. It is difficult to think outside of the past because my history is documented in who I am as a person. Scholars say that a child's personality is shaped by the time he is five years of age. I'm beginning to think there is some truth to that. I was dealt a pair of incompatible, strong-willed parents and confusion, chaos, and abandonment before the age of five. I sometimes wonder how I got through four years with Jim and Marcy's family—misbehaving in school, missing my mother, and all the while feeling I didn't belong.

When my mom finally came to get me out of that tiny niche on Whitney Road when I was eight years old, I didn't know then that I would move twice more before the fifth grade. I moved next to Astoria, Queens, in New York, where I lived with my mom's friend, Kyoung. I attended parochial school for the third grade and just as the school year ended, I moved back to Ohio.

This time Ohio was different. I stayed with a Korean woman named Young. She lived with a Tae Kwon Do instructor and her two sons, Tony, age sixteen, and Andy, age fourteen. The few months that I was with this family, a number of things came to light. I found out that my mother was paying for me to live there when Young became increasingly angry with me for no reason that I could see. Tony pulled me aside one day after I had been yelled at and told me that his mother wasn't angry with me but was angry with my mother because she hadn't paid. Hadn't paid? Why hadn't she paid? I wondered. I understood that raising someone costs money, but why hadn't she paid? Young once told me that she was raising me because my mom didn't know how to take care of me. She said that if my mom left me I would have nothing to worry about because she would take care of me. As hard as I found that to believe since the lady was always angry with me, I wanted to believe that I had nothing to worry about. Her offer, though strange and twisted to me, sounded somewhat inviting since I hated moving and I didn't know what to believe.

Young's words seared my ears, and the thought of mom not returning haunted me. As it turned out, mom also had paid Jim, Marcy, and Kyoung. This new information forced the connection in my mind between my mom's missed payments and the treatment I was receiving. I resented both my foster families and my mother. It was difficult enough to comprehend these families being paid for my care, but I really resented the thought that my mother would dare miss a payment. My resentment was twofold. First, the untainted perception I had of my mother began to soil. Then, when I began questioning my mother, I began losing faith in my own judgment and trusted no one. In a matter of months, Mom came back and moved me once again.

It was in the middle of the fourth grade that I arrived in New York City for the second time. This time it was the Woodside section of Queens where I stayed with the Kims until I went away to college. At this house were the head of the family, "Uncle," his wife, and their two sons, James and John. The Kims had six other foster children in addition to me. All of the kids in Uncle's care attended Public School 11 only five blocks away. Most of the class dismissed me as the new kid dressed in hand-me-downs until people noticed that I was artistically inclined and athletically adept—which was at least a start and more than I had ever had before. School didn't mean much to me until I reached the sixth grade where I met Mr. Meadow. He was the first person to take a genuine interest in my abilities as a student, athlete, and scientist. His charisma would fill the room, and the amount of passion and energy he devoted to his students was peerless. Mr. Meadow motivated my curiosity, intelligence, and creativity. He changed my outlook on school and on myself.

Mr. Meadow was about five feet ten inches and had what I can only describe as a white Afro, only his hair isn't thick and he isn't black. He looked a lot like pictures I had seen of Mark Twain. He let me sit in the back of class with the microscope. I would bring in samples of dirty water that I had retrieved from various sources in the neighborhood. When my face was in that microscope the world around me did not exist. I watched in awe the paramecia and other microorganisms swimming around in the water. The truth is that I was teacher's pet, and I liked it even if some other people didn't like it. Mr. Meadow's spirit was very apparent to me, and I basked in his presence. He used to tell me to train for the decathlon before I knew what one was. He always asked that I remain true to myself and taught me not to be influenced by others. One conversation we had shines above all others. We had been talking and then he looked into my eyes. "Tony, don't ever change. I'm serious. Don't ever change. OK?" I didn't know how to react to the solemnity behind his words, so all I could muster was a simple nod of affirmation. Don't change? I couldn't understand the full meaning of what he was trying to say or how to take it truly to heart. His investment in me was matched by my desire to learn from him and the genuine respect I had for this man who respected me and believed in me. He helped to erase a great deal of my self-doubt, and he built my confidence.

I wish my life at school were even remotely representative of my life in the Kim residence. Perhaps it would be asking too much of life to have things go well in both worlds. During my stay with the Kim family, I never once felt as if I was a part of the family. Aside from the mistrust they had of the world in general, the way in which they ran a family was not healthy. According to the Korean old school of thought, children were commodities and were to be seen and not heard.

I distanced myself from everything in the Kim's household except from Uncle's son James. He was the only member of that family with whom I felt I had any connection. The Kims owned two apartments on the same floor of the building. James and I stayed in apartment 4D with his grandmother while the rest of the family lived in apartment 4B. James and I would stay up late playing video games or watching television. Sometimes, we'd play basketball together and for about a year, he was one of my Tae Kwon Do instructors. James also tutored me in math. He was my older brother and I looked up to him. We never spoke about what I was truly feeling except for once.

"You know bro, I've never really felt at home here," I said to James softly.

"I know. I can understand that."

"It's like . . . well, it's not like I'm very upset that I wasn't a part of this family because, well . . . you know. . . ."

"Yeah," he said as he shook his head.

"It's kind of sad, bro," I said.

"It is. That it is," he said softly.

A moment of silence overtook the room and he gave me an understanding nod, as if to say he understood my discomfort of never feeling "at home" and my struggle to get away. I was sad that I had lived with a family for almost a decade and never felt truly welcome there. Beyond not feeling welcome, I was so uncomfortable I didn't like being in the physical presence or close vicinity of Uncle or Auntie. So that I could spend the least amount of time at home with the Kims I would go out as much as I could and stay out late, and I was as active as I possibly could be in high school. Looking back I can see the irony that at age six I was always upset at being made to stay out of Jim and Marcy's house, twelve years later I was doing everything I could to stay out of the house. "Men don't run from their problems." Who could have taught me this? Jim? The Tae Kwon Do instructor? Tony or Andy? Uncle? James? I wouldn't know. Though I picked up pieces of manhood from each of them along my path of development, I am unclear how to apportion to what extent these male foster figures have affected me.

With loneliness as my companion and introspection my bedfellow, I brooded over the questions that challenged my understanding of my circumstances, my mother, and the world around me. The changes happening to my body only contributed to my confusion and lack of understanding. While undergoing these changes in my life, Mom was still a sporadic beacon of light, and while I took her for granted, I resented my predicament and wanted more from her than just an escape from my current environment. I wanted attention and to belong. The difficulty of dealing with my loneliness was more than feeling I didn't belong in my various foster homes—it was complicated by my developing racial identity. I had lived with one white family, a single Korean woman, and two very different Korean families. But I am Korean and black. No one I lived with could fully understand what it was to be a mix of two separate minority worlds, and until later in my life, neither could I.

I always knew that I was different. With the tangerine family it was very obvious, especially when they would pick me up from school. Everywhere I went, including New York City, I managed to warrant a second look. This made me so terribly self-conscious that I was embarrassed by my heritage. I remember once, Mom and I were on the subway. I sat next to Mom who was dressed in a white linen outfit and sat reading the latest volume of Korean Health Digest. As I sat there, I stared around me and secretly hoped that no one was staring back. I don't know whether it was the book she was reading or the clothes she was wearing, but I felt like everyone on the train was looking at us. My uneasiness at her presence was displayed on my face. I was so unused to being in my mother's presence that it was as if she were some strange foreigner reading her magazine right next to me. Then she turned to me and began speaking Korean in front of everyone. As her native language entered my ears, perfectly intelligible, I wanted her to stop. My brusque responses to her were in English, *my* native language. But she was happy speaking to me that way, showing her affection, and I should have been too, but instead I was overwhelmed by feelings of embarrassment. I was certain that everyone on the train could see that I was not fully Korean and so was wondering why this woman was speaking to me in that tongue. Not coincidentally, that is exactly what I was wondering, too.

I will never forget that painful train ride with Mom in which the most important thing to me was not wanting a subway car full of strangers to know that I spoke or understood my mother's native language. I felt as if she were determined to make me fully Korean. The language barrier that exists between us has really hindered our relationship. On the one hand,

Mom is this loving person, her caring and warmth just flowing over me. On the other hand, my mother is a person whom I've had very little time to get to know. My mom has been absent nearly all my life, yet strangely enough she knows me a lot better than I have given her credit for. That day on the train she looked deep into my eyes as she was speaking to me and then stopped and went back to reading her magazine. It was as if she had sensed my innermost thoughts; the discomfort and conflict I sat with. So for the rest of the journey we rode in silence.

I have always prided myself on being different, but for a long time, I felt funny. The type of "funny" that I felt the first time I heard someone call me a "Chink," an experience only matched by the first time I was called a "nigger." As the hapless victim of the synergy in being the biracial new guy, I have always been conscious of my differences, externally and internally. To my Korean friends I always felt like the token black guy. To those two black men who passed me on 43rd Avenue one indelible night, I was a "Chink." The powerful feelings of contempt and racism are vivid and lasting. So permanent, that I revisit them every now and again. What is it that people see when they look at me, and why do their furtive stares make me uncomfortable? As I attempt to answer these questions, I find myself caught in life's gauntlet of self-discovery.

During my years in high school I had not fully come to terms with my racial identity, but at least my relationship with my mother was getting better. It was no consolation that we couldn't be together, but I began to realize that she had really wanted the best for me all along. The sacrifice my mother made transcends human emotion and reason, at least to any American or any non-Korean way of thinking. My mother gave up her life so that I might have a better chance at success than she. In my selfish adolescence, I was unable to recognize her strength, humility, and sacrifice. After my freshman year at college, however, I was blessed with the opportunity to fully appreciate my mother's gift of life and my responsibility for it.

By the time I had finished my first year at college I had not seen my mother since my high school graduation. I spent the summer working to raise enough money to visit my mother in Houston, Texas. I had changed since I last saw her. My first year of college had filled my life with new academic and extracurricular experiences, and I had braided my hair in cornrows and put on fifteen pounds. What would she think? As I disembarked the plane my mother stood at the gate anticipating my arrival. I saw her radiant five foot five inch frame tiptoeing, almost hovering. Her caring eyes scanned each passenger with X-ray precision and surprisingly looked right through me. I nearly passed her before she recognized who I was. In an instant, her eyes lit up and her smile increased tenfold and her arms reached out for me. "Oh my goodness! I almost didn't recognize my Tony—so handsome and tall. Oh my goodness!" she exclaimed. It certainly had been a long time.

When we arrived at the apartment my mother had been living in for some time, I couldn't help but notice it looked like she had just moved in, because of the lack of any furnishings. In the living room there was a table on which was a small pewter picture frame with a picture of us on my sixteenth birthday. The kitchen had not been touched. My thoughts echoed off of the bare walls as I helped to put away the groceries we had bought for dinner. I asked my mother why there wasn't anything in her house. I could almost hear her response before she answered: she spent so much of her time working that she had no need for an apartment to look and feel comfortable. Before I could even enjoy having spent twelve hours with Mom, she had to go to help out at the store where she worked.

When she came home she began cooking. I helped her for a short while, then relaxed and sat watching her in action from the living room. We finally sat down to a feast, and I gorged myself and we spoke. It wasn't the kind of hapless chatter that you might expect two people to have after a long separation. Every gesture and word was a conversation in its own right. The synergy of mother and child contributed to the regenerative air in that humble room. We finished our meal, and I remember her teasing me about my hair. She didn't want me to have long hair, and she also didn't like my cornrow braids. Seeing through my snappy excuses she said, "You don't always have to wear your culture out like that." I spent all night thinking about her insight.

My last day in Houston came quickly. I packed quietly and wore a smile of satisfaction on my face. I was happy that I had the opportunity to see my mother. She offered her motherly words of wisdom as the taxi pulled up to her door. I asked the driver if he would take pictures of my mother and me together. He took a step back and aimed the camera at us. I told Mom to get on my back and when she did, I carried her around the parking lot. Her laughter was so pure I almost collapsed. When I let her down, I hugged her as the driver snapped another picture. After giving my mom the biggest hug and kiss any son could muster, I called on the Lord's strength to prevent my tears from surfacing. It wasn't that I was afraid of being unmanly, I just chose not to cry all the tears behind the ones on the surface. If I started, she would too, and I don't think the taxi driver was prepared to deal with a bawling mother and equally torn son, so I stared out of the taxi window and smiled. She stood there waving back with the same painful grin on her face. As the car pulled away I felt as if my brain was saturated from holding back all of the contentment and tears. I made small talk with the driver during the ride to the airport.

I thought about her meager living conditions and how blessed I was to have a mother who cared about me so much. I have been asked why she didn't keep me by her side. Other people have questioned her motives for placing me in the foster care of other families. This visit answered my own questions. It is difficult to put into words what my mother's burden is. Like many traditional Korean parents she wanted for me all that she had missed in her own life. She dropped out of college to work to support me when I was six or seven. And although I moved many times to different foster families, I was uprooted less often than she was during that time. As the object of her love, I felt obligated to my Korean heritage and how important it is to her that I don't lose what little I know. I thought about her words of advice that I don't always have to "wear my culture out." I felt as if I did in order to remind myself of my own background. It was a constant struggle. The pride I had for my mother's heritage was countered by the overwhelming negative feeling I got when she would overemphasize my Koreanness. At one point, she asked if I would change my last name from that of my father to her own. I was torn up by the powerful nature of that request. It was as if she wanted me to discard my blackness or to destroy the traces I had of my father's heritage. On one hand, my father was absent from my life so why should I carry his name? On the other hand, my name has been my basic identity since I was born. In the end, I didn't change my name and my mother understood.

Race matters. And it doesn't. I cannot detach myself from the biracial aspects of my background. Though I state this obvious fact about my racial identity, I sometimes wonder how my life would have been different if I were just of a single race. I have been told that I have benefited by having received the best of both worlds. And while I have been exposed to both the ugliness and benefits of multiracial life, I have not felt the need to choose one side of my racial background over the other. I have reached a level of comfort where I am proud of all that I am. In some respects I would say that I am more of a New Yorker culturally than either Korean or black. For me, the distinction is important. Race and culture are synonymous when people with a similar history or genetic make-up share common life experiences unique to their heritage. There is no singular black experience in America that I can identify with. Neither is there any definitive Korean or multiracial experience. To say the very least, growing up multihued has never been dull. But my racial composition is deeply intertwined with all the important relationships in my life. My relationships with my mother, with friends, and with the opposite sex all reflect the intricate connections between different parts of my life.

An important illustration of this connectivity is how I have interacted with the opposite sex. I have not had much difficulty attracting women because of my physical appearance, which undoubtedly has to do with my multiracial look.

But physical attractiveness has not been the only source of my appeal. Because I have craved the attention of women from the day my mother left me with the tangerine family, over the years I have developed a personality and demeanor that commands attention. Merely attracting women, however, has not solved my loneliness or other interpersonal problems. The obstacle to my having more meaningful and satisfying intimate relationships is rooted in all of the baggage I bring to the table when I get involved in a relationship. Since everything is connected, many of the ways in which I interact with my mother have carried over into my intimate relationships. It therefore makes sense to me that I am an emotionally difficult person to get to know. It seems reasonable and rational to me that I can love someone and then leave her in a heartbeat.

These patterns are a reality in my life. I believe that the lack of family and maternal stability while I was growing up has fostered my pick-up-and-go mentality when it comes to intimacy. I have had to be somewhat callous emotionally to avoid breaking down. My perspective has undergone a number of changes with each new relationship. In the past year I have made conscious efforts to dim the glowing lack of faith I have in womanhood. I feel betrayed in many ways by girls I date. Perhaps I am holding them accountable for my subconscious disappointment with my nomadic lifestyle, and because everything is so short-lived.

It is easier for me to become physically involved with a woman than to invest any serious emotions or real love. The few times that I have really trusted and loved, the relationship failed to survive long distances and miscommunications. Emotional self-preservation outshines my desire for true companionship and so I have closed off parts of myself. In addition to repressing parts of my personality, at the start of a new relationship I determine just how much feeling I am willing to put into a particular relationship, and I seldom deviate from that plan. Some people say that a person should love like they've never loved before, but what about hurting like never before? A guiding truth is that I don't want to hurt like I have before. Every time I grow close to someone, thoughts of long distances and miscommunications remind me of past pains. Many of my friends, past girlfriends, and sexual partners have questioned my dead-end response to them:

Why don't you just let go of your past?

Why can't you just enjoy us right now?

Can you stop dwelling on what went wrong before?

Why don't you want to be with me?

Why don't you just open up?

How could they not know that, of course, I have asked myself the same questions a thousand times over.

"My future wife is not enrolled at this college" is how I euphemistically put the lack of companionship in my college experience. My desire to transcend my personal history and emotional limitations has been nullified, and I am presently torn between sexual attraction to multiple females and meaningful co-existence with one woman. College life is not conducive to long-distance relationships. Consequently, I am ill prepared for what it is I am wishing for. I come to the relationship table with baggage. All of my unsolved and unanswered problems and questions stay packed up, and I expect these females to magically shed light on something they know nothing about—the deeper me.

With each encounter I either find out something new about myself, or I am reminded of some undesirable quality in my personality. In short, I am still searching for myself. I am afraid of being hurt again. My relationships with the opposite sex have left a stone in my heart. I have weathered self-induced loneliness because of my closed nature. And, through understanding, I have broken the stone in my heart. It's a healing process. I don't think that I will be able to have a meaningful and healthy relationship until I have rid myself of all of these smaller stones. Mistrust, fear, anger, and resentment must fade behind love for me to move on.

Even the longest journey begins with one step. Over the years the stride, pace, and frequency of these steps have all changed. Now, twenty-two years later, my journey continues. I feel as if I have revealed as much about the journey as I have about the traveler. The words and stories I have shared highlight the most powerful memories I have of people and experiences that helped determine my path in life. However, they are only fractions of my entire story. I have not mentioned my true friends who have been my surrogate family and support every step of the way. I am eternally grateful for having them in my life. Neither have I mentioned my involvement in student organizations, dance, my fraternity, or my academics. One can imagine the gamut of things I found to enhance my only-child existence. My search for a complete me is undying. The motivation it generates is eternal.

For my narrative to be complete, I need to know the full story for myself. So, I have begun to search for my father, who was my age when my mother conceived me. The thought that a man out there somewhere is the provider of half my genetic code, and that his presence in my life before the age of five has influenced my growth, sparks insurmountable curiosity. My search has begun with the help and support of my mother and my friends. I have no expectations, but whether I find him or not, the search itself can only further my journey of self-discovery.

Anthony Luckett earned a BA in engineering sciences/studio art and a BS in mechanical engineering from the Thayer School at Dartmouth College. After graduation, he volunteered as a teacher in the Marshall Islands, teaching elementary English (EFL), math, and science. In his second year in the central Pacific, he was the principal of the elementary school. Anthony currently lives in Boston and teaches high school math.

EMERGING DIVERSITIES

Johnny Lee   No Such Thing . . .

The church is an integral part of being Korean, at least in my family. Although I was born here in the United States, my immigrant parents have always taught my two siblings and me to see ourselves first as Korean, then as a child of God, and lastly as American.

"The *hiyan* peoples, they are very different from Korea," my mother would always say. "We are not the same way as them. They think we are not equal either. We have to be the smarter, work harder, and pray to the *hinanim* every day so we can make it."

With Christianity playing such an integral role in my upbringing, internal conflicts quickly arose as soon as I hit puberty, which was when I realized that I was more interested in penises than vaginas. Afraid of eternal damnation, I tried for years to repress any and all thoughts of sex as much as I could. As a result, my early teen years were filled with guilt and shame over my inability to resist the "lure of Satan." In all of my misery, I spent a lot of time huddled in a closet praying to God in repentance for my bad thoughts. Back then I did not tell anyone what I was going through because I did not want to be seen as evil. I also genuinely felt that God would one day transform me into a "normal" person if I believed hard enough.

Right around the same time, I made a discovery that completely changed my life: online gay chat rooms. As a sexually inexperienced and depressed teenager, these chat rooms became my saving grace. It was the one thing that kept me sane through all my years of dating girls and contemporaneously masturbating to male underwear ads. Although these chat rooms only added to my contrition, they also became an amazingly refreshing release for me. For the first time I found a way to talk to other people like myself. And best of all, the fear of being discovered was never an issue because I was hidden behind a computer screen. Most of the identities I created in these chat rooms were fabrications, which gave me the excuse of never having to admit to myself that I was really gay.

During the course of my chat room addiction I met someone whom I will call Peter. Peter and I became immediate friends, and for about six months we kept up with each other's lives, sent pictures back and forth, and even gave each other birthday gifts. He admitted early on that he was a great deal older than I was, which bothered me at first, but we managed to become close nonetheless because he made me feel comfortable about my sexuality.

Talking to him felt liberating and easy, because I no longer had to lie about my interest in men. I didn't have to alter the pronouns I used when referring to people I was attracted to, nor was I fearful of admitting to him that I liked gay porn, and that I felt sick to my stomach whenever women came too close to me. He was the first person I met who didn't feel that being gay was such a bad thing. Therefore, he became a welcome change from all the other straight friends I had in my life.

As time went on, Peter began to grow impatient with our anonymous friendship. Our conversations gradually began to end with talk of when we would see each other face to face. As much as part of me wanted to, I was not ready to take such a big step. Gay life was still a very frightening and evil thing in my eyes, and I did not want to surrender to it yet. Therefore, I shyly denied his request for several weeks. Keeping this arrangement was very difficult for me, because my craving for men grew more and more powerful. I wanted so badly to be touched, to have the strong arms of a man wrapped around me, and to feel his lips pressed against mine. My hunger for the male body was becoming uncontrollable. Yet I had absolutely no idea how to satisfy this need without feeling ashamed and without outing myself to my family.

Peter and I never spoke directly about being with each other, yet there was a subtle flirtation underlying every exchange we had. For instance, we always told each other whether we had masturbated that day. From what I could gather, I was almost certain that he wanted to sleep with me. As exciting as this prospect seemed, Peter's experience and age made me incredibly nervous. I was a clueless teenager with an enormous sex drive who knew nothing about how to satisfy someone. There was no doubt in my mind that I was too inadequate for him.

Worse than the fear of inadequacy was the constant anxiety I had of being caught by my parents. This had been a concern of mine for as long as I could remember. Therefore I went to great lengths throughout childhood to make myself as typically male as I knew how. Partly due to my efforts, and partly through their own denial, my mother and father managed to convince themselves for years that I was straight. For them to admit I was gay back then would have completely ruined the perfect image of our family they had tried to uphold in the face of God and the entire Korean community.

Life at home functioned under the watchful eyes of my insanely demanding mother. She raised my siblings and me under strict discipline and expected us to act appropriately at all times. We were taught at an early age that every action we made affected not only ourselves but all *hangooks*. As Koreans, we were responsible for upholding the dignity of our people. This meant doing well in everything and abiding by God's rules.

Since my earliest memory, I can remember my mother telling me about her dreams for my life. When I was twelve, she was convinced that I would be the first Korean President of the United States or, more modestly, a highly esteemed medical doctor. As I grew older, the dreams only became bigger and more idealized. However, never did they include anything like homosexuality. Homosexuals were despicable in my mother's eyes. I knew this because she had often cracked bigoted jokes about the gay men who worked with her at her clothing company. She was the main reason why I had to resort to gay chat rooms and to secret friends like Peter whenever I needed attention.

Peter seemed to be the only ticket out of the repressed life I had been leading until then. Frustrated, sexually curious, and in desperate need of a man's affection, I therefore broke down and told him that I was interested in getting together. My sexual desires had become so insistent that I no longer cared about concealing myself. My only concern was in satisfying a need that had been unfulfilled for too long. Without giving another thought, I e-mailed Peter with my phone number, and in a matter of seconds the phone was ringing.

Peter lived in a small apartment complex in Lower Manhattan. I initially wanted to meet in a more public space like a coffee shop or a restaurant, but Peter complained that he had a lot of work to get done at home. Therefore, we made plans to meet for a while at his place, and then go out to eat after he was done. Although this made me feel a little uncomfortable, I figured that his excuse was a viable one, and that I had nothing to worry about. Strangely enough, Peter also added that instead of having me ring his buzzer from the stoop of his building, I should wait across the street wearing a red shirt and jeans. He said that when he saw me from his rooms, he would come to the front door and prop it open so that I could slip inside unnoticed. I brusquely agreed to his request and left quickly for the subway.

As I sat, impatiently waiting for the train to arrive at his stop, all I could think about was how it was going to feel to finally be with a man. My excitement was so great that it far overshadowed the worry I also felt in taking such a bold step for the first time. When I arrived at the front of his building, I allowed him to act out his mysterious ritual of letting me in. I stood on the street for about five minutes before finally hearing the door creak open slightly. My forehead began to sweat profusely as I slowly inched inside. Peter's apartment was dimly lit and music was playing softly in the background. The apartment was in slight disarray, but it looked as though he had tried tidying up while I was on my way over.

I gazed around the room and finally saw Peter standing in the corner. He was a tall, burly looking man with thick shoulders and no neck. His face was heavily scarred with remnants of acne, and he had a heavily receding hairline. Immediately, I realized that the pictures he had sent to me were obviously not of him. He looked a great deal older and chunkier than the blonde, blue-eyed athletic type he had fooled me into believing he would be. Upon looking at him, my first instinct was to leave. But for some reason, I didn't. Although this man was not who he said he was, he was a man nonetheless and that alone was oddly exciting.

As I walked inside, I told him that his dishonesty was making me feel uncomfortable, but he didn't respond. He simply kissed me, first on the forehead, then on my mouth. Next, he picked me up off the ground with his thick arms and proceeded toward the couch. I know I should have stopped him right then, but for some reason his bold act seemed unusually exciting. I became struck with an overwhelming sense of longing and fear, which rendered me immobile and mute. As idiotic as this must sound, perhaps you will be able to sympathize if you think back to those times when you felt like doing something bad, simply because you were sick of being right, sick of obedience and of always taking orders. I felt all of those things. My desires were boiling over, leaving me a pathetic fool. I didn't care about what the consequences were; all I wanted was to feel a man's touch.

As Peter laid me down on the sofa cushions, he slowly began rubbing his massive body up against mine. One of his hands held down both my arms, and the other was placed heavily on my chest. He straddled me tightly, gripping both of his legs around my body so that I was pinned to the sofa like a wooden board. As he proceeded to gyrate and rub up against me, he suddenly put his hand around my neck and squeezed slightly. Immediately, I became frightened and wanted to stop what we were doing. I turned my head away from his kiss and asked him to get off of me. He responded in a rasp, "You're so beautiful, you're so fucking beautiful."

In a sudden panic, I tried to remove my arms, but this caused him to grip them even more tightly with both hands. When I began to roll around underneath him, he put the full force of his body weight onto my pelvis. I tried my best to squirm away from him, but he held me so firmly that my hips began to ache. At one point, I managed to free one of my hands and began pushing him away and screaming. But with one sudden motion, he grabbed my throat and squeezed firmly. With his other hand he gripped my arm so tightly with his nails that he pierced my skin. Blotches of blood began to appear on his couch. His massive body clasped onto me so tightly that it felt as though he could easily break me if I made a wrong move. When I stopped struggling with him, he began rubbing up against me, harder and more frantically this time. I could feel his hard-on against my stomach. It felt like a weapon, ready to harm me at any moment. I was trapped and more frightened than I had ever been in my entire life. I could hardly believe what was happening.

There was a large mirror that hung over his sofa, and I remember looking at myself, thinking that I would be killed by this man if I didn't do something. But because I was so much smaller than he was, I was even more fearful of what he would do if I tried to stop him. I felt like screaming and yelling, but my immense fear silenced me. I managed to muster up enough courage to hit him once across the face, but he only became more forceful and even more excited. "So, little faggot boy likes to play rough?"

At one point, as he was nearing the peak of his excitement, he grabbed my red shirt and tore it down one of the seams. When I heard the sound of my shirt ripping, I broke. Tears started pouring down my face, and I began to sob hysterically. I thought my life was going to end right there in his apartment.

Surprisingly, hearing the sound of my crying made Peter turn extremely sympathetic. In an unexpected twist of fate, he stopped grabbing me and began wiping my tears and apologizing softly in my ear. His facial expression suddenly changed from one of extreme desire to immense guilt. Seeing this as my only opportunity to get out, I pushed him aside and ran out the door as fast as I could.

I tell you this personal story from my life not only for dramatic effect but also because it represents one of the biggest turning points in my life: I realized that hiding my homosexuality from the world was only going to bring me grief. This also made me realize that I had to quickly come to terms with who I was. After this experience, I wanted so badly to run into my parents' arms. But I couldn't. I couldn't tell anyone, because I was too afraid of what they would say after they found out how I had gotten into that situation. I knew that I could not go on lying forever to the people I love. I needed help. But I was deathly afraid of revealing the truth. This is the story of how I managed to stumble my way out of the closet, and how I eventually succeeded in becoming myself.

Even at the early age of six, I was fully aware of the fact that I liked boys. Most kids that young are too busy playing with toys or eating glue to even realize they have genitalia. I, on the other hand, remember having my first erection while sharing a seesaw with a boy in the backyard of my school. At the time, I never connected my feelings with any larger picture. I certainly did not think of myself as gay. I merely thought that this was how I was and that my interest in girls would develop as I grew older.

My mother began to suspect that I was gay right around the time of my thirteenth birthday. A music teacher at school had tried to make a pass at me and after getting ratted on, he claimed that I was "the little faggot who flirted with him all semester." A few months following that incident, my mother caught my eyes lingering a bit too long on an underwear ad for men. From that point on, she began waking up occasionally at dawn to pray by my bedside and weep about her worries for my life. As this was going on, I had no choice but to pretend I didn't see what was going on. I was deathly afraid of telling my mother that her suspicions were correct. My mother also had no intention of speaking to me directly about this topic; therefore, we existed in denial until my first year of college. At this time, she was finally forced to face the truth.

During the summer after my freshman year at college, a friend of my father's had pulled a few strings and found a job for me at a lucrative law firm in DC. Unfortunately, the landlord of an apartment I had found in DC through a listing in a gay classified ad called my house to confirm I was taking the apartment. I was not home, and in the course of speaking with my mother, she determined that he was gay. That was all it took.

I came home at two in the morning that night, completely unaware of what had just occurred. When I walked into my room, I found my mother sitting on my bed with a Bible on her lap and used tissues scattered across the floor beneath her feet. From the strained look in her eyes it appeared that she had been crying for quite some time. Confused, I asked her what was wrong and why she was upset. She didn't answer. During that brief moment of silence, as I looked at my mother sitting a few feet away from me, I suddenly realized what she was about to say. Perhaps it was the Bible or the strange expression on her face that gave it away. I don't know for sure. She looked down at the book in her lap and then up at me. Slowly words began to form in her mouth, and she finally asked, "Are you . . . the gay?" She spoke softly, but in a way that I knew not to answer her.

"For so many year, I try so hard. I try to raise you right way. I pray to God about this every day . . . e-very e—very day I pray so much about this. How can you do this? . . . You embarrass us like this . . . you cannot be this way. . . ."

I stopped her before she could finish. "What are you talking about?" I asked. "Why are you asking me this all of a sudden?"

"ARE YOU THE GAY?" she demanded. "Tell me! Answer me! Is my son the gay, the little fagboy wearing the tight clothes talk like girl?" She proceeded to prance around in a fit of anger, trying her best to mimic what to her was an accurate impersonation of all gay men.

"Umma, please. Please don't do this, Umma," I pleaded. "I'm tired, and I need to get some sleep. You look tired, too."

I looked into my mother's eyes, and I could see that she was not being rhetorical. This wasn't like past instances, when she had asked me in passing why I didn't have a girlfriend, or why I didn't like to play sports like my brother. This time, she needed an answer. My heart began to race as I quickly tried to come up with the best response for her. But before I could even think, she asked again, "ARE YOU THE GAY?"

I didn't know what I was thinking at the time. I'm not sure that I actually was. Without another moment of hesitation, I said, "Yes, Umma. Are you happy now? I am!" Tears began to flow down my face.

As soon as those words left my mouth, I become overwhelmed by a combined sense of relief from having shared this enormous secret and regret for allowing those words to escape from me. In a panic, I held my breath and wished that I could somehow press some kind of retrieval button so those words could slip back into my mouth before they reached my mother's ears. As I stood in front of her, I felt more exposed than I ever had before.

Her hands started trembling frantically as she slid slowly from the bed and onto my carpeted floor. Her eyes began to water and with all the strength she could muster she whispered, "I don't believe . . . I don't be-lieve. No such thing as the gay Korean. You are lying. There is no Korean gay. . . ."

At that moment, I knew that I had to make one of two choices. I could either tell her that she was right and that I was not really gay but only go-ing through some problems, or I could speak honestly and tell her the truth. If I denied my homosexuality, I knew I would continue living a lie in front of my family and that I would have to go through the pain of pre-tending just for the sake of making my parents happy. If I spoke the truth, however, I knew that I would have to face severe consequences.

I hesitated and tried stalling simply by not responding and looking at the floor. Before long, my mother broke in and proceeded to say, "You can-not." In addition, she affirmed that I was not like those gay men she saw coming into her ladies clothing store, wearing makeup and speaking with androgynous voices and bent wrists. "It's impossible . . ."

My chance to liberate myself from the lies I had been telling all my life was quickly beginning to pass me by. I knew that if I didn't say something soon, I would lose the opportunity to reveal who I really was and would probably have to wait at least a few more years before the opportunity came up again.

Finally, I spoke and said, "Yes. I am gay. There is such a thing as a Ko-rean gay person. I have always been gay, Umma. Now you know."

I will never forget the expression I saw on my mother's face after I spoke those words. A mixture of extreme anger, shock, sadness, and fear, con-densed into her little eyes and in every little wrinkle on her face.

For the rest of that night, my mother and I spent hours crying and ar-guing with each other. She told me that I was not to move into that man's apartment anymore, and that I was going to live with Mr. Khim, the man who had gotten me the job at the firm.

"Why?" I asked. "Why can't I live where I want to live. I don't want to inconvenience Mr. Khim. And besides, he's probably going to think that I wasn't responsible enough to find my own place."

"No, you don't worry about that. I already call Mr. Khim. He know that you are coming tomorrow. You cannot live with that bad man. He going to have sex with you and try to stick his penis in you. You cannot live with the gay. No, I will never let my son live in the gay house."

"Umma, not all gay people are bad. He won't do that."

"Yes! Yes they are all the bad! How do you know that they are not bad? Don't you know that God said so about the gay. God HATES the gay. They are all bad. They are all going to hell!"

My mother's opinions were made clear. She was not going to tolerate having a gay son, nor having a son live with someone who could corrupt him. In her final words, she stated that since I was going away to Washington, she would let the topic go for the time being, but as soon as I got back she would find a doctor for me and have me stay home for the fall term of next year so that I could "fix" myself. Although I disagreed with her wishes, I knew that it was not appropriate for me to argue with her any further. No matter what I said, she was not going to listen.

As she stood up from the floor to leave my room, she looked directly at me and said, "You have to pray to God. I will pray for you. But you have to pray, too, if you want to change. God will not punish us because he loves us. Don't worry, OK? If you pray, you will not think like this." She smiled, trying to look as encouraging as possible, and walked slowly back to her room.

A million things were rushing through my brain at once. All my life, I had been dreading this moment, and now it was finally here. What was going to happen next? I looked over at my packed bags and suddenly felt relieved that I was leaving tomorrow morning for DC.

For the next few hours, I slept soundly in my bed, perhaps because I was so exhausted from all the things that had just occurred. After just a few hours had gone by, however, I was awakened by my father whom I saw kneeling beside my bed. When he saw that I was finally awake, he grabbed a hold of my hands and nervously began to rub them in the awkward way he always does when he wants his children to know he cares. I asked him what was wrong, but before he could speak, he began sobbing.

That was only the second time I had ever seen my father cry. The first was at my grandfather's funeral; and even then, he had held back his tears until the very end when the coffin was being lowered into the ground.

I looked away from him quickly, realizing that my mother must have told him about the conversation she and I had a few hours ago. A sudden sense of fear began to consume me, because I had always been most afraid of how my father would react if he found out that I was gay.

He was, what most would call, the stereotypical Korean male. He came home from work everyday, plopped himself in front of the television, turned on the sports channel, demanded his food, and was perfectly content for the rest of the night. Because of his seeming lack of interest in the family, he and my mother have always had a very rocky marriage that appeared close to ending on several occasions. Like most Korean fathers, he was stern, unemotional, and always kept his distance from his children so as to maintain our respect. He and I never really spoke all that much, but it never bothered me because that was the type of relationship I was used to.

As he continued to rub my hands, he gently brushed the hair away from my face and said, "Johnny, I want you to know, I am not going to get mad like your mother." I looked at him, surprised at what he was saying.

"Thanks," I said awkwardly. Since I had spent my entire life never really sharing a deep conversation with him, I found myself at a loss for words. I could sense that both he and I had absolutely no idea how to express ourselves to each other.

"The reason I'm not going to get mad is because I know how you feel. I know what you going through."

Upon hearing those words, I automatically became defensive because I didn't want him to brush this off as a silly passing phase that I would be able to overcome as long as I listened to his advice. I had heard comments like this coming from my parents before, like back when I was having rough times at school and when my mother was trying to convince my brother and me to stop smoking.

"No. This isn't a dumb phase. You don't know how I feel. You can't possibly know," I said firmly.

"Yes. Yes I do, Johnny."

I tore my hands away from him, and I rolled over on my bed and faced away from him. "Go away, Ahbah!" I moaned.

"Just listen to me," he said. "Before I marry your mother, I never want to be with a woman. I was virgin before I meet her, and I was happy being with friend . . . like you. The reason I marry is only because I want a family. I want the children. You have to think that way, too. Please don't tell Umma I say that, OK? Please."

As he gave his final plea, he quickly slipped out the door and left me alone in my room. I lay in bed completely still, aghast at what I had just heard. Was my father hinting at what I thought he was, or was I making an unfounded assumption? As I thought back to all the fights my parents had with each other, things began to take on a whole new meaning. Often times, months would go by when my mother would sleep on the floor in my room, and use the excuse that my father's snoring was keeping her awake. There were also instances when my father would stay up in my brother's room and play computer games until the late hours of the night, or come home at dawn and say that he was having drinks with his friends. Moment after moment began playing out in my mind, and I suddenly saw things so differently. Was my father homosexual or at least bisexual? If so, perhaps homosexuality was genetic after all.

I could hardly believe how quickly things were beginning to change for me. Within the last few hours, I had lost my apartment, gotten kicked out of the closet by a stranger, and now I had discovered that my father was possibly gay. The thought made me cringe, simply because I hated thinking about either of my parents in sexual terms. Strangely enough, I also began feeling angry with him, because I didn't think it was a fair thing to do to my mother. I promised myself that I would one day tell her what my father had confessed, just so she would know why her marriage was not working out. However, I have yet to gather enough courage to speak those words to her.

My parents insisted I stay with their friend in DC who had found the summer job for me. This was an awkward situation, and at one point he called my parents to tell them I was going to Vermont for the weekend. They immediately contacted me after work and asked whom I was planning on visiting. When I told them it was just a friend, they demanded that I give a name. I refused and said that they probably didn't know who the person was. Suddenly, my dad's voice overpowered that of my own and my mother's combined, and he said, "I KNOW who you are going to visit. You are going to visit Jonathan, aren't you?"

How did he know about Jonathan? He said that Jonathan's name appeared several times on the phone bill he had just received. I kicked myself, remembering how frequently I had called him during my brief time spent at home.

"Is he your boyfriend?" he asked in a loud tone. "I know he is."

My mother began to join in at this point, and the two of them probed over and over about whether or not I had a lover. After hesitating for a few seconds, I eventually answered, "Yes, yes, he is my boyfriend."

As soon as I spoke those words, my parents moved from being mildly upset to absolutely infuriated.

"I can't believe you," my mother yelled. "You are having sex, aren't you? You are sucking his dick, aren't you? You make me sick. How could you find a boyfriend?"

"Do you like dick up your ass?" my father added. "Should Umma start picking out your wedding dress for you? My second child is a *boy*—he is not a *girl*. I don't want the faggot. I hate the faggot son."

Was I living in the damn Twilight Zone? His harsh words confused me. What had happened to his promise not to get as upset as my mother? Was he merely doing this to keep up appearances? It all seemed very strange to me.

I decided to visit Jonathan despite my parents' threats to disown me if I did.

Jonathan and I had met several months ago at a gym where he worked as a step aerobics and spinning instructor. A friend of mine who was a regular in one of his classes had urged me to meet him, because she knew that both of us were looking for people to date. Just having entered college, I was eager to be introduced to new people, especially ones who were attractive and gay. So, I agreed to go along with her. When we finally met for the first time, however, there were no church bells or sirens going off in either of us. As a Filipino American, he had never found other Asian men attractive. I held the same sentiment. But my attention was quickly diverted from his ethnicity to his strapping body. Previously, my disdain for dating Asian men had always been due to my preconceived notion that they are all scrawny or effeminate. Jon, however, was far from either of those things. He was the first Asian gay male I had ever met who was not only masculine but who had an amazingly chiseled body. His large pecs and defined arms, which were not covered by the tank top he was wearing, were an immediate turn-on for me. For Jon, a seven-year age difference between us was an added reservation.

After dating for a short while, however, he and I took a liking to each other, and our worries seemed to no longer matter. We were both fairly experienced at sex; therefore, he did not have to spend any time teaching me or acting as my mentor. We developed an equal relationship, and no longer looked at each other along the lines of our age.

Jon picked me up from the airport and we made our way back to his house. To our surprise, three police cars were parked alongside the sidewalk in front of his home. As Jon slowly parked the car, we did not say a word. Both of us had a feeling that my parents had something to do with this. My heart began to race, and I swung my head in all directions to see if my parents were hiding somewhere behind the bushes.

"Your roommate called and told us about some threats made over the phone. Perhaps you should go inside and listen to them," said one of the police officers to Jonathan.

Jon and I walked toward his house, holding each other's hand. When we got inside, he immediately went for the answering machine. In red blinking letters, it indicated there were twenty-two messages.

The first one began to play and, as I had suspected, it was my mother. "Hellooo, this is Misesse Yoo calling for Jonattan Cruzze. Please call me back; this is berry serious."

After a long beep, the next message began to play.

"This is Misesse Yoo again! Please! Please! I need talking witthe you, Mr Cruzze. Please call me back! If you do not, then serious trouble!"

Message after message began to play, and I soon realized why Jon's housemate had called the police. The next few messages were from both my mother and my father, and they all said the same sort of thing. By the seventh message, things began to sound very strange.

"CALL US BACK! We have to talk! If you touch our son we going to KILL YOU! We will hire black killer to go to the house and KILL YOU! Watch out for us! We are coming there right now to the your house! Do not try to fucking touching our son—you FAGGOT GAY bastard!!!"

From that point on, the messages grew worse and more frightening. In the latter messages, my parents not only threatened Jon but also began threatening me. As I sat there with him, listening to my parents talk about murdering us, my knees began to shake violently and tears ran down my face. An uncontrollable feeling of despair came over me, and I shrank into a ball on the floor.

The policemen stood back, unsure what to do in a situation like ours. One officer walked over to Jon and patted him on the back. A female officer came over to where I was slumped and tried to console me by saying they had dealt with a situation like this before and it all worked out in the end. "All worked out," I thought to myself. Lady, you obviously don't know my parents at all.

"Do you want to press charges?" one officer asked. "I think that we have enough here to have your parents arrested, if that's what you want."

I looked at him in disbelief and said, "Of course not! They are my parents. I can't have them arrested."

After hearing my response, the officers looked at each other and decided that it was time for them to leave us alone. Before they left, they offered to have someone watch over the house, but I told them that it wasn't necessary, so with a quick thank you, all three of them left in their cars.

Jon stayed by the door and peered outside to make sure no one was creeping around behind the bushes. Meanwhile, I paced around the room biting my fingernails into nubs and sweating profusely.

I could tell by the expression on Jon's face and by the way he kept avoiding eye contact with me that he was angry. He had probably never expected to be thrust into this situation in such a dramatic way, yet it now seemed he was just as involved as I was. Although I knew he didn't blame me for what was going on, I felt incredibly guilty. Jon had done nothing wrong and did not deserve to be in this situation, yet my crazed parents had somehow managed to drag him down with me. Being the nice guy that he was, he reached over, gently squeezed my shoulder, and forced a smile on his face.

I had always known that my parents were not going to be happy after they found out that I was gay. It was a fear I carried with me throughout childhood. Even so, no matter how much I was aware of my parents' hatred of gays, I never truly believed they would respond so harshly. After all, I was their son. Part of me thought that after living in America for so long, they would grow accustomed to the idea that being gay wasn't a bad thing. I was quickly discovering my assumption was very wrong.

Jon and I felt like sitting ducks. Although we were five hours away from my home in New York, we both knew that my parents were crazy enough to take the long trip up to Vermont to collect their son and to give him a good reprimand. What else they would do to him was what we were both afraid of.

What had I done wrong? As this question kept repeating in my mind, rage began to build inside me as I realized over and over again that the answer was nothing. I had done nothing to deserve this treatment from them. I couldn't take it anymore. I walked over to the phone and dialed home with determination. As it began to ring, however, I hoped that my mother would not be the one to pick it up.

"Hello . . . ? Hello?" It was my brother.

"Kenny, Kenny, thank God it's you." My voice began to tremble, and I was still out of breath from having cried for such a long time.

"Johnny, what the fuck is going on? Are you all right? Calm the hell down. Breathe . . . I can hardly understand you," my brother barked.

Before I could answer, his voice suddenly turned into a hushed whisper, and I could hear the creaking of the floor as he rushed to get as far away from my parents as possible.

"Where are you right now? Are you with that guy? Please tell me you're not at his house." I paused, wondering how he knew about Jon. I suddenly realized that my parents must have told him about my secret. For some reason, it hadn't occurred to me that they would actually take the liberty of telling my siblings that I was gay. Of course, this would have been consistent with how things normally go in my family. Most of the time, there are never any secrets kept among us. Whenever something happens to one person, everyone somehow finds out about it. For instance, when my sister had gotten her first period, my mother announced it to all of us a few minutes after my sister had just finished telling her how embarrassed she was. We were all raised to believe that no secret was too big to be kept from family. Nevertheless, I had still hoped that something as big as this would be kept private and that my parents would give me the opportunity to come out to my brother and sister on my own.

"Yes, you mean Jon. . . . He is here with me now." My voice stammered and there was a brief moment of silence. I wasn't sure what my brother was thinking. I wanted him to laugh and tell me he supported whatever I decided to do, but I knew that hearing this news was very hard for him to deal with. I had been almost as afraid of coming out to my brother as I was with coming out to my parents. Growing up, he had clearly expressed his dislike of gays on several occasions, joking crassly with his friends about faggots and dykes and mocking any guy he knew who had the slightest effeminate mannerism. Along with my parents, he too had suspected that I was queer for a very long time. But like most people, he didn't want to accuse his younger brother of something he felt was so despicable and worthy of mockery. Not knowing what to say, I shyly asked, "So, what do you think about all this?"

"I don't fucking know. Umma . . . she says you're gay. Whatever. I don't want to talk about it now." His answer was as I had expected. Like my father, Kenny never liked to talk about anything more meaningful than who should win the next World Series or what he should eat for dinner. He quickly tried to change the subject. "I'm gonna get in a lot of shit if they pick up the phone, you know that?"

"I know, I know. I just had to call to see what was going on. I want to know if . . ." I was suddenly interrupted by the sound of my mother's voice in the background.

I held the receiver close against my ear and listened as intently as I could for a response, a question, or even a noise from my mother that would indicate what she was thinking at that moment.

"Does she look pissed?" I asked nervously.

Hearing this question said aloud made me wonder why I was suddenly so scared of my own mother. This was someone who had raised me, whom I was supposed to love and who was supposed to love me in return.

Five days went by before I finally returned home to face my parents. When I walked through the door, my entire family was seated together in the living room. My mother and father sat next to each other and both had stern expressions on their face. For the first few minutes, a silence fell over the room that was so thick with tension that even my brother couldn't help but squirm around in his seat. Finally my mother looked toward me and said, "Johnny-ya, Ahbah and I decided that no more yelling anymore. No point. We want you to go see a special doctor. You have to be cured right away. They have to fix—we cannot fix. We have to help you. . . . God will help you, too."

"What, a special doctor? You mean a psychologist?"

My brother suddenly broke in. "No, she means a psychiatrist. She knows someone who can help you, I think. We all feel that you should do this, too."

I looked at my brother and sister and couldn't believe they actually bought into my parents' bogus plan. How could they think this was a good idea? Why were they siding with my parents?

"Are you guys all crazy? I am gay. You've all known that for a long time, you just never wanted to accept it. This is the way I am, this is how I will always be. You're just going to waste money trying to fix me. I just don't like girls. God, can't you understand that? Girls do nothing for me. In fact, they make me sick. How do you expect me one day all of a sudden to wake up and go from liking dick to pussy?"

"Don't worry about money. I will take care of everything," my father said, trying to interrupt me before I went any further.

"Nothing is going to happen. This is who I am, I can't help that."

My brother spoke up once more. "How the hell do you know? You never know what could happen. I am not a freakin' expert, but neither are you. Don't be so damn closed-minded. If you had even the slightest chance to change, wouldn't you want to take it? It would make life so much easier for you. This is fucking the smarter thing to do."

The conversation went on for three more hours, without the slightest hint of resolution. I tried my best to convince my family not to send me to a shrink, because I just knew that my visits would amount to nothing more than a big hole dug deep into my parents' pocket. Unfortunately, my family remained firm in their opinions, despite my constant attempts to dissuade them.

I ended up visiting three different "specialists" that summer. The first person I went to told me after the second session that she was not going to try and change who I was but that the purpose of my visits would be to help me cope with the trauma of coming out to my parents. The following day, however, I learned from my sister that the doctor had called my mother as soon as I had left her office and told her over speakerphone that she thought I was curable. She also added that she really didn't think that I was gay, but that I was only rebelling against my parents' wishes for attention. Her comments single-handedly made my situation at home immensely worse than it was before because, instead of dissuading my mother, this doctor had confirmed all of my mother's deluded suspicions and made her more convinced that I was only going through a problem stage. After hearing what she had said, I refused to see her again because I was afraid I would lunge at her from the across the desk and rip her hair out for lying to my parents.

The second person I went to was a small, chubby Korean man who specialized in family counseling. The only advice he was able to give me was that people can change.

"You are too young to make any clear-cut distinctions about yourself. Everyone changes. For instance, one day you may love vanilla ice cream, and the next day you will hate it. In the same way, you may think you like men today, but it can very well change tomorrow. That's the beauty of life, the beauty of being human."

After three more visits with him I felt I had wasted enough of my time, so I told my parents that I no longer wanted to go. Before they agreed, however, they joined me for one session and found out for themselves just how incompetent he was. During the meeting, my parents and I got into an argument that became so intense we almost broke the furniture in his office. The psychiatrist was so clueless as to how to moderate the situation that he simply left the room until we finally decided to leave as well.

The last specialist was a man in whom my parents had placed the most hope. Our pastor had recommended him to us, because he was not only a psychiatrist, he was also a Christian pastor himself. Assuming that he would automatically be anti-gay, my mother eagerly set an appointment for me to meet with him and even skipped a day of work to come along.

His office was on the top floor of a large building in midtown Manhattan. When my mother and I walked inside, I was surprised to find that he was not Korean. He stood about six feet tall and had slicked back white hair. At the start of our session, he first asked me to explain what was going on, and why I was brought to him. I explained, as best I could, all the events that had gone on that summer. When I finished speaking, he then asked my mother to describe my story from her point of view.

"Well, Pastor Richards, I know my son, and he says he is the gay. But I really do not think he is the gay. The gay men do not look like him. I need you fixing him please. To change him. God is not happy. He hate the gay, you know that too, right, Pastor Richards?"

When my mother finished with her explanation, Mr. Richards thought for a while. His face looked perplexed, which made me think that he was getting ready to scold me. Resigned, I sat back and waited for him to tell me how wrong I was and how I could change as long as I prayed hard enough or read the Bible. But surprisingly, when he gave his assessment, instead of offering a cure for my homosexuality, he completely sided with me and began reprimanding my mother for treating me so harshly. His response was so unexpected that it didn't hit my mother until much later that he was actually disagreeing with her. At first, she simply nodded her head at every comment he was making, thinking that he was giving me advice on how to be straight.

"I am a pastor. I have been one for thirty-five years of my life. I don't know why God would create gays and also say that being gay is wrong. Perhaps no one will ever know. But we have no right to judge or say that this lifestyle is wrong. This is not your son's fault. In all honesty, Mrs. Lee, your actions repulse me. You should be ashamed of yourself."

I was in complete disbelief at what he was saying. I had expected to hear more of the same old rhetoric from him about changing myself but he was actually very supportive. My mother became completely silent. As I looked at her sitting in her chair, red with guilt, I suddenly felt a sense of hope for the first time.

When the session ended, my mother left the office in a hurry, with the excuse that she had to get back to work. Later that day, she spoke to me briefly and tried to convince me as to why Mr. Richards was not a capable psychiatrist. She came to the conclusion that I would no longer see him, because "He looked like bad man, and he probably the gay."

That was the last attempt my parents made to seek professional help for me that summer. This was mostly due to their costly expenditure of more than two thousand dollars in fees, which gained them nothing. After having gone to these "special doctors," my outlook on our society became decidedly more grim, and I felt more disillusioned then I ever had before. Although the last person I visited was in support of me, the others were clear indications that there was still a great deal of ignorance and homophobia in existence, even among educated tiers of our society. Before this time, I never thought legitimate psychiatrists in the United States would feel that homosexuality was something to be changed. It seemed so ludicrous to me. I looked at Jon and all my other gay friends and wondered how anyone could ever think they were sick or needed help. Who comes up with these rules?

Two more incidents occurred that summer, which forever changed the way I viewed my family and the relationships I had once felt were so vital to my life. These events both involved arguments with my mother and father, respectively. The first involved a scenario in which my mother became convinced I "had the devil in me" and attempted a spontaneous exorcism that led to her trying to prevent me from leaving and wound up with her tackling me, causing a serious cut to my foot and sending me to the emergency room.

A week later, my father and I had an argument that ended with me punching him in the face. Before this time, I had never hit anyone before; I couldn't even comprehend it. But after his fifth attempt in one week to "beat the gay out of me," he left me with no other choice. When the fight ended, I was not the only one left severely bruised. My mother tried to protect me from my father's wrath and ended up getting herself battered by him as well. My father locked himself away in his room, treating the small cuts he received from having fallen into a glass coffee table after I punched him square in the chin.

His final words to me were to forbid me from ever returning home again. "Do whatever you want," he said. "Get the AIDS. Just don't come to me. You are no longer my son. You shame us."

That night, I packed up my belongings as quickly as I could and had my brother drive me back to Jonathan's house in Vermont. This final episode had broken me and made me realize there was no use in fighting anymore. After leaving home, more than four months passed before I was able to speak to my parents again.

Recently, I bumped into a friend from high school whom I hadn't seen since graduation. His father was a close childhood friend of my mother's and had immigrated with my parents around the time of the large influx of Koreans in the late seventies. Since we had not seen each other for years, we spent the evening talking about what was new in our lives. When he asked how my family was doing, I told him about coming out to my parents and how difficult it had been. Based on the reactions of all of my other friends, I had expected that he too would be appalled by my story. However, instead of reacting in shock, he actually sympathized with my parents' point of view. None of the details of that summer were surprising to him. In fact, he even attempted to rationalize their behavior. "You have to see things from their perspective," he said. Interestingly enough, after hearing his response, I began to notice similar ones from my other Korean friends. They have all been unexpectedly understanding of the way my parents reacted that summer. As much as I hate to generalize, it is almost impossible to ignore the glaring conclusion that this trend points to.

Korean society, as many will tell you, is generally not accepting of gays. It's a fact I have grown to understand and live with. However, I do not tell my story to have Korean culture criticized as backward and antiquated. Even through all the sadness, I never once damned my parents, nor my Koreanness. If that is what you thought I was getting at, then you have missed the point. No one should fool themselves into thinking that the United States is a great deal more sympathetic to the GLBT (Gay, Lesbian, Bisexual, Transsexual) cause than are my parents. If that were the case, then there would be fewer "closet-cases" and Matthew Shepard incidents in this country. It is very easy, as an outside observer, to react with amazement and anger at what my parents have done. It is even easier to brush my story off as a tale about a dysfunctional Korean family. Before you take this route, however, it is perhaps necessary to ask yourself this: What would happen if I were your son/daughter, brother/sister, cousin . . . and came out as gay? Would it be so unreasonable to think that you or your family members would respond in the same way as mine did? Although this is only a guess, I am assuming there are only a handful of families who would genuinely be unaffected by it and even supportive. Having a gay relative would make no difference whatsoever?! To those who do not judge, I applaud you. But to those large numbers of you who would be bothered, the only thing I have left to ask is why? What is it exactly you fear?

Today, as I stand on the threshold of my twenty-first birthday, I look back at the events of that summer and realize that my life will never be the same. Sadly, after all that has been said—the threats, and the insults—I find it difficult to feel the same love I once felt for my mother and father. It is impossible to take any of it back. Although I consider each new day a time to forget, I know there will always be scars. My parents are still far from reaching the point of accepting my homosexuality. In a way, I think they never will. My mother still asks me when I will bring home a girlfriend nearly every chance she gets. She is bothered by the distance I have kept from her since then and is now trying to have fewer confrontations with me. My father, surprisingly, has become more understanding and is frequently the one to quiet my mother when she begins to argue with me about how I am living my life; however, the lack of communication between us has grown acutely worse. I doubt there will ever be a time when

I can speak freely to him about any new boyfriend I acquire. And as much as I would like to ask him about that morning when he tried to communicate to me, I do not think I will ever be able to. But my life is not unlike anyone else's. We all exist with scars that seem too deep and too painful. I guess that is the one thing I have come to learn from my coming-out experience.

Since graduation from Dartmouth College, Johnny Lee has worked as a marketing manager for a jewelry designer and lives in a "fabulously small, yet amazingly expensive, apartment" back home in New York City. His parents and he maintain a relationship; however, their interactions are limited. He is hopeful that over the years the relationship will improve.

Vincent Ng   Farewell My *Tung-Tew*

"Would you put down the dishes and just fucking listen to me!!!"

"Well . . . all right then, Derek. What is it?! We're listening," Mother responded in an agitated tone with more than just a hint of impatience. . . . Silence . . . I took one long hard swallow and made the best effort I could to articulate myself as clearly as possible, even as I felt my body tensing up, my heartbeat pounding with anxiety, and my eyes on the brink of watering.

"I'm gay . . ."

There was another long, drawn-out silence. I could feel the shock settling in—my mother desperately searching for words on which to grasp for emotional stability. After a few painful seconds her gaze clawed its way over to Howard. My eyes also shifted at that moment toward my father. They immediately became fixated on him with a longing, desperate plea for help, for support, for acceptance. In the background I could hear mother as she gasped and in a panic-stricken tone said, "Howard, don't just stand there. . . . Call the doctor, will you?!"

Father held his position for just a few seconds before the tension was too much for even him to hold on to, and as he turned away from me, I felt as if he were discounting the only son he had ever had—completely and utterly rejected.

At that point I disengaged my gaze from him and directed all my energy away. My stare immediately became focused instead on a five foot eight inch, slim, Chinese man in his late fifties sitting in the last seat in the second row—my real father as he sat watching the play. Through my eyes I told my father of my own pain, the very same feelings of isolation and abandonment, which I hoped filled him with remorse. In my mind I begged of him, "Why can't we connect on a more authentic level? Why can't we talk openly about things that really matter for a change? Why won't you just pay me some goddamn attention?!" At that point I was certain this was not just a theatrical performance but rather that the whole play itself, all the preparation and all the character development, had been rooted somewhere in my own personal experience. This performance was a rehearsal for my own life, and now it was time for my father to finally take his first step into it.

Early in the summer after my freshman year of college, I had decided to participate in a week-long "Theater of the Oppressed" (T.O.) workshop. As an interactive participatory style of theater used to create social change, T.O. draws its themes and ideas from the performance group's collective stories of oppression, conflict, or struggle. From a large group of more than forty participants we split up into five smaller focus groups, and I chose to be part of a focus group specifically addressing homophobia. Together in a group of six people we shared personal stories in which we had encountered homophobia and created a single-act play that incorporated personal struggles from our collective experiences.

Although the story was not based directly on my experience as an ambivalent twenty-one-year-old Chinese Canadian still exploring my sexual orientation, I willingly offered to play the role of the protagonist, a gay male fifteen-year-old, who endures a painfully rejecting coming-out experience with his peer group, and who later returns home to have the experience further aggravated by a complete rejection by his parents. I knew that in many ways the young man's struggles to gain acceptance, recognition, and attention from his peer group were no doubt experiences that paralleled my own life, and I knew I wanted to be able to explore dimensions of my own relationships: the fears, the voices, and the internal monologues, through my character, Derek. I also found that the struggles Derek faced in his life, particularly in the relationship with his parents (most particularly with his father), resonated with my own struggles to develop a positive identity as a Chinese male confronting, wrestling with, and coming to terms with many of the traditional values and limited definitions of race, ethnicity, sexuality, and masculinity that my father had modeled.

Though the story itself was outlined, in many ways the unscripted, improvisational format of the play allowed me to develop Derek's character based on my own lived experiences and relationship with my parents. As soon as we started rehearsing I began to feel ownership of the play, and through every quirk, every gesture, every movement in every limb, the play came alive for me, intertwined with the innermost thoughts and hidden emotions within my character: the suppressed anger and rage as a result of not being heard, the burden of shame for not having lived up to my father's expectations of an ideal son, and the yearning for a true connection rooted in a genuine relationship.

Later that evening, I followed up the performance by initiating a discussion with my father—one unlike any we had ever had before. I pulled out the sofa bed in the guest house we were staying at, and as I lay down next to him, propped up on my side, with a hint of curiosity in my voice I casually asked him, "So, Dad, what did you think of the play tonight?"

The evening had created the ideal situation to have this conversation with him. There was nowhere to leave to, and the play had served as a convenient introduction into a dialogue on sexuality. I purposefully decided not to tell him whether I identified with a particular sexual orientation, nor that I was exploring my own sexuality, but rather decided to see where his own assumptions about my desire to talk would lead the conversation. Would he assume it was an indirect way of telling him I was gay? If so, I could challenge his homophobia. Part of me felt very safe, since many of the emotions and fears around rejection, abandonment, and shame had already been laid out on the table during the performance. I purposefully phrased my questions from the perspective of the characters, as I tactfully asked him, "How do you think the father in the play felt when his son came out?"

He waited for a moment. I noticed as he uneasily shifted, crossed his arms across his chest as he lay, and stared blankly at the ceiling.

"Well . . . a man and a man are just not meant to reproduce. It is biologically unhealthy," he answered, simply reciting his way through the same arguments on homosexuality that he had always cited. After prodding him further with my persistent line of questioning, however, it suddenly became apparent to me where his own fears really lay. "Well . . . you know it would really be a disgrace to the Ng family name—to have a gay son that is."

He then proceeded to tell me stories about the black sheep in the family: distant relatives who had fallen victim to alcoholism and gambling in Hong Kong. My curiosity was piqued, as I keenly wanted to know more about his relationship with his father and the values that had been instilled in him growing up.

"So, Dad, did you ever do anything that your father wasn't proud of?" I asked.

"No, . . . " he said, then paused for a few seconds; his eyes again shifted uneasily. "Well, . . . just this one time . . . I was climbing on the rooftops of our apartment back in Hong Kong. I was quite a naughty boy back then, I'll tell you. My father told me never to climb on the rooftops and one day he caught me."

"What did he do then?"

"Well . . . *tung-tew* of course!" *Tung-tew* was a Chinese feather duster used for corporal punishment. "And he really hit me that time, I'll tell you."

"Where did he hit you?"

". . . on the legs. The back of the legs."

"And what did he say?" I looked directly into his eyes, and I could see them begin to water as he choked on his words.

". . . it's better I break your leg with this *tung-tew* than have you fall off the rooftop and break your own leg, you stupid boy!"

My body froze in numb shock. I felt devoid of feeling, wanting to console, to reach out, to support my father; yet all I could do was sit there. I had no words to say. All I could do was imagine being him. . . . and how horrendous it would have been to have had my own father say that to me. The pain I felt made me feel like my body had shriveled down to the size of a walnut. My body was gripped by anger as tears started to come to my eyes. It's no wonder he blames himself for getting beaten even to this day.

For a split second, I could not help but see him as an amazing survivor. He was one who made it through growing up in a physically abusive family environment with a non-present father. He was someone who genuinely tried to give his own children a better life, yet still felt the pain that dwelled deep down inside him. I began to see how the patterns of coping through physical abuse had been passed down through the generations; his parenting styles had been learned through his own destructive role models. Now I realized why, when I was ten years old and had slipped and fallen down the stairs at home, his response had been to yell and swear at me, "You see! *Tew!* (Fuck!) I should give you the *tung-tew* for falling down those stairs since I told you not to run in socks. *Mo-lun-yung-a-lay!* (Fucking useless!)"

I had sat at the bottom of the stairs crying as my mother held me in her arms and embraced me without saying a word, protecting me from his abuse. My mother has always been there for me. I feel it is through her that I have learned genuine empathy. She has always been the one who has encouraged me to pursue new programs, to greet challenges and new ideas with an open mind. Through my mother I have learned to reject traditional sexist gender roles and to embrace a broader definition of masculinity. It would be easy to assume that simply because she was my mother she naturally possessed a maternal instinct to provide unconditional love in all situations; yet, as I began to learn more about my mother and father's history and their family relationships growing up, I really began to see and understand where it was that I came from.

From a poor farming family, my mother had grown up with loving parents and strong female role models—namely her grandmother, who was particularly radical for her time. As an adolescent, she had rejected the Chinese tradition of foot binding and had run away from home to lead her own life. My father, in contrast, had grown up around an abusive, diabetic, gambling-addicted father who died a slow, bitter death. I could see how we had both been shaped by the practice of shaming as it had been meted out to my father and passed along to me as a young boy. I began to see myself as a generational product of a historical lineage of fatherlessness, and I had vowed to myself that I would not subject my own children to the same painful pattern of absenteeism.

I could see the loneliness that he felt in his life at times. I could see how his style of parenting made it difficult for my younger sister and me to relate to him on a personal level. I could see how the unhealed pain from his relationship with his father had become the recycled content for his role as an oppressive male in his relationship with my mother. I longed for openness in our relationship, yet I instead received a very limited definition of masculinity that excluded vulnerability. It occurred to me that my father was never taught and as a result did not understand or value the role of emotional literacy in human development. Perhaps this explains why I have never felt comfortable disclosing personal thoughts, talking about sexuality and relationships, or sharing my true hopes, fears, and aspirations with him. Instead, with my father, I learned to fear judgment, rejection, and shame.

The night of the one-act play my father witnessed the performance of my life. I had never felt so in touch both in a physical and an emotional sense with a character I played—particularly in the scene where I broke down emotionally and had to yell at the top of my lungs to get my father's attention. I needed him to hear how much he had hurt me in the past. I needed him to hear how frustrating it was to live my life always feeling like I had never met his expectations. It felt as if he never wanted to listen—perhaps because he himself had never been heard. After all, it's much easier to run away from one's problems. Unfortunately, however, there were times when running away was not even an option for him, and I soon learned that rage had an alternative outlet: violence.

I can still clearly picture that night. I was fifteen years old; we were driving home down a highway and an argument had erupted between my parents. I remember that it became heated very quickly, and the next thing I knew my father picked up a cellular phone battery in the front of the car, turned around, and threw it at my mother's head.

My mother burst out screaming, "Stop the car! I'm getting out!!" And before I knew what was going on, we had swerved over to the shoulder of the road and screeched to a stop.

My father yelled back, "*Tew-lay-lo-mai!* (Fuck your mother!) Get out!" And my mother scrambled out of the car slamming the door behind her as she bolted out on to the highway into the darkness. I remember breaking out in a panic that a car might hit her; I watched clinging to the edge of my seat as she flailed her arms in the air dashing out in front of the headlights of an oncoming car. It stopped, and within a split second she had climbed in and was whisked off down the highway in the other direction. My thoughts scattered like an ice cube tossed into a blender, splintering in all directions. "Where the hell is Mom going?!" I screamed in silence. My father waited for what felt like an eternity, though it was probably only a few minutes before he pulled back on to the highway and drove home. It was a silent ride, and I recall walking into the house feeling empty inside, utterly lost as I tried to hide in isolation in my room. About an hour later I heard a knock at the door, and when I answered it, to my surprise I encountered two policemen.

"Would you mind if we just had a quick word with your father," one calmly asked. Anxiously, I went to fetch my father, then waited as he stepped outside and they closed the door behind them. Lifting myself up by the fingertips to peer out the high kitchen window, I watched with horror as the two policemen handcuffed him and pushed my suddenly limp father into the back of the police car without mentioning even a word to me. I felt the blood drain from my legs and a lonely pale fright overcame me as I collapsed into a crouched ball on the floor. . . . my father didn't even look back at me. I sank to the ground as my sister came up to me a few minutes later wiping the tears from her eyes as she sat down on the chair next to me and through tears and sobs begged me to tell her where they were taking my father.

"I don't know!!" I abruptly spat back. Void of answers and not knowing what to do, I wrestled with the frustration of being expected to know what was going on. A creeping feeling of being completely alone caressed my body, as I sat there, helpless, trying to calm both myself and my sister through the night—until my mother returned several hours later, tired and emotionally exhausted. My father was released the following day, but no reconciliation efforts were made, and still to this day he blames my mother for everything that happened.

I had to come to terms with not only my father's emotional distance and occasional violence but his demands with respect to living up to traditional Chinese values as well. Growing up, I always had odd notions of what exactly it meant to be Chinese. To me, the notion of being *Chinese* encompassed everything bad about living with my father. Images of him swearing at my sister and me and threatening to punish us with the *tung-tew* crop come readily to mind. When I was thirteen years old he implemented a "speak Chinese only" policy at home, yet both my sister and I refused to speak Chinese. In fact, it was nearly impossible for us to communicate in Chinese having grown up with English around the home and having gone to international private schools where the majority of our friends were white expatriates' children from the United Kingdom or Australia. Our father assumed that the Chinese language was somehow automatically programmed into us—in a sense he made the classic immigrant mistake of assuming that his kids would retain all of their "heritage," including language, even after he and my mother had decided to put us through a Western educational system.

To me, *Chinese* was Nick Cheng, the dorky kid with glasses who spoke with an accent, whom we never let play soccer with us. *Chinese* was going on a trip to our ancestral village in China when I was thirteen years old to pay respects to our ancestral graves and having all the villagers—even the men in the restrooms—make fun of me because they thought I was a girl because I had long hair. *Chinese* was sitting in a loud, crowded dim sum restaurant with old distant relatives whose company I dreaded because I couldn't communicate with them, and I regularly suffered their ridiculing comments criticizing the Chinese boy who couldn't even speak his own language. In fact, I hated the language. Most of the time I heard it spoken was either when my parents were arguing or when it was forced on me by a bitter, unreceptive, old Mandarin teacher in elementary school who was overly critical about our pronunciation. In general, I tried to dissociate myself from most things that appeared to be Chinese—after all, I just wanted to fit in with my white friends.

The first time I became consciously aware of needing to fit in was when we relocated to Canada in anticipation of the fragile political situation surrounding the British colonial handing over of Hong Kong. It was during high school that I can first recollect that race was made a salient issue to me. We had moved to Toronto, Ontario, which has a fairly large Asian population—mainly recent immigrants from Hong Kong, Korea, and Taiwan. I attended an elite all-boys private school that was probably 40 percent Asian, 40 percent white, and 20 percent other minorities. I remember sitting in French class during the first week having a conversation with a Canadian-born Chinese guy.

"Oh, you're a Honger, eh? Yeah, one of those F.O.B.s," he snickered.

"What do you mean, F.O.B.?" I asked.

"Oh, you know, Fresh Off the Boat," he answered gloating with a wry smile. I did not know how to respond. Part of me was shocked, part of me was offended, and part of me was somewhat anxious. I was from Hong Kong—yes, that was true—but I certainly did not arrive on a boat. Part of me was thinking, is this really someone whom I want to associate with? But another part of me was also thinking, well, if he knows a bunch of white kids, and I don't really want to become associated with the "F.O.B. Hongers," then perhaps he might be someone I want to get to know. I would soon come to understand that F.O.B. and Honger were derogatory racial slurs laden with all the negative Asian stereotypes of speaking with an accent; being a nerd, unathletic, and smelly; having no Western manners; and bringing stinky chinese-sausage fried rice to school in your lunch box and being scared to eat lunch in a public place where people might be offended by its odor. Being a Honger meant having no confidence, interpersonal skills, or leadership abilities. And though I would never admit it to myself in high school, it was also about being asexual or sexually invisible.

I found myself having to fight hard against all of these cultural stereotypes. I was not a computer geek; I was not a violin prodigy; and I did not wear glasses (and for the longest time refused to get glasses even though I needed them). Yet, as much as I distanced myself and tried desperately to define myself in opposition to these cultural stereotypes, in frustration I still found myself bound to them. Matters of sexual attraction did not escape my stereotyping: I had always been physically attracted to white girls. Until I was fifteen, I had never found Asian girls the least bit sexually appealing; for some reason, all of my preadolescent and early adolescent crushes were on white girls. I guess somewhere in the back of my mind I had a small Asian man, white trophy girlfriend complex: that if I could date a white girl, well, hell, that would prove that I was white—or at least not a Honger. Ingrained in my psyche was the idea that all Asian girls were boring, dull, and demure, and subconsciously, I had bought into the dominant popular culture definition of female beauty: I wanted Barbie, someone who had unrealistically big breasts, a thin waist, and blonde hair.

By sophomore year, however, my racial readings had to be adjusted. I started attending the boarding school program, and in this new environment about 80 percent of the students were Hongers. My roommate, Tommy Wu, was from Taiwan, and my two suitemates were from Hong Kong. I quickly found out that I really enjoyed the company of all of them, and we ended up bonding over cooking midnight snacks of rice, noodles, and *daw-see-leng-yu* (Chinese canned fish). I realized the stupid small things we did together captured an element of nostalgia that brought me back to home in Hong Kong. Indulging in the familiar foods and the smells, I felt comfortable not having to hide my customs and cultural practices. We would play pool together after school, and during our pickup basketball games, I would even joke around by throwing out random obscene Chinese slang words—*jo-ma-lun-yeah-ah-lay*—as my friends would smile and laugh at my pronunciation. Undoubtedly, they appreciated my making the effort to relate through Cantonese.

Back at school during the day, however, I acted as if I barely even knew them. They became the confidentially filed friendships in my secret drawer, only to be opened at night when no one was looking, since there was no way that among my white friends I could be seen to be friends with Hongers. Consequently, it was hard for me to make friends with recent immigrant Asians and maintain those close friendships, and it was also hard for me to ground myself in a strong Asian identity.

Barely aware of my own ethnicity, I drew my closest four male friendships from a variety of ethnic and racial backgrounds. During elementary and middle school, my best friend was a tall, introverted British guy named Jim. In high school, my best friend was a tall, spunky, Chinese-born Canadian called Graham. Though I would describe my best friendships as close, they were primarily activity-based and fairly competitive in nature, and it was rare that we would connect through personal sharing or feel comfortable discussing whom we had crushes on or our relationships. My close peer group in high school was fairly diverse along ethnic lines, activities, and interests: we were two Asians, two white guys, and a brown guy, and since we were so hard to categorize we avoided any reputation branding.

As a group, we entered the dating scene late, and it was not until senior year that we began to consistently socialize with a group of girls. I never really felt the pressure to start dating, let alone pursue any sexual exploration, until late senior year, and as a result I entered college not having had any experience with a long-term romantic relationship or with sex. Furthermore, I had never had anyone whom I could talk to openly about sexuality. It seemed far too awkward and shameful to do so with my parents, and my sister seemed too young and immature. But in fact, this changed when I went to college and my sister started dating before I did. Then, it was not my multiethnic friends to whom I turned to talk about girls, but instead to my sister. Chelsea gradually became the knowledgeable one when it came to romantic relationships; thus she was no longer just a little sister but someone I could go to for advice, and my own maturing views on gender roles allowed me to begin to see her as an equal. Slowly, we began to open up and share more personal thoughts. We further bonded by making light jokes about the generational and cultural tensions in our relationships with our parents. Most important, however, we began to provide emotional support for each other at times when our parents would engage in heated arguments, and I have now come to view her in many ways as my best friend.

My concerns about my race and the absence of any romantic or sexual relationships even of the most fleeting kind had somehow remained tacit throughout high school; yet they were forced into the open upon my arrival in college. I was confronted with a barrage of sexual stimuli, a multitude of attitudes toward sexuality and experimentation, opportunities for dialogue on race issues, and liberal, avant-garde teachers. The deeper friendships I began to form led to more honest self-disclosure, and I really began to question what it meant to be both a Chinese Canadian male and a sexual being. It became legitimate to express my feelings through action and find out where my sexuality lay, since I had come out of my high school years unclear. College thus allowed me to come into my own, and instead of walking through certain set paths based on a narrow script, I began to break molds that my Chinese father had set down, exploring things in dramatic and even ostentatious ways. Rather than remain an inhibited and repressed Chinese father's son, I pursued my dormant sexual interests and the plethora of scripts available to me. One groundbreaking event in the formation of my sexuality was a retreat I attended the summer before my junior year entitled "The Gendering of Power," in Oregon.

One of the goals of the workshop included acknowledging, recognizing, and coming to terms with our worst socialized fears. Though I initially felt extremely nervous, in a private counseling session with Joanne, an open, accepting, twenty-four-year-old, I eventually felt comfortable sharing with her my fears around public speaking and even my anxiety about penis size. I remember Joanne looking at me, and as a smile crept across her face, curiosity and trepidation simultaneously overcame me. Her eyes brightened as she suggested that I take the opportunity at creativity night that evening to write slam poetry about my penis and present the piece while wearing nothing but a G-string! I immediately burst out laughing as I visualized the absurd image; my emotions oscillated between ridiculous bemusement and the fear of absolute humiliation. I laughed again so as not to permit the emotion of fear to overcome me—and decided that I had to do it.

The image is still crystal clear. I am almost completely naked, in all my vulnerability standing on stage in front of fifty people having just ranted, raved, and displayed a full range of emotions through a poem about my penis, when the audience erupted into overwhelmingly supportive applause. I could see tears breaking through smiles; a powerful sense of reclaiming myself, my body, and my own freedom to express my sexuality seized me.

I still wonder what exactly prompted me to fully expose myself in such a flamboyant, out-of-character performance, but the results were undeniably positive. On one hand, the physical and verbal exorcising of my fears through a penis monologue had helped me to realize that these fears were simply emotions; since the emotions did not compose my personality or my true self, I could be liberated from them. On the other hand, empowerment came from the incredible validation I received from the wonderfully supportive audience. Thus, the process itself was an important step toward accepting myself and being accepted by others as a fully sexual being.

The entire experience provided me with a different framework to look at both my sexuality and my personality as a whole. I came to realize how entrenched my fears about my own sexuality were. Why was I desperate to prove that I was a sexually confident person through streaking challenges, yet deathly afraid to have anyone see my penis in any public setting, even the changing room? Why did I always feel so left out in conversations about male sexual bravado? Why was I so afraid of sexual intimacy? I began to realize just how ingrained my fears of public speaking and leadership were. Why was I always so afraid of speaking out in class? Why was I so afraid to take on leadership roles in high school? I began to realize how negative a Chinese identity I had adopted. Why, for example, over the past five years, had I bought into pronouncing my last name not like it was supposed to be pronounced, "*Ng*" (tongue wedged to the back of the throat), but rather with an anglicized adaptation, "*Ing*" (tongue slightly curled and placed behind the lower teeth)? Why was I ashamed for so many years to say that I was born and raised in Hong Kong? I finally realized that I was ready to confront my two worst fears: those regarding masculinity and ethnicity.

Consequently, I felt a strong desire upon returning to college for my junior year to share my insights with my closest friends. The experience had such a profound impact because I was able to break away from many of the limiting stereotypes, particularly around sexuality, which I felt had strait jacketed me as a young Asian man. I yearned for a more genuine, intimate connection with my friends. I wanted to invite them to share their own personal narratives and struggles after I had shared mine. I wanted to be able to feel comfortable enough to cry with my closest friends, especially male friends, and break past any gender-based rules about emotional displays. I had gained a newfound sense of confidence, grounded in provocatively challenging traditional roles.

Perhaps most significant, I could now remind myself, "I am a sexual being!" Part of this realization was the fact that I was potentially capable of arousing other men or women through intimate physical contact. One attractive younger woman had come up to me after my reading and whispered in my ear that she liked men with small penises. "Wow!" I remember thinking to myself, excited that I was establishing my own confident definition of what masculinity meant to me. Having challenged many of my own assumptions of masculinity, and having begun the process of confronting my own homophobia, I found myself motivated by the momentum of the workshop to begin to explore where my sexuality would unravel with a close male friend.

In some ways an unlikely partner, in other ways an ideal one, Justin, a short, loquacious, Jewish senior was both available and very receptive to my advances. Early on I sensed he harbored a strong admiration for me that gradually continued to build as our relationship progressed, and as I developed more trust in him I realized that Justin would never tell anyone about the intimacy I foresaw would occur. I trusted Justin, and I felt extremely safe. Furthermore, since he was naturally more effeminate and passive, I noticed myself taking most of the initiative to act on sexual impulses and move our relationship into more intimate waters. Thus, through the experience of leading, I suppose my own masculinity felt affirmed.

As I saw it then, I was not really gay. I was just a heterosexual male experimenting with other guys, so open about his sexuality that he was free to have sexual partners of both sexes. Yet, there existed a strange eroticism about the clandestine nature of our relationship: we would sneak off to the study rooms in the basement of our dorms where no one would ever study to have our midnight rendezvous. With the door jammed shut, books dispersed on the table to suggest that we were studying, and the lights off, we fumbled around to pull each other's clothes off and touch each other in places that we had never been touched before. The whole experience was all so novel, so spontaneously teenage, pubescent, and awkward, so secretly "dirty," so unscripted. At times I felt lost and confused, at times I felt guilty, and at times I felt simply curious. Eventually, I ventured an explanation as we reflected together on our relationship—I viewed sexuality as a spectrum, and we were just two liberal guys trying to figure out exactly where we fell on that spectrum.

Determined to branch out, I did not limit my sexual activities to Justin, and within a few weeks I had grown even more confident in myself and my ability to act on my sexual impulses. Over the next summer, a friend named Parker had flown out to Toronto to visit me. The timing was rather opportune, as I had recently met Annette and Carissa, two French Canadian girls, and I had invited them to spend a night with Parker and me up at a ski resort two hours away from town. I may have been partly motivated by a desire to prove my masculinity to Parker. Later that evening after a romantic dinner and a few glasses of wine, we found ourselves all deciding to take a nude dip in the hot tub. Surrounded by a sea of bubbles and the gentle purr of the water jets, I became increasingly self-conscious as I listened to the inner voice in my head. It began to say, "Okay, now's your chance. All of you are nude in the hot tub, you've got to make a move—make it suave, offer to give Annette a massage. This is an amazing opportunity. For heaven's sake, she's beautiful and naked! Oh, for crying out loud . . . come on, take some initiative! Show her what a *real* massage feels like." With a wide grin on her face, she gracefully accepted the offer I finally made, at which point Parker and Carissa decided to make their way up to the bedroom.

The experience that followed was rather surreal and in some ways almost seemed like a reenactment of a chapter out of *The Latin Lover's Guide to Sexual Secrets*. I was determined to prove my masculinity by helping Annette come to orgasm and to be the most sensual lover I could be. Though I was very attracted to Annette physically, I felt that the experience was as much about performance as it was about pleasure. In contrast, with Justin the sexual experience was about exploration, play, affection, and respect. In my mind raged a constant debate as I tried to satisfy the masculine ideal, the pressure to act dominant, as if I knew exactly what to do, yet also balance an emotional connection. I realized that an emotional connection is ultimately what makes sex transcendent—something my father had never really taught me. But with Annette, intimacy was suddenly replaced by what I now see as a gender-based cultural script, as I found myself strangely avoiding eye contact with her. The situation may have been *too* intimate, as I felt myself becoming too vulnerable. Then again, perhaps it was my own inexperience. Perhaps it was my nervousness in assuming I was expected to "perform" at a certain level, or perhaps it was my maleness and the implicit gender assumption that men are supposed to be stoic and nonemotive.

Nevertheless, I distinctly remember her commenting to me after two hours of having done just about everything short of sexual intercourse, "You are not like the guys back in Montreal. You are so much softer, you give much more attention—almost as if you were my steady boyfriend."

I sat there quietly brimming with self-satisfaction, affirmed and pleased on a certain level that I could bring as much satisfaction to a woman as I could to a man; yet I was confused the next day when she appeared aloof and conversation was limited to a minimal exchange of a few words over breakfast. As I paused for a moment to reflect, I wondered if the greater degree of satisfaction that I had derived from my relationship with Justin was due to the fact that I had in fact a greater inclination toward homosexuality than heterosexuality; but then I questioned whether this was true.

What I have learned is that intimacy is most profound when experienced hand in hand with emotional displays of affection and constant communication about feelings; whereas sexual attraction expressed physically, absent of these other factors, does not mean as much. I realized that the problem with only exploring sexuality on a physical dimension is that the sexual experience often gets paired with stress. I needed to bring my partner to orgasm, and I needed to be able to sustain an erection and have my own orgasm—at the right time, of course. In the process, I was ignoring my own needs. I could not allow myself to be absolutely vulnerable, to trust, and to connect not just on the physical but also the emotional level— I felt harnessed by my maleness, emotionally chained down.

Thus, after much pondering, discussion, and self-reflection, I have come to develop different theories on sexuality to explain not only my own behavior and thought processes but also those which I have seen and experienced in others. At one point in time, I genuinely thought that every single person on the planet was bisexual. I justified this by theorizing that it was simply the case that most people were actually living in denial. On a certain level perhaps I still ascribe to this fluid, polymorphous theory on human sexuality; yet part of my inclination to believe this may arise from my own insecurity in choosing a firm sexual orientation.

The problem for me with identifying myself as gay has always been that I have never really felt like I was gay. Stories by gay friends describing critical markers of growing up gay do not resonate with my experience. Furthermore, I have been and still am very physically attracted to females. At the same time, identifying myself as heterosexual does not seem like an ideal fit either, since I do find some men physically attractive. Having experimented sexually with both sexes, I feel that I am capable of connecting on physical, emotional, and spiritual levels intimately with both men and women. Perhaps I would be most comfortable now in identifying myself as a bisexual male still working through my own homophobia while simultaneously struggling with my own definition of masculinity.

All of the different aspects of my identity that I had been grappling with—my ethnicity, masculinity, and sexuality, as well as the deepest concerns I had about my relationship with my father—all came to the forefront of my life in the weeks approaching my college graduation ceremony. Just two weeks before the ceremony was to occur, I sat down with Chris, a close mentor who was also a college administrator, to have a late evening private conversation. It occurred to me that night that I was sitting on a tremendous amount of anxiety and fear around inviting my father to attend my graduation ceremony. I knew that my mother could not attend since she was attending my sister's high school graduation abroad, yet I was surprised at how reluctant I was in inviting my own father to attend the ceremony.

The fears I was sitting on around graduation were intertwined with fears of rejection and embarrassment. I wondered, was I still Chinese enough by his standards? Would he still find something in me to be proud of if I told him I wanted to become a teacher rather than go into business to make money? Would he accept me if I told him about my feelings around sexuality? I began to realize that I didn't know if I had ever lived up to what my father's expectations were. I was scared of his disowning me, his utter disappointment shadowing my glorious day to be proud of.

I made one of the hardest phone calls of my life that night inviting him to my graduation, and my father did attend the ceremony two weeks later. I had decided that I was going to make every effort to make him feel like he was welcome, to be proud to introduce him, and to challenge my fears.

In fact, he was so proud of me when he came over that he didn't even mind when I pretended he was the graduate as I took off my graduation gown and hat, placed them over him, and encouraged him to walk around with my diploma in his hand.

Graduation, in some ways, was a major step toward reconciliation in our relationship. I had the opportunity to have an honest dialogue with my father about my fears of rejection and failure in the face of high parental expectations. I also seized the opportunity to discuss acculturation in the context of race and ethnicity since it had always been a salient issue in my life. Part of coming to terms with who I was involved reconciling the distant personal relationship I had with my father, but I also realized that I needed to reconcile with myself what it *really* meant to be Chinese, since that was the source of much of our conflict. So much of what I had written off for years was beginning to surface; I was beginning to make sense of cultural values passed down through the generations, but I still did not understand my own ethnic heritage.

With regard to my ethnicity, my sexuality, and my masculinity, sometimes I wonder if I am simply going through phases of trying on new identities and roles—a kind of *moratorium*, as identity theorist Erik Erikson might suggest. However, I tend to phrase my current state more as a continuous cycle of creation and exploration; and as I embark on a career path in the field of education, I hope to be able to share some of my personal stories and struggles to help future generations begin the process of intrapersonal discovery—examining oneself in depth.

Looking forward, I see the primary challenge in my life being the continuation of a progressive transformation in my relationship with my father. I take pride in the strides I have made in my own personal development, as I shift away from the more traditional views of masculinity and ethnicity, and at the same time incorporate a more mature view of my own father, as I see how he is but a prisoner of his own upbringing. While I see my roots as an important connection to my past, I do not see them as defining my future. I feel, therefore, that it is important to find out more about Chinese history, Chinese American/Canadian history, and my family, in an effort to ground my identity though not to define myself completely. I have sat down with my father and looked at my family tree to try to understand my generational roots, and I recently watched a Chinese film about a father and son relationship following which my father and I had a discussion about core Chinese values such as respect and family honor.

I am developing an appreciation of the things that make me different and unique from my Caucasian friends. The personal significance and value I attach to family has in many ways been shaped by the close relationship I have with my uncles and aunts on my mother's side. My Chineseness is now about claiming pride in the foods that I grew up eating, introducing my Caucasian friends to dim sum, teaching them how to use chopsticks, sharing our unique holidays, festivals, and traditions, such as giving red *lai see* packets, and even learning Mandarin again so that my friends do not simply assume for me a default white identity.

Still, there is nothing I see myself focusing on more than my relationship with my father. I would like for him to be able to acknowledge the past pain and hurt that has come between us and to fully embrace the identity I have built for myself. I want him to see that my desire for an honest, emotionally intimate father and son relationship is not in opposition to the values that are most dear to him. I want him to understand that I do see myself as the end of a long ancestral lineage, and that I value everything for which he and his ancestors have struggled. I am tired of constructing layers of social identities that do not communicate a consistent core self across space and time, and I want to disclose an authentic version of myself without having to face the wrath of shame. Shame begets silence, and it is the silence that truly hurts in the end.

After spending three months in the Marshall Islands as a volunteer high school social studies and math teacher, Vincent Ng moved to Shanghai where he taught poetry and music appreciation at the elementary level at the Shanghai American School. The intersection of film, environmental, and educational interests then lured him into teaming up with a documentary film crew in rural northwest China working on a feature length documentary film, *China's Sorrow: Earth's Hope*. Intrigued by alternative educational practices, he is now teaching at a Montessori school in Beijing.

Afterword by Vernon Takeshita   Revolution and Revelations

THE PERSONAL JOURNEY AND THE DEFINITION OF COMMUNITY

Early into the twenty-first century, we can all be amazed that Americans continue to hold on to, use, and perpetuate the nineteenth-century concept of race. Race has been a rationale for enslavement, segregation, and imperialism. As an idea to rally communities around a larger shared identity, nearly every instance of extreme nationalism since the dawn of the last century has had some racial component, convincing believers that their interconnection was innate and that their political goals were consequently self-evident. The belief that race was "scientific" gave the concept a sense of being a fact of nature, even an expression of God's plan.[1]

By the 1980s, however, critics realized that race had more to do with belief systems than science. It became fashionable in academic circles to describe race as "socially constructed." Yet, if the concept of race is quack science, why do Americans find this way of thinking so hard to change? Why do they continue to apply such an outdated concept to millions of Asian Americans?

This book provides some insight into the changing American concept of race, and it does so in an unusual and somewhat surprising manner—by picking the minds of young Asian American adults still in the process of defining their beliefs, their identities, and their connection to the larger society.

When I began to read the diverse essays in this collection, I wondered what meaningful observation or conclusion could I gain from writers barely out of puberty. Although full of enthusiasm, eager to tackle new concepts, and deeply earnest in every new revelation, these writers lack much worldly experience and show even less comprehension of larger contexts—social, historical, or political. And yet, in the stories they have chosen to tell and the epiphanies they have shared, I believe there is an important critique of the nation's promise of equal opportunity and, more specifically, a benchmark to gauge the progress hoped for by the late civil rights movements, which included the birth of the first national movement for Asian American rights.

What Difference Does Three Decades Make?

In the spirit of the times, Asian American students during the 1960s and 1970s followed the example of the Black Panthers and devoured the teachings of Martin Luther King Jr., Malcolm X, Che Guevara, Mao, and others, in search of a strategy to create a new and better society. The Left in America spoke fervently about inevitable and necessary revolution: the new age, they predicted, would see the end of racism, sexism, classism, imperialism. Revolution was everywhere. It was your duty to choose sides.[2]

For minorities, the very notion of race needed to be transformed from something shameful to an idea that could be acknowledged with pride. Perhaps the pain of growing up, of being embarrassed by what white Americans thought of you, could become a source of strength to challenge the prejudices of the majority. Black Power found echoes in Red Power, Brown Power, even Yellow Power. In fact, the label Asian American found its first widespread acceptance during the early 1970s.

Who were the advocates of these radical manifestos? Who were the leaders of the new organizations that mushroomed into existence—political activists, labor organizers, arts and culture rebels? Who were these writers grappling with the meaning of society and identity and community? They were young adults. But where did the revolution go? To find out, we could talk to its aging participants, but we can also listen to their contemporary counterparts: the twenty-year-olds who have written these essays. Their writing screams out to be compared with the reflections of their predecessors.

The Song Remains the Same

Americans often pride themselves on the rapidity of change or "progress" in national life. For example, many people argue that racial prejudice was discarded by most Americans along with legal segregation. While acknowledging extremist groups and some white backlash to the demands of the civil rights movement, conservative Dinesh D'Souza warns that "these sentiments cannot be taken as representative of whites in general."[3] Racism has been relegated to the fringe of society, and therefore complaints of racism must be an irrational pathology in the minds of minorities themselves. The consensus among many is that minorities should focus on changing their minds rather than on changing American society.

And yet in these pages, testimony after testimony demonstrates that American society has not changed so radically as some purport. Writers from diverse parts of the country and from entirely separate Asian immigrant communities catalog experiences that show many Americans unrepentant and unreformed. A white student calls a Vietnamese student a Chink. Many report a constant feeling of being judged according to race: "I was certain that everyone on the train could see that I was not fully Korean." "To me, Chinese was Nick Cheng, the dorky kid with glasses who spoke with an accent, whom we never let play soccer with us." and "I was sad that I could never really be 'American' because I looked so unlike one." Adolescent insecurity inevitably feeds into such attitudes, but this alone does not explain why an apparently consistent message of racism appears to be communicated from very different parts of American society. How different are these testimonies from that of a seventeen-year-old boy who complained in 1972 that "the white man looks upon the Chinese as very humble, a short little guy with buck tooth, glasses, round thick glasses or something like that. Isn't masculine at all as far as the guys are concerned."[4]

Many of these students grew up feeling ambivalent about their Asian identities. One writes, "Growing up, I always had odd notions of what exactly it meant to be Chinese. To me, Chinese was everything bad about living with my father." Another noted that "being Korean was a liability that I felt I had to overcome. I thought that others were constantly conscious of the fact that I was Korean and therefore different in some way." Relatives contributed to their sense of cultural failure with "ridiculing comments criticizing the Chinese boy who couldn't even speak his own language." Acknowledging that he failed to meet the expectations of others, the young man admitted, "In fact, I hated the language." These complaints can be found not only in the accounts of third-, fourth-, and fifth-generation Asian Americans but even in the tales of second-generation Chinese and Japanese Americans from the 1920s through World War II. Americans have been remarkably consistent about expecting Asian

Americans to be foreign, timid, and exotic, the opposite of what it means to be American.[5]

Values from traditional cultures weighed heavily on the choices made by those second-generation Asian Americans. How many of their priorities would become those of these students? One student notes that her parents' preference for arranged marriages was "one of a number of values that my parents and I disagree on." As an American, she tries to imagine "what my mother's feelings [about her own arranged marriage] must have been. Wasn't she scared? Was this what she wanted? How could she know he might be right for her?" Yet as alien as arranged marriages appear to this daughter's eyes, she later bemoans the result of having her desired freedom of choice, explaining that on "some nights, my walls and pillows soak up soul-filled cries and tears as I slowly surrender to faith and sleep. I want to care about someone who also cares for me. However, I cannot get past the wall of finding a second person for this relationship." By her own account, her parents' arranged marriage was successful and yet she wants no part of the tradition.

Over and over these writers reveal moments when they are technically insiders (that is, as a family member, a member of the ethnic community), but their judgments about that culture are seemingly the judgment of an outsider. Values learned in American schools, from the media, from simply not accepting the practices of their parents uncritically take priority, much to the disappointment of the older generation. More troubling, these students question whether their choice away from tradition represents ethnic disloyalty or perhaps a deeper self-hatred, or if it's simply a matter of being "modern." Their struggle to find answers reminds us over and over of the courage required to tackle such broad questions about tradition, culture, and identity. These are topics that academics spend a lifetime studying, but for these students, an answer is needed not just for intellectual satisfaction but for the practical reason of living.

Adding to the complexity, many of the ideological tools young Asian Americans use to judge their families' traditional cultures are not unbiased and, in fact, reflect racial and ethnic stereotypes that stretch far back into U.S. history. The notion that Asian cultures are inherently abusive to women and that this is a point of contrast with American society is repeated uncritically by many of the authors. According to one, his mother "gave into her misogynist traditional culture." Another writes, "The practice of Confucian ideals led to decreased communication and ultimately to feelings of isolation," and "It occurred to me that my father was never taught and as a result did not understand or value the role of emotional literacy in human development." What is astounding is that these observations come from students who admit that their knowledge of their families' homeland is limited at best, and yet they do not hesitate to proclaim the backwardness of these old practices.

It is not surprising that a student could write condescendingly, "I have also been able to incorporate a more mature view of my own father, as I see how he is but a prisoner of his own upbringing. While I see my roots as an important connection to my past, I do not see them as defining my future." These students are apparently unaware of the divisive debate in the late 1970s between Frank Chin and Maxine Hong Kingston, among others, which explored the issue of traditional culture, artistic freedom, and gender and racial stereotypes. The question of abandoning "backward" traditions for "modern" American values will be very familiar to readers of second-generation writers such as Jade Snow Wong.[6]

The youthfulness of the authors must be considered when evaluating the accuracy of their stories. As participants in the narrative, they present subjective evaluations rather than objective history. Firsthand experience with the Asian cultures can vary remarkably among Asian Americans. Observations about parents may present a very narrow or skewed representation of what living in Asian countries is actually like. Economic status, regional variations, urban compared with rural, type of education, religion, and more, contribute to this complexity in life that cannot be reflected in reductive contrasts between the American and Asian. It's no wonder that abandoning traditional practices seems so appealing. Who wants to voluntarily become a flat stereotype?

A Different Path

As striking as continuities between Asian American youths may appear, changes in priorities can also be found in these essays. Perhaps the most obvious contrast with the attitudes of civil rights activists is the absence of a sense of a larger racial community. Asian Americans/Pacific Islanders have never had a shared language, religion, or history. They do not look alike, as the label includes not only East Asians but Indians, Pakistanis, Native Hawaiians, and Maoris. Other inhabitants of Asia have been arbitrarily excluded from the label; for cxample, Israelis and Saudi Arabians are counted by immigration as whites. Prior to the 1960s, the effort to group these diverse peoples together had little to do with what they had in common and was more a reflection of the American desire to exclude them from legal immigration and naturalization.

Activists in the Asian American movement hoped to bridge these divisions by constructing a political movement that united diverse communities through similar interests. As a consequence, Chinese parents may have hated the Japanese for the atrocities committed from the 1930s through World War II, but younger Chinese and Japanese Americans sought to form a coalition to combat American racism and discrimination. From this beginning, a loose coalition of Asian American advocates formed and began to have a larger impact on American national life. Early leaders became not only academics but also politicians including Washington State's governor Gary Locke, Clinton civil rights administrator Bill Lan Lee, and President Bush's transportation secretary Norman Mineta. Such individuals and their organizations succeeded in getting reparations for the World War II internment of Japanese Americans, continued the fight for immigrant rights, and won recognition in the arts, including the National Book Award and the Tony and Academy awards.

Nevertheless, in all of these essays there is hardly a mention of prominent Asian Americans. Inspired by the sense of pushing back boundaries, the activist generation carried the Asian American label prominently. It was understood that adopting this panethnic identity would raise the prominence of otherwise small immigrant communities and translate into actual political power. The essays in this collection show a striking lack of awareness at all of these accomplishments.

What happened? How can such a high degree of national success be followed by a near lack of recognition by a next generation of young people actively searching for role models? How thinly did the Asian American movement penetrate into American consciousness?

One of the difficulties Asian Americans faced in the 1960s was an attempt to start a civil rights movement at the very time a whole new wave of immigrants from Asia arrived in America. A civil rights victory, the Hart-Cellar Act of 1965, ended the racial barriers that had excluded Asians from legally entering the United States. From 1965 to the present, new immigrants from Asia have accounted for the majority of U.S. immigrants. Two-thirds of all Asian Americans today were born outside of the United States. The problems encountered by first-generation immigrants, such as language, poverty, and acculturation, seemed to be fading by the late 1950s but reemerged stronger and on a larger scale by the 1970s. Economic and skill requirements in the new immigration laws created unique pockets of immigrants who had significant capital and higher education and skills in places such as Silicon Valley. The result of the laws was to create more generational, class, and ethnic diversity within a racial community that was already hard to define.[7]

In these essays, young Asian Americans repeatedly write as if their generation is the first Americanized generation. The sheer size and force of the new immigrant wave could overshadow the important work that the older communities had undertaken in the past. Failure to engage some of the newer Asian immigrant communities in a political dialogue also means that not all new immigrants feel comfortable in the tag "Asian American." Throughout these essays, students show this ambivalence. One announces, "I am a Korean American. More accurately, I am an American with a limited Korean background."

Other new identities arose simultaneously with the Asian American movement—some of which appear to have greater urgency than the racialethnic tag. A young man calling himself "an ambivalent twenty-one-yearold Chinese Canadian still exploring my own sexual orientation" admits that his breakthrough came about when "perhaps most significant, I could now remind myself, 'I am a sexual being!'" Discovering his sexual identity is a liberating experience but he remains ambivalent about his ethnicity. What sort of complex or composite identity must now be taken into account when dealing with any individual? How is any political movement supposed to reflect this new complexity?[8]

There is also a self-consciousness about this dilemma that the authors recognize. Even at their young ages, they often see that the answers they seek may be constantly evolving, and they are preparing themselves for the journey. "As a teenager, I felt that I was first and foremost an American, and that my Korean background was only of marginal importance in my personal makeup." But this writer now hopes to explore the topic in order to understand both himself and his family. Another student is confident she "will continue to remain both Pakistani and American." She writes that she is proud of the "sense of permanency this community provided [that] also helped build a strong sense of identity within me." Of course, as she has reaffirmed her connection to her homeland, it has been constantly changing—perhaps in ways she might not approve of.

Another student places the problem of identity in the postmodern context of perspective. He writes that "the real effect being Korean had on me was not a product of others' direct perceptions of me but of my own perception of others' perceptions." If so, where does perception end and reality begin?

The search for meaning in one's personal history and the connection one maintains to family and community cannot ultimately be resolved in a single moment or a single essay. These are complex questions for any individual. But add to that the difficulty of living between traditions and cultures, the dislocation of immigration, the contested authenticity of all things "American" and "Asian," and the relatively new legal and political identity of "Asian American," and it becomes clear how formidable a task was handed to these young writers.

The burden of reinventing the wheel could be lifted somewhat from many of these students if they researched preceding generations of Asian immigrants and Asian Americans. Such research is readily available by fine authors and historians. Nevertheless, these authors have written honestly and successfully in enlightening the reader. If you are interested in where these young people are now, you hold the record in your hands. These essays raise difficult questions, and in this book we experience a glimpse of life journeys that often retread old paths while entering new and uncertain territory. It is undeniably fascinating.

Notes

1. Matthew Frye Jacobson, *Whiteness of a Different Color: European Immigrants and the Alchemy of Race* (Cambridge: Harvard University Press, 1999); Thomas F. Gossett, *Race: The History of an Idea in America* (Dallas: Southern Methodist University Press, 1964); Stephen Jay Gould, *The Mismeasure of Man* (New York: W. W. Norton, 1966).
2. William Wei, *The Asian American Movement* (Philadelphia: Temple University Press, 1993); Amy Tachiki, *Roots: An Asian American Reader* (Los Angeles: University of California Press, 1971); Emma Gee, *Counterpoint: Perspectives on Asian America* (Los Angeles: University of California Press, 1976); Yen Le Espiritu, *Asian American Panethnicity: Bridging Institutions and Identities* (repr., Philadelphia: Temple University Press, 1993).
3. Dinesh D'Souza, *The End of Racism: Principles for a Multicultural Society* (New York: Free Press, 1996).
4. Victor Nee and Brett De Bary, "Clifford Fong," in *Longtime Californ': A Documentary Study of an American Chinatown* (1973; repr., Palo Alto, Calif.: Stanford University Press, 1986).
5. Mary Paik Lee, *Quiet Odyssey: A Pioneer Korean Woman in America* (Seattle: University of Washington Press, 1990); Jade Snow Wong, *Fifth Chinese Daughter* (Seattle: University of Washington Press, 1989); Frank Wu, *Yellow: Race in America Beyond Black and White* (New York: Basic Books, 2002).
6. Maxine Hong Kingston, *Woman Warrior* (New York: Vintage Books, 1977); Frank Chin, "Introduction: Come All Ye Asian American Writers of the Real and the Fake," in *The Big Aiiieeeee!: An Anthology of Chinese-American and Japanese-American Literature*, ed. Jeffery Paul Chan, Frank Chin, Lawson Fusao Inada, and Shawn Wong (New York: Meridian, 1991); Wei, chapter 3.

7. Peter Kwong, *The New Chinatown* (New York: Hill and Wang, 1996); Jan Lin, *Restructuring Chinatown* (Minneapolis: University of Minnesota Press, 1998); Bill Ong Hing, *Making and Remaking Asian America through Immigration Policy, 1850–1990* (Palo Alto, Calif.: Stanford University Press, 1994).

8. Some proposals can be found in the anthology by Karin Aguilar-San Juan, *The State of Asian America: Activism and Resistance in the 1990s* (Boston: South End Press, 1993); Russell Leong, *Asian American Sexualities: Dimensions of the Gay and Lesbian Experience* (New York: Routledge, 1995).

Andrew Garrod is Professor of Education and Director of Teacher Education at Dartmouth College, where he teaches courses in adolescence, moral development, and contemporary issues in U.S. education. He currently directs a teaching volunteer program in the Marshall Islands in the central Pacific and has conducted a research project in Bosnia and Herzegovina over a number of years. His recent publications include two coauthored articles "Forgiveness after Genocide? Perspectives from Bosnian Youth" and "Culture, Ethnic Conflict, and Moral Orientation in Bosnian Children," and the coedited books, *Souls Looking Back: Life Stories of Growing Up Black* and *Learning Disabilities and Life Stories*. With Robert Kilkenny and Christina Gómez he has coedited an anthology on growing up Latino. In 1991 he was awarded Dartmouth College's Distinguished Teaching Award.

Robert Kilkenny is Clinical Associate in the School of Social Work at Simmons College in Boston. He is coeditor of *Souls Looking Back: Life Stories of Growing Up Black* and of *Adolescent Portraits: Identity, Relationships and Challenges*, which is in its sixth edition. With Andrew Garrod and Christina Gómez he has coedited an anthology on growing up Latino. He is the founder and Executive Director of the Alliance for Inclusion and Prevention, a public-private partnership providing school-based mental health, special education, and after-school programs to at-risk students in the Boston public schools.

Russell C. Leong is the chief editor of *Amerasia Journal*, the national interdisciplinary journal of Asian Americans published by the UCLA Asian

American Studies Center. He also edited *Asian American Sexualities,* the first book on the gay and lesbian Asian American experience, and *Moving the Image,* the first book on independent Asian American film and video. Leong is an adjunct Professor of English and of Asian American Studies at UCLA. *Phoenix Eyes,* his book of short stories on sexualities and migration garnered the 2001 American Book Award and his poetry, *The Country of Dreams and Dust,* received the PEN Josephine Miles Literature award. His work has been included in many anthologies, including *Charlie Chan is Dead* and *The Open Boat,* and has been translated and published in Shanghai, Nanjing, Taipei, and Hong Kong. Leong lectures and teaches in the United States and in Asia.

Vernon Takeshita was born and raised in the San Gabriel Valley and did his undergraduate work at Yale where he double majored in English Literature and History. After graduation, he worked with Nancy Araki in California collecting oral histories of Japanese American farmers. These histories were used to raise funds and to add to the collection of the Japanese American National Museum, which opened to the public in 1992. Concurrently Vernon worked at the Los Angeles Theatre Center; his plays *Performance Anxiety* and *The Rising Tide of Color,* were produced by East West Players in 1990 and 1992 and have subsequently had productions elsewhere. Vernon attended graduate studies in American History at Columbia University. He has taught in various capacities at Columbia, Cornell's Urban Semester Program, and most recently at Dartmouth College.